Praise for

Invest Like You Give a Damn

Invest Like You Give a Damn turns the dull topic of personal finance into a fun, thought-provoking page turner. One of the most insightful personal finance books of the past decade, it shows how to vote with your wallet for what you care about. It reveals how to channel your savings, investments and pension, whether a mountain or a molehill, into fuel for the burgeoning new sustainable economy. Investing for good is not a sacrifice; you can have your ethical cake and eat its returns, too. A must-read for everyone who wants to align their money with their values and make a difference with every dollar.

— Bob Willard, author and speaker, *Sustainability Advantage*

Marc de Sousa-Shields has written a masterful argument for why and how investors can and should use their voices in addressing issues of social and environmental well-being. From his position as a 30-year practitioner of using investments to achieve positive and impactful results, he introduces us to a broad range of successful approaches and urges us to join in the effort. His is a global approach, one that can be adapted for local regulatory or practical concerns yet through it all his focus is clear: investors must have a voice if the planet is to achieve anything approaching universal human dignity and ecological sustainability.

— Amy Domini, founder, Domini Impact Investments and
co-author, *Ethical Investing*

From college graduate to retired Boomer, this is *the* investment guide for everyone with a pension or portfolio, no matter how modest, wanting to change the world for the better. Get it, use it and give a damn about what your money does!

— Joel Solomon, author *The Clean Money Revolution* and
Chairman, Renewal Funds

Marc de Sousa-Shields is urging greater action from us all in an area in which we can all participate — socially responsible investing (SRI). Unfortunately, with SRI, the reality can be far from the theory. Since all firms are mixes of good and bad (rather than all good or all bad), identifying those that are the most "socially responsible" is not for the faint of heart. Marc tackles this challenge head-on, surveying this essential area of SRI with insight, flair, and humor. The result is recommended reading for all those who care about shaping business practice, while striving for a decent (both morally and financially) retirement.

— David Chandler, author, *Corporate Social Responsibility: A Strategic Perspective and Strategic Corporate Social Responsibility: Sustainable Value Creation*, and contributor, United Nations Principles for Responsible Management Education book collection

Finally, a primer on SRI, financial planning and the true meaning of life all in one entertaining, insightful, thought-provoking and factual book. This is a must-read for anyone trying to understand sustainable investing and how to get their financial life in order. I plan to share copies of this book with all the graduates in my life so they can learn in a few hours what took me years. Marc de Sousa-Shields' *Invest Like You Give a Damn* unpacks the potential of SRI and should be read by every young person starting their career and the parents who love them.

— Coro Strandberg, President, Strandberg Consulting and award winning corporate sustainability pioneer, consultant

This new book by Marc de Sousa-Shields gives the lie to Rhett Butler's most famous line. True, the history of conscious, green, responsible and sustainable investment suggests that helping investors see the wider consequences of their choices and portfolios be a Sisyphean challenge — but it's one that Marc de Sousa-Shields gives a real run for its money.

— John Elkington, Chairman & Chief Pollinator, Volans and co-author, *The Breakthrough Challenge: 10 Ways to Connect Today's Profits with Tomorrow's Bottom Line*

A quarter of a century ago, Steve Lydenberg (KLD's "Master Researcher," as reverently and accurately depicted by Marc in *Invest Like You Give a Damn*) shared with me that his greatest fear was that "One day I'll wake up and we'll be mainstream and nothing will have changed." While we still have some distance to travel until SRI can be considered mainstream, it's clear that institutional investors have embraced the concept more enthusiastically than individuals. In his book, Marc takes direct aim at the retail sector with the understanding and force that only someone of his experience and passion can — for he knows that as long as individuals sit on the sideline we will be unable to leverage capital to extent required to ensure the transition to a more just and sustainable global economy. As Rush, the Canadian rock band extraordinaire, told us in the 1980 classic Freewill — *If you choose not to decide, you still have made a choice.* Thanks to *Invest Like You Give a Damn*, individuals now have the motivation and practical tools to proactively decide — and to make a difference.

— Michael Jantzi, founder and CEO, Sustainalytics

A call to arms in the investing revolution, *Invest Like You Give A Damn* is a user-friendly guide to socially responsible investing for investors of limited means and unlimited conscience. Marc de Sousa-Shields' book provides a history of the revolution and a guide to its tools, aspirations, and purposes. There's no reason any reasonable person couldn't read this book and then reorganize their portfolio to make the world a better place.

—Bryan Welch, author, *Beautiful & Abundant: Building the World We Want,* and former publisher, *Mother Earth News, Utne Reader* and *Mother Earth Living*

INVEST
like you GIVE A
DAMN

INVEST
like GIVE A
you GIVE A
DAMN

MAKE MONEY,
CHANGE THE WORLD,
SLEEP WELL AT NIGHT

Marc de Sousa-Shields

new society
PUBLISHERS

Cover design by Diane McIntosh.
Background image: © iStock (92098495); Globe ©iStock (465061766). Sidebar image: Adobestock_96096859.

Printed in Canada. First printing October 2017.

This book is intended to be educational and informative, and does not provide specific actionable investment advice or recommendations for any investors. Always consult a financial and or legal professional to determine what may be best for your individual needs. As such, the author and publisher disclaim all responsibility for any liability, loss or risk that may be associated with the application of any of the contents of this book.

Inquiries regarding requests to reprint all or part of *Invest Like You Give a Damn* should be addressed to New Society Publishers at the address below. To order directly from the publishers, please call toll-free (North America) 1-800-567-6772, or order online at www.newsociety.com

Any other inquiries can be directed by mail to: New Society Publishers
P.O. Box 189, Gabriola Island, BC V0R 1X0, Canada (250) 247-9737

LIBRARY AND ARCHIVES CANADA CATALOGUING IN PUBLICATION

De Sousa-Shields, Marc, 1963-, author
        Invest like you give a damn : make money, change the world, sleep well at night / Marc de Sousa-Shields.

Includes index.
Issued in print and electronic formats.
ISBN 978-0-86571-848-7 (softcover).--ISBN 978-1-55092-643-9 (PDF).--ISBN 978-1-77142-238-3 (EPUB)

        1. Investments--Handbooks, manuals, etc. 2. Finance, Personal--Handbooks, manuals, etc. 3. Portfolio management--Handbooks, manuals, etc. I. Title.

HG4527.D46 2017   332.67'8   C2017-905833-9
                                           C2017-905834-7

Funded by the Government of Canada
Financé par le gouvernement du Canada

| Canada

New Society Publishers' mission is to publish books that contribute in fundamental ways to building an ecologically sustainable and just society, and to do so with the least possible impact on the environment, in a manner that models this vision.

MIX
Paper from responsible sources
FSC
www.fsc.org   FSC® C016245

Certified
Ⓑ
Corporation

new society
PUBLISHERS

There is a spirit weaving indivisible a deep desire for blessed harmony within and among ourselves, inexorably binding us to all that is wondrous and natural.

Contents

Acknowledgments

THANK YOU TO ALL MY FRIENDS AND COLLEAGUES from whom I have learned so much and whose dedication to things sustainable brings hope, inspiration, and energy to the many challenges at hand: Michael Lent, Frank Coleman, Amy Domini, Steven Lydenburg, Cheryl Smith, Steve Schueth, Alya Kyal, Joe Dougherty, Margarita Saravia, Jesse Fripp, Heather White, David Chandler, Coro Strandberg, Juan Jose Laura, Polly Kelekis, Eugene Ellemen, Janice Astbury, Carlos Perez Verdia, Michael Jantzi, Robert Walker, Darrell Ross, all the great professionals at the International Fund for Agricultural Development, and of course, Peter Kinder, among many, many others. Thanks as well to the 50 plus interviewees whose inspiring thoughts helped greatly with the inertia to do this book. Thanks to Rob West of New Society Publishers for his exuberant confidence and encouragement.

Books are family affairs. Thank you Mateus, Zoe, Brennen, Rita, Mom, Dad, Sam, Kellie, brothers Patrick and Leo, Maricela, and Jackie R. Most of all thank you Tonia, no better partner in life and sustainability could there be.
— Cuernavaca, Morelos, Mexico, Spring 2017

Part One

You and Sustainable Investment

CHAPTER ONE

Great Green-Gray Icons

I MAGINE THE FATE OF THE PLANET being held in thirty-two crypt-like coffers, row upon row of pale gray and gray rectangular metal boxes, three-quarters the height of the average American woman.

Worn and battered from years of hard use by a combat-ready military unit, these great boxes landed most ironically in an odd-shaped room of a rambling Georgian style home in Cambridge, Massachusetts.

In them, nothing less than the seeds of salvation, from which would grow a towering testament to what a small cadre of prescient, seemingly nutty priestesses and priests of information can accomplish.

Clothed in khaki, some inevitable Birkenstocks, and the occasional suit and tie, these dedicated few collected and disseminated data....

That's all: data. Information.

But not just any data — data that has changed and continues to change the world. Incredible bits of analogue memory, proof, evidence, rumor leading to fact. Thousands upon thousands of newspaper articles clipped, medical articles photocopied, court judgement reports, public policy documents, ciphers, and observations, all exposing the good, the bad, and the nasty of the health and safety, treatment of labor, air, water, biodiversity, trading practices, and other practices of one public company after another.

The goal of this floorboard-warping data? Turn data into information, and information into insight, insight into action. They had the twin objectives of piecing together profiles of corporate sin and virtue and, almost ironically, making money.

These iconic containers held one of the first comprehensive efforts to systemically judge the social and environmental impacts of Corporate America.

The insights?

Which American companies made money screwing the planet, and which made money while making it a better place. It was information to intelligently guide investors wanting to profit from a making a more sustainable world. Not just to hold companies accountable — though that has happened as a result — but to punish and reward the bad and the good by withholding or investing capital, as the case may be.

Many SRI Pioneers

By now some of those lucky few, like myself, who were there circa 1990 may have guessed these crypts of data were secondhand filing cabinets stuffed full by Amy Domini, Peter Kinder, and Steven D. Lydenberg of Kinder Lydenberg Domini (KLD), one of the first social investment analytics firms in America.

Notable among the many pioneers of what was then called "ethical investment," KLD and other firms began to systemically dissect the sustainability impact of corporate America. I first met the Cabinets in 1990, when Peter Kinder unceremoniously introduced me to them as they stood guard in the elegant dining room of what was then Peter and Amy's home.

Somewhere in the depth of that room, I heard drawers opening and closing, mutters of muted conversations. That was Steve Lydenberg, Master Researcher, who, like obsessive others in the early years of ethical investment, had a passion for evidence that was to become the bedrock upon what we now call sustainable and responsible investment (SRI) has since evolved. To Steve, it was an unconscionable, incalculable error to theorize without data, to judge without facts — an almost naive philosophy given all that has happened in U.S. politics recently.

No matter your political inclinations, facts still drive investments. Even so, the underlying theory of change that makes sustainable and responsible investment such a powerful tool for change is that investments are made only if data informs and inspires those able to make a difference in this world.

Are these your people too? I hope so.

Back to history.

Many other brave souls had similar goals to those at KLD, some with crypts of their own. Others bought and applied the parchment offered up by KLD. Companies and organizations like Clean Yield, Franklin (now Trillium), EthicScan, the Social Investment Forum, Progressive Asset

Management, First Affirmative Financial Network, Pax World Funds and more.

There were efforts in other countries too. Michael Jantzi, founder of Sustainalytics, who briefly shared office space with the Social Investment Organization I co-founded in Canada (renamed the Responsible Investment Association, or RIA), is an example, as are others in the UK and other European countries. Each deserving of merit and praise themselves: All hail to them!

The Cambridge Mass Flood: A Pivotal Moment in SRI?

Some years later, the Cabinets were moved, some by hand trolley, to a new home in KLD's below-grade office. A step up and down from their former Georgian abode. During a late winter storm not long after, the office was flooded with the very best the Cambridge city drainage system could provide. Some claim the flood was the result of an Ayn Rand-inspired capitalist conspiracy to flush the disruptive force of SRI down the drain, so to speak.

Me? I see it as fate in biblical proportion. For far from slowing the SRI movement down, the flood caused a rapid advance, moving KLD from parchment to digital (and to a fifth-floor office in Boston), greatly expanding its already sophisticated means for parsing and assessing data.

Perhaps I exaggerate to make a point. Many other SRI data providers were switching to digital at the time, but it makes for lovely theory. Anyhow, around that time, a bunch of equally zany and prescient investment professionals got together to form the US Social Investment Forum. It was to be the first professional association of SRI investors in the world. Led by a cohort of determined professionals, they created one of the most determined professional movements of the day, a hallmark of SRI to this today. Folks like Steve Schueth, Alisa Gravitz, George Gay, Milton Moskowitz, Joan Bavaria, and so many, many others set out on the mission with a single goal: to prove sustainability investment is better in all respects than conventional investment.

At the time, there was a mere $200 billion in SRI, invested by individuals and institutions — foundations, unions, universities, and the like. Then, as today, SRI could be defined as a strategy to profitably invest in ventures that have some form of social or environmental objective. It can be as simple as not investing in so-called sin stocks — companies that produce armaments, tobacco, porn, or gaming. Investments at the time were mostly focused on publicly traded companies, or companies traded on stock markets.

Today there are over $6.7 trillion in SRI assets. And not only in stocks and bonds but in many special-purpose vehicles from community investment funds to, wait … hedge funds!

Who can resist the just-too-great-to-ever-be-cliché observation of Margaret Meade: *Never doubt what the determination of a small group of people can do to change the world.*

It's been my great fortune to have known many of the pioneering SRI actors, and in a modest way participate in the evolving story of SRI over the past 25 years. At times, I have been in the thick of things, but more often standing on the sidelines, either as a corporate sustainability consultant, a researcher trying to encourage SRI in emerging markets, or, as I am now, a commentator trying to make heads and tails of all that is economic and sustainable.

It has been both amazing and disheartening to have deeply re-familiarized myself with SRI for the writing of this book. It has been amazing to see what the pioneers have accomplished and what emerging new standard bearers are building. Wow…. $6.7 T, as in trillion!!! All that without anyone even knowing (or at least agreeing on) what "sustainable" really means!

1 million seconds is about 11.5 days; 1 billion seconds is about 32 years while a trillion seconds is equal to 32,000 years.

It is a bit disheartening that SRI has made incredible strides to systemically identify the best, highly profitable sustainability investments yet has largely failed to move past the very basics in the public's mind. Most popular press articles about SRI in 2017 are depressingly similar to the ones published in the early 1990s. Usually led by the utterly irrelevant question, proven time and time again, over and over, repeatedly, *ad nauseum, ad infinitum*: "Is SRI as profitable as conventional investment?"

The answer is simple, and if you promise to never, ever entertain any other response than mine, I will answer the question: *No investment strategy can promise any return greater than another.* If an investment professional guarantees this, run, prepare to lose money, or eventually go to jail.

What we can undoubtedly say about SRI is that despite hundreds of independent academic studies proving that sustainable investments are equal to or outperform conventional investments, many stubborn, uninformed investment professionals and media pundits continue to believe that investing with sustainability in mind costs returns.

Just ask Lloyd Kurtz. For over 22 years, Lloyd and others of his colleagues have been responsible for managing the Moskowitz Prize, the global award recognizing outstanding quantitative research in SRI, much of which establishes the very competitive performance of SRI. Better yet, trust a 2015 meta-study by Oxford University that reviewed over 200 investigations in SRI performance. The study found that 88% of companies with robust sustainability practices demonstrate better operational performance, and another 80% of the studies reviewed showed "prudent sustainability practices have a positive influence on investment performance."[1]

Despite the $6.7 trillion in assets, and despite evidence that would convince even the most cynical of cynics, corporations in America are not stampeding toward having greater sustainability performance. The threat of divestment for crappy sustainability behavior or the promise of more capital for better has done nowhere near enough to change corporate habits. Nor has SRI yet to significantly alter the investment behavior of most investors.

Short story: SRI has not ignited an enduring excitement among mainstream investors, many of whom would chafe — to say the least — if they, their families, and their communities were directly exposed to the worst and all-too-common standard operating practices of most companies.

An uprising of individual investors: That's what we need. Nothing begets change faster in a free market economy than demand. Nothing. The Social Investment Forum (SIF) of America investigated this. What did it find? It found that individual investors requesting SRI services, even from the most *conservative financial organizations*, often led to the provision of SRI services.

If you muck about on the SIF's fine website, you will also find that institutional SRI investors have been carrying the SRI load. Bless their souls. But don't get me wrong — while this puts up great asset numbers, its individual investor engagement has lagged, and it's individual investor engagement we need to incite an SRI revolution.

Can institutional investors ignite passion, like Greenpeace or Bernie Saunders? Probably not. Like constituents calling their congressperson, individual investors who believe our world is in desperate peril and in need of a sustainable fix need to get off the proverbial couch and let their advisers know about SRI, and let them know they want SRI options.

My discussions with institutional investors and SRI professionals lead me to believe that an individual investor-led movement may be coming. Public demand is finally echoing in the halls of most investment houses.

Will SRI catch fire and burn the underbrush of conventional invest-ment to be just "investment"? Before I answer that, imagine for a moment that all the $20 trillion or so of capital of the New York Stock Exchange was put behind our sustainability dreams. If this is possible, and many think it is, the question then becomes, what will it take to get *You, yes, You,* off the couch and using your capital for sustainability?

Now, I can't say for certain that aligning your investments with your so-cial, environmental, or economic world vision will make the world a better place. But I can say this: If you don't try, the world will certainly not be-come a more human, more habitable place for our kids and theirs. Cliché, I know. But metaphors are hard to find when global temperature records are being smashed faster than my sixteen-year-old evades doing dishes.

Where does that lead us?

What is in *Invest Like You Give a Damn*?

I would like to say this book attempts to find the key to your heart and mind. But my Buddha has sharp elbows and pointy boots which aim to kick your butt off the couch and into sustainability investment. We both know your values are the kind we need to put to work to secure your own financial future and the future sustainability of the world. So why not?

My hope is that the research and the fifty or so interviews I did for *Invest like You Give a Damn (ILYGAD)* causes something to jump out at you, hopefully something that excites you enough to make more and better SRI investments. But more than this, I hope that you become an incessant-ly broadcasting sustainability investor. You know, the cocktail party, BBQ, after-church social SRI proselytizer type!

Less hyperbolically, *ILYGAD* is about how YOU can shape a new world through YOUR investments, be they for retirement, saving for your kids' college, a home, or whatever you have in mind.

Because *ILYGAD* is about individual investment, the book looks in de-tail at the specific needs of the two biggest economically active investment cohorts, **Generation X** and **Millennials.** Gen Xers control about $7 trillion of investment assets, while Millennials control about $3 trillion and will soon inherit another $7 trillion: That's more than enough to reshape the investment world in their image.

ILYGAD provides a guide for you, the individual investor, to make more and hopefully better sustainable and responsible investments. It provides loads of stories, opinions, and examples throughout, many taken from interviews with investors and investment professionals. *ILYGAD* also has tons of hard facts from investment and sustainability investment research targeted to the economic and investment challenges of Gen Xers and Millennials.

Part One looks at you as a person and an investor (both Gen Xers and Millennials), and how powerful personality traits can help or hinder your ability to invest sustainably. It's a bit new agey but hopefully insightful, because, despite what Adam Smith would have you believe, our economic decisions are often far, far from rational or destined to maximize profit.

Part Two is all about financial planning. What? Yes, financial planning. *ILYGAD* is about igniting a storm of SRI, so the more money you can invest, the better. This means good household financial management. Initially this was going to be a smaller focus of the book. But after many interviews, I learned that financial management and investment are so clearly and closely related and folks wanted insights on both. And as I said, if you save more, you can invest more.

Part Three is about making great SRIs. It reviews investment basics and presents what I like to think of as a groundbreaking tool, the Sustainable & Responsible Investment (SRI) Allocator, a simple method to match your desired SRI impact with your defined Financial Asset Allocation.

ILYGAD Investment Philosophy

Do not seek more than you need to live well and sustainably. Place experiences over products; time over money; and friends, family, community, humanity, and a vibrant environment over all.

That is the ILYGAD Investment Credo. Translated into an investment philosophy: $70,000 and 7%.

People are happy if they are financially secure, and an annual income of $70,000 in secure, disposable pretax income has been proven to maximize Happy (not including health care and education costs). There is no need for more, apparently. Don't get me wrong — if you want or need more than this, and want a sustainable life, that's your business, and this book still has lots to offer you. It's just my own perspective and belief that more than this makes for too much consumption. That some people have too much and some too little does not encourage the communal (and political) will and effort to create public health, education, and other systems required for full and true economic and social sustainability.

I would add two caveats to this. One is savings for kids' education. (Although expensive, education contributes to economic inequality and should, in my mind, be near to free.) The second is savings for health care. Until these basic human rights are secured for all people at a very reasonable cost, the reality is $70,000 doesn't cut it, so we need to plan for more.

As to 7%, the 100-year annualized average return on the New York Stock Exchange (by various measures) is about 7%. Forget 30%, forget 20%, forget 10%. Aim for 7% and you should get it. More importantly, you will send a signal to companies that long term is fine, that life on this planet is a game of centuries, not fiscal quarters. Wanting more is to want unsustainable returns, which only stands to fuel unsustainable production and consumption.

SRI is a Game of Centuries

How much can you change the world with SRI? I'm not sure, as it was thirty years ago that I first got into this game. But this I can say with certainly: SRI as an investment strategy can fulfill your financial goals and is a powerful part of a broader sustainability movement that is likely something you are or want to be a part of.

ILYGAD, I hope, will entertain, inspire, and educate. But most of all, I hope it gets you off the couch and investing sustainably.

What you learned in this chapter

- The *ILYGAD* Sustainability Investment Credo: $70,000 annual income (not including education and health care costs) and a goal of 7% investment return.
- Sustainability is a game of centuries, and we need to invest that way.

Chapter Two

SRI Definitions Disguised as History

I'LL NOT TELL A LIE: the history and evolution of sustainable and responsible investment (SRI) is personal for me! I am vested, ecstatic, and
jaded all at once, and my story will neither be complete nor necessarily jibe
with those of others. But it's mine.

Let me explain.

When I graduated with my MA from the University of Toronto in 1989,
I had visions of doing a PhD, but my supervisors saw fit to recommend me
to any *other* school besides U of T. I am not entirely sure why, or if it was a
badge of honor or shame.

At the time, I couldn't understand or forgive them. In retrospect, they
were Three Wise Supervisors. I suspect that they knew the incremental
change approach, which is so much a part of academia, was neither ready
for me nor I for it. Neither of the two prevailing intellectual schools of
thought at the time — the ascendant neoconservativism or the still kicking
but definitively ailing social democratic Marxism — had any compelling
pull for me.

Rather, like many tail-end Boomers/beginning of Gen Xers, I felt
vaguely Hippy and certainly Rebellious. The labor versus capital canard
seemed too cobwebbed, too ineffective, too inefficient to get the job done.
We didn't want to just protest and get government to change things. There
was a new idea afoot, one more conventional and disruptive at the same
time. What if, we thought, we could use the power of capital to change the
very nature of consumption and production? Not an entirely new idea, but
it was a new twist to powerful currents of social and environmental advocacy swelling from the protest movements of the 1960s and early 1970s.

It was a market-based approach to sustainability. The fiercest environmental and social development advocates eschewed it as traitorous, while

most others simply thought saving the world was the responsibility of government and civil society, not business — if they thought about it at all.

We believed different.

Our first instinct was that there is nothing more powerful than capital to move people to act. We also reasoned that even the most hardened conservatives would at some point want to pick up the crap in their own backyard, even if they had been complicit in putting it there in the first place.

Absurd proof of this abounds, none better than the former CEO of Exxon, Rex Tillerson, now U.S. secretary of state. As boss of Exxon, he led one of the most ambitious fracking for oil and natural gas programs in the U.S.A., while covering up the company's own research from as far back as the 1970s that found climate change an imminent threat to humanity! More absurd yet, while Exxon defended fracking as safe and good, Tillerson was behind a lawsuit to ban fracking from his own neighborhood![2] Seems even the most capitalist of capitalists shares some of the values underlying sustainability. We all want natural environments to enjoy; dignified, fairly paid work; basic human rights, etc.

Okay, I may be stretching an example to make a point, and Exxon along with most major companies remains almost entirely focused on profit. Yet companies respond quickly to demand. If enough of us want something, they will change to provide it. That's why the *commoditization* of sustainability values has such great promise. The more we price sustainability into the way we consume, the greater our impact can be.

It's not crazy when you think about. We have come a long way toward doing just this. Sustainability value has modern origins in the form of *The Green Consumer Guide*. This was the definitive guide for those of us wanting to consume with maximum positive impact on the planet. From using newspaper and vinegar to clean windows to choosing the least-harmful shaving products, this was the bible.

First published in 1988 by the sustainability lions John Elkington and Julia Hailes, *The Guide* showed what to buy or not but also how companies could make money while caring for the environment. It sold a fantastic number of copies despite the fact that almost every product promoted as "environmental" was either astronomically expensive or only sort of worked. Environmental products still enjoy that brand. But the notion that consumers can affect how producers produce and how products impact the planet has only grown in popularity and sophistication.

Demand for "sustainability value" in what we buy has risen dramatically. It's like brand value, or the portion of a product's selling price that consumers are willing to pay beyond its basic functionality. Consumers pay for this type of value all the time. Consider a top-end Citizens watch. It tells the time and can look as good and last as long as a Rolex. But many people are willing to pay much more for the Rolex simply because it is a Rolex. Same for a Toyota Prius in the early 2000s, when one cost far more than any car its size ought to have cost. Hollywood actors were particularly fond of the Prius, paying a premium price of $40,000 plus, when a comparable non-hybrid car would have only cost $25,000. We pay more for local foods, we pay more for fair trade coffee — you get the picture.

If you buy the occasional product for its sustainability value, you are hardly alone. Multitudes of surveys tell us more than 75% of American consumers actively look for "sustainable" products. This is good — but sadly, less than 20% tend to buy sustainable regularly, and less than 5% buy that way often.

Much like sustainable consumption, sustainable and responsible investment asks us to buy into companies providing both tangible and intangible sustainability-related benefits. Tangible benefits include how the companies treat labor, whether they pollute or not, whether they advance women or not, etc. Intangible benefits include the pride of owning solar, boasting rights over running shoes made entirely of recycled material, etc. — not things you can always see or touch, but like the Rolex, the value is real.

Sustainable and responsible investment (SRI) is an offshoot of this free-market, change-the-world-for-the-better tree, only less well known than its consumer counterpart. Why? For many reasons, but let's face it — sustainability is a confusing term. Throw in investment and, well, the cloud of unknowing just gets bigger.

Overlaying all this is the worry, fear, and *ennui* investment invokes in many people, which causes them to break out in sweat and rashes or enormous streaks of procrastination. SRI, as a result, is not as easy a sale as local potatoes or recycled shoes.

A Short History of SRI

Both conditions of "sustain-unknowability" and "investo-phobia" are completely understandable. If you are a painter, a teacher, a human resource manager, or a barista, your job isn't to understand investments and sustainability to the nth degree. But the basics you should be familiar with.

So let's take a little walk through SRI history land, hear a story or two, and hopefully learn a thing or two.[3]

SRI has antecedents in biblical traditions, in the Quran, indigenous spiritual guidance, and pretty much every spiritual tradition. The Quakers were among the first to systemically practice what we might call SRI ... in 1758(!), when at their annual Quaker Philadelphia gathering they decided to ban members of the church from owning slaves or engaging in the slave trade.

Modern SRI got rolling in the mid-1960s, when anti-war protesters and civil rights leaders started pointing fingers at all the not-so-good things companies did to violate human rights. It was then that two of my heroes — Luther Tyson and Jack Corbett, Methodists with a history of working for affordable housing, peace, and employment rights— decided to launch an SRI mutual fund. The idea was to give investors a way to align their investments with their values. Pax World Fund was born in 1971. (*Pax* is Latin for *peace!*)

The following year the inhuman treatment of the Vietnamese during the Vietnam War was crystalized in Nick Ut's photo of nine-year-old Phan Thi Puc fleeing her burning village, back ablaze from napalm. Many Americans began to think that dumping chemicals on innocent Vietnamese villagers wasn't a good thing and that they ought to discourage it by divesting their money from Dow Chemical, the producer of Agent Orange.

Around about the same time, the Reverend Leon Sullivan — a member of the board of directors of General Motors, no less! — drafted a business code of conduct for South Africa. The Sullivan Principles, as they came to be known, asked foreign companies in an apartheid state to not support racial discrimination or segregation.

From then until 1991, when apartheid was repealed in the country, many large institutional investors avoided investing in companies operating in South Africa. The successful divestment movement was led in the United States by political pressure from universities, faith-based institutions, city and state governments, and pension funds large and small. The impact was impressive; the outflow of capital helped influence major South African employers to call for the end of apartheid.

SRI Negative Screening Takes Off

SRI didn't bring an end to apartheid alone, of course, but it had a big hand in it. Ridding the world of that scourge was something else! And it showed those in power what the prescient Quakers, Tysons, Corbetts, and others knew all along: Money can move seemingly intractable objects.

The Pax World Fund was soon followed by numerous others, but it took dozens of more years for SRI to really take off. And when it did, it did so on the coattails of tobacco.

For years, Big Tobacco managed to spin, spin, spin, like a precision top, the horrid lie that tobacco smoking was a good thing. Seems incredible today, but Big Tobacco, like the equally evil climate change deniers after them, spent years spewing tobacco and health misinformation. All for a dollar, or rather, many, many billions of dollars.

The deception continued into the mid-1980s — when, astoundingly (or not?!), Big Tobacco was found out to have known the awful truth of their cancer-causing product for decades. But by the early 1990s, the jig was mostly up, as the combined pressure of health advocates, cancer survivors, devastated families, and the generally sane among us managed to convince the world that tobacco smoking was indeed very, very bad.

All through the tobacco wars of the late 1980s and 1990s, SRI provided investors the option to avoid investing in tobacco companies. This is **negative screening**: the conscious decision to a keep a company or companies making things you don't like out of your investment portfolio.

Negative screening can be a one-off decision; for me, sadly, this includes Volkswagen, a company that makes great cars but recently got caught first-degree lying on emission standards (heaven and Earth will move before I will buy a Volkswagen or invest in their company — if you own one older than 2016, don't feel bad; they fooled us all!) Or it can be a sector busting, such as all tobacco or defense companies.

The theory of negative screening is that if enough investors strain out a company or companies producing something evil, the price of capital increases such that it becomes difficult for them to operate, causing shareholders to look elsewhere for returns. That's the theory. In practice, it doesn't work that well.

A quick glance at the stock market today shows that the same terrible smoke stacks are still standing. Sure, Big Tobacco took a huge hit considering how they *could have profited* had SRI and others not taken them to task. But it still has tremendous net worth and lots of happy shareholders: Worse, it remains a terrible plague to society and a horribly profitable business. Sadly, much of the Big Tobacco venom was simply exported overseas to developing countries, where the anti-tobacco movement doesn't always have the support of government, legal systems, or empowered citizens to fight the lies, half-truths, and omissions of the huge, well-funded tobacco companies.

The SRI tally of anti-tobacco assets — the total number of assets held in investment funds screening out tobacco companies — continues to be a substantial volume of SRI assets under management. It is testament to what is possible and to what still needs to be done.

The focus on tobacco also tested the patience of many SRI professionals, who saw SRI as a tool with bigger potential than simply taking on a single industry (and some might add, cynically, to symbolically grow SRI assets). Tobacco is a huge health issue, which no one can deny. But the fight against it didn't contribute all that much to the systemic change needed to address complex sustainability challenges — nor in the end has it taken out Big Tobacco.

Ultimately, the real force SRI brought to bear on tobacco was tactical. It helped popularize SRI as a lightning rod of what is possible. But like many other issues, the fight against the tobacco companies needed broader public outrage to mobilize the support required to shut them down, particularly state governments suing the hell out of them. SRI provided much stirring of the public support pot, and as with South Africa, got a noticeable amount of investor money to steer clear of Big Tobacco.

Shareholders Unite in Activism

One of the ways SRI did this was to support dozens of fund companies, individual investors, faith-based institutions, and others to file dozens of very difficult and often embarrassing questions to answer at annual Big Tobacco shareholder meetings.

This is called **shareholder activism**. As you might know, publicly traded companies have annual shareholder meetings. The business at these meetings is to report on company performance, issues affecting business, and how the company might deal with them. Electing the board of directors, executive compensation, and other issues related to company management are also on the docket.

Many of these agenda items require a vote of the shareholders. Now, as you may also know, most companies have millions of shareholders, only a few of whom bother to go to the meetings. Most fail to show up, either because they don't know they own the company (e.g., stocks are held in pension funds or mutual funds, which investors don't take the time to familiarize themselves with) or because, if the company is doing okay, why bother?

If a shareholder feels inclined to vote but can't go to the annual meeting, they can instruct a third party to vote on their behalf. This is a called a **proxy vote** and is usually given to the fund in which their shares are held. The fund managers attend and vote on their behalf.

The proxy vote is a sharp arrow in the SRI quiver, made sharper by SRI's platoon of even sharper proxy warriors. These are dozens of SRI analysts whose job it is to represent sustainability-minded shareholders. They have two main tasks. The first is to proxy represent at AGMs. The second — and this takes place long before the AGMs and requires an incredible amount of work, dedication, and talent — is to get company to put a sustainability-related question on the AGM agenda.

Now, to say companies don't fight tooth and nail to avoid rabble-rousing SRI activists from filing these embarrassing questions would be to denigrate the work of SRI analysts. For years, AGM were rubber-stamping, chicken dinner affairs where the Big Boys got together to give themselves large, uncontested raises and generally pat themselves on the back for a job well done (even if it wasn't).

The moment the single-share-owning Greenpeace activist strolled down the aisle at a big chemical company AGM and unceremoniously slapped a dead-from-mercury-poison salmon on the podium and demanded an explanation spelled the end of the AGM as a boys' clubhouse meeting.

Urban myth or real event?

I can't say, but from the late 1970s on, the activist investor was someone to be feared, forcing many more than a few companies to address social, environmental, and economic issues they would rather deny at worst or rationalize as a cost of doing business at best.

The success of SRI shareholder activism continues to be less than forcing actual change. In the beginning a "win" was simply getting an issue on the AGM agenda. Then it became a measure of how many votes an SRI question got; as a wise Hollywood character once said, "It's all about the numbers." Okay, maybe he said all about the "money." But in activism, votes are money, and at an AGM, it's all about the votes.

Shelly Alpern, formerly with Clean Yield and now with CERES and a heroine of mine, is one of those steely strong sustainability proxy warriors. She once told me that in the early years, activists could barely manage 1% outstanding share votes. Today they often get 25% or more. Incremental vote grabbing is the modus operandi: Get 1% this year, 5% the next, and before you know it, you have 25%.

We can thank the hundreds of dedicated SRI proxy voting experts for their resolve in winning what could be a disheartening 10%, yet steadfastly keeping critical issues like gender balance, LGT rights, and climate change on the shareholder AGM agenda year after year.

From a put-sustainability-on-the-radar perspective, the SRI industry's success has been outstanding. From 2012 to 2014, over 200 U.S. institutions and investment management firms controlling over $1.7 trillion in assets filed or co-filed SRI-related AGM proposals. Issues addressed ranged from LGBT rights, political contributions to climate change and other environmental issues such as biodiversity.[4]

SRI (Largely) Fails Cocktail Party Test

Nevertheless — and I hate to say this — the incredible effort of Shelly and her many SRI colleges rarely passes what I call the **SRI Cocktail Party Test (CPT)** — becoming the topic of a conversation people are eager to engage in at a party. Same with negative screens. I've yet to hear of anyone rushing to their investment adviser demanding divestment from British Tobacco because of what someone said at a party.

Any good social movement requires sparks, which light fires and lead to fireworks so powerful they move people to move. The CPT is a simple measure of that level of excitement.

Imagine yourself at a cocktail party (or the gathering of your choice). You and your friends and colleagues of a like mind are all milling about chatting of things of interest. Bring up your most recent SRI purchase, say the five hundred shares of a 250-million-share company you divested from because they won't put the question "Will you reduce the carbon emissions at manufacturing operations" on the agenda at their annual general meeting.

It could happen that this becomes incessant cocktail chatter — I await the day, beer in hand. The paradox and the singular challenge of SRI is that it's a damn sexy name and concept, which on the surface seems simple and exciting. But because much of what SRI does is proxy voting and negative screens, in practice it just doesn't light the social change matches of regular folks.

If anybody at the party is listening, it's because they pity you, hope you'll change the topic soon, or happen to be one of the few, proud sustainability investor geeks on the planet, like me. Sadly, most are looking around for the next drink.

We need to face the facts. Getting people excited about something they know little about and is not grab-you-by-the-lapels interesting is the real SRI challenge. Giving a Kickstart donation for an independent movie showing that Apple is exploiting and poisoning young Chinese factory workers — now that's exciting. And that's SRI's competition.

Fortunately, shareholder advocacy and negative-screened investment funds are not the only games in the SRI town, even if they account for most of SRI assets. The two other options you may know are **positively screened investments** and **impact investment**, both far more promising CPT material.

Smashing TVs & Connecting to Our Souls

Around the late 1990s, many in the SRI industry found ourselves wanting more than assets driven by "tobacco." So we formed the Morelos Forum, named after the state in Mexico where I live. Among our ranks were SRI professionals from Canada and the United States, and occasionally other countries.

We met annually for 15 years to address one question: how to take SRI mainstream, beyond negative, beyond activism, and make it a huge, inspiring force for sustainability. Our goal was to un-puzzle why so many people want to make the world a better place but don't exploit one of their biggest leveraging tool — investments.

The group thought hard for three days a year to resolve this conundrum. At one point Eric Steedman, a Morelos Forum founder, jumped up in frustration and encapsulated our dilemma in a single phrase: "Smash TVs"! He was referring, of course, less to the medium than to popular culture, which encourages the very thing that is killing us: our incessant consumption of stuff made unsustainably, which, like junk food, causes habitual lethargy, poor health, and bad thoughts.

Consumerism is only getting worse. We consume like rabid bandits and expect the world economy to expand every year, not just to accommodate a growing population but to somehow improve our "welfare." Except it's not about improving welfare, it's about improving purchasing capacity.

People can get a bit crazy when I suggest this. But I believe that if we took some time to examine our collective navels we might realize our penchant for converting desires to *needs*. The gods know I am guilty too, but they also know it's *our* responsibility to resist the big-screen, new-phone, third-car demons that plague us all. Remember, though, that no snowflake ever feels responsible for the avalanche, and, as John E. Lewis once famously said, "If not us, then who? If not now, then when?"

But I digress.

The Morelos Forum never did break the code to setting the SRI excitement bonfire alight. We did coin the phrase Sustainable and Responsible Investment in 2003, consistent with the now-common understanding that environmental, social, and economic injustices are intractably interlinked. It's simply not a single-issue play, which is the complex Achilles-heel that SRI has to explain and put into practice. Which poor farmer in Kenya will you ask to go organic and give up the certainty of a chemically induced yield that is slowly poisoning land, communities, and consumers alike yet feeds her household of ten? She certainly gives a damn about the environment but can't do much if it means even $10 less to her annual income of $1,200.

When we looked at the SRI through this lens at the Morelos Forum, we saw the resolutions of its complexity in a different light. Two things stood out for us.

One, growth economics doesn't work for sustainability. Always growing our economies to meet never-ending material desires is a no-win proposition. We already use our natural resources four times faster than they are replenished (i.e., we need four planets to sustain ourselves). No-growth economics must be the ultimate focus of SRI. Two, to maximize SRI's potential it must connect with the values and needs of people; that is, resolve the challenges of the Kenyan farmer and our sustainability goals at the same time.

All this came together at the Morelos Forum when Amy Domini, founder of Domini Social Investments, started on about "slow" this and "slow" that. At first, we thought she might just be getting ready for retirement. Turns out, she was talking about how "less" makes for a "more" enjoyable life, and isn't that the point anyhow?

The "slow" she was referring to was the Slow Food movement. Take time to find the best and most natural ingredients, shell peas and cut onions with friends and family, enjoy wine, eat slowly, discuss, laugh, connect....

Of course, Slow Food is a metaphor for a less time-stressed, stuff-cluttered lifestyle. The very act of slowing down, buying natural, and cooking together is clearly more sustainable than slamming back a Hungry Man or Lean Cuisine dinner could ever aspire to be.

Many people agree, and the Slow Food movement has grown in leaps and bounds, as have the organic food, natural health and beauty markets, among many others. Connect an issue to our personal interests; find meaning; act. As Jennifer Boynnton, the sage managing editor at Triple Pundit, points out, the formula for connecting to people is simple: It's all about what we put *into ourselves*, put *on ourselves*, and what is *around us*. Tap that, and change happens.

The menu of investment options around the turn of the last century hardly captured the compelling pull of connectedness. SRI couldn't pass the cocktail party test let alone viscerally grab at our values and souls. Nor can it easily compete with late-night appeals asking us to save a child's life. The immediate "happy" these things give us remained broadly elusive for SRI.

Kristen of New York is an investment professional and has yet to make SRI investments. But she does volunteer for a microfinance foundation that helps entrepreneurs in developing countries access credit. Kristen does this knowing that she is directly helping people; she can imagine, feel, sense her impact through colleagues she shares time with and stories sent back from the field. Kristen sometimes feels her investment can't compete at this level. Charity, giving, altruism, these evoke powerful, selfless connectedness — and to paraphrase, this gives us a Huge, Uncomplicated, and very Gratifying feeling — a HUG!

HUG an SRI Mutual Fund or Least Worst Company?

One step closer to that HUG are **screened mutual funds**. There are some 350 SRI mutual funds which mix positive and negative screening. With over $2.6 trillion in assets, these funds, like their conventional, non-SRI peers, invest in portfolios of stocks and bonds based on fund-specific risk and return objectives. SRI funds employ similar financial strategies as conventional mutual funds but also have "sustainability" strategies. Some focus on a mix of social and human rights and environmental and economic justice issues. Others invest in a single issue, such as alternative energy, the advancement of women, or alleviating poverty.

Many SRI funds often use a **best-of-sector approach**. As you may have guessed, this employs negative or positive screens to select companies with the best, or "least worst" (depending on your viewpoint), sustainability performance. This approach often causes great surprise among first-time SRI investors, who, when first peeking into a best-of-sector portfolio, find, to their great dismay, companies they would have never expected to see in a sustainability fund.

The best-of-sector approach is about lesser evils. But we must remember that until very recently, SRI analytics was such that it was hard to do much more than avoid companies in the news for having done bad things.

Without getting into the thickets of SRI data analysis, prior to the mid-2000s, SRI data was limited to surveys filled out by the companies themselves, triangulated with information from public sources. This simply did not allow for the kind of sophisticated analytics done today, which correlates comprehensive sustainability data with financial performance.

This limitation led to a lot of "bad" companies that we thought were "not bad" slipping into portfolios. British Petroleum, for example, was often held in "best-of-sector" portfolios. BP seemed to have a great sustainability program and, for the most part, stayed out of the news. That was, of course, until all their rotten eggs broke in the Deepwater Horizon oil platform explosion. BP had hoodwinked a lot of us into thinking they had some sustainability game, when in fact all they actually has was good public relations.

Sustainability investment information and rating companies, and the funds themselves, have since developed some fairly spectacular analytical models that can pinpoint beyond best and least worst sustainability performance. And the holy grail sustainability and financial performance algorithm is now within sight.

Something else to know about "best of sector" is that it allows fund managers to allocate your capital across different economic sectors, as a method to control portfolio financial risk. If the transportation sector tanks after the crash of coal (yeah!), technology or consumer durables can hold your portfolio's financial performance.

If you are like me, it's hard to bear hug the least offensive companies. The "best-of-sector" approach may excite some conversation at cocktail parties, but is unlikely to easily pass the CPT. Jessie Fripp, *ILYGAD* interviewee, summed it up for many: "Best-of-sector sounded great until I thought about it, then it struck me that it was like keeping the axe murderers out of the party but inviting the thieves and gangsters."

While perhaps not as dramatic, an interviewee from New York said, "it feels like the companies in SRI funds just haven't been caught yet." Given the recent spate of corporate sustainability lying, it's hard to argue — VW and emissions, Mitsubishi and fuel efficiency, Exxon suppressing climate change data since the 1970s, Walmart caught in a massive corruption scheme in Mexico! The list goes on.

Divestment more HUGable?

Ten years ago, climate change was just coming on the SRI radar. By 2014, climate-change assets controlled by SRI reached $551 million. Some $43 billion, a tiny speck of traded stock in the greater scheme of things, was diverted from fossil fuels companies in 2014. In the gathering momentum of the coal divestment movement, fed by months of record high temperatures around the world, this number had grown to over $4 trillion by the end of 2016. Impressive!

My good friend Professor David Chandler likes to chuckle when he sees the SRI community get all frothy with asset divestment numbers. "The only true barometer of success," he argues, "is a steadily declining share price of Big Carbon producers." He insists quite logically that as divestment funds exit a stock, other investors simply buy them up cheaply.

He is right. Divestment has had little effect on Big Oil company stock prices or on the market fundamentals underlying oil. Regional conflicts, wildfires around the Canadian tar sands, and OPEC policies drive fossil fuel economics more than anything else. Even BP, heinous purveyor of Deepwater Horizon, has seen relatively stable share prices over the past several years.

Investors still have little impact beyond the symbolic from a market perspective. Symbolism has its place, perhaps a higher place on the HUG-ometer than many might think. Today's fossil fuel divestment movement is energizing hundreds of thousands of students, universities, and some public pension funds to walk away from fossil fuel investments. That's something. In combination with other progressive market, civil society, and government forces, change is blowing in the wind ... remember South Africa!

Impact Investing, HUGging Yet?

Positively screened investments have always been a part of SRI. They are companies or investment opportunities included in a portfolio because they promote or support the advancement of a specific sustainability issue, or sustainability generally.

Over the past several years, positive screening has become known as **impact investment**, or capital that proactively targets specific sustainability challenges. Same thing, different words, so don't be confused.

An impact investment can be in companies, organizations, or funds with the intention to generate a measurable, beneficial social or environmental impact. Some claim the term has been usurped by conventional investment companies and basically means positively screened investments

Sounds pretty much what SRI industry has been doing for decades. Right? But if you parse the definition, you find there are two types of impact investments, one more passion-inducing than the other.

High Impact and Definitively HUGable

The first type of impact investment has been around for a long time and was once commonly known as an alternative or community investment. This is oxytocin for sustainable investors, the investment that makes our pulse shoot past the Moon and makes us go looking for cocktail parties just to sing its praises.

The Calvert Foundation, Community Development Financial Institutions, Oikocredit, Shared Interest, Blue Orchard Finance, and many other funds are the pioneers of this investment type. Hundreds more opportunities have followed with their own take on things, some more SRI than others. High-risk social venture capital, microfinance investment funds, social housing projects and small-scale farming cooperatives are other examples of this type of investment.

Some high-impact investment opportunities pay market returns, others below market, and some require long-term capital commitments. All make tangible connection between the lives of the people your investment supports.

Among the most sustainability minded funds is Triodos Bank of Holland. Triodos offers a family of high-impact funds some with near-market returns, some less. The sustainability impacts are, however, quite astounding. One of its funds invested in a coffee-growing cooperative in

Quillabama, Peru, which I had the opportunity to evaluate. This was no or-
dinary investment. Located high in the Andes mountains, the cooperative
was known both for its incredible coffee and for the five-hour, moun-
tain-edged, switchback-filled, stomach-churning drive it took to get their
coffee out!

If this type of investment doesn't induce a HUG, I am not sure what
will. (I know I certainly hugged our driver when we finally arrived.) Yet it
is exactly this type of HUG middle-income investors are hard pressed to
find or get from other types of SRI. Even once found, such investments
can be challenging to understand and, often, too risky. Compared to simply
volunteering or donating to an organization with the same sustainability
objectives as the investment, all the trouble of impact investing may not
seem worth the effort.

As a result, and despite the promise of a great a big HUG, this type of
high-impact investments have seen only modest growth from $41 billion
in 1995 to around $64 billion in 2014, with over half being in community
credit unions of one type or another.

New Wave Impact Investors, not as HUGable?

Where the real "impact" investment growth has taken place, perhaps ironically, perhaps sadly, is in funds sponsored by what many view as the villains
of finance, aka the Goldman Sachs, Blackwaters, and Morgan Stanleys of
the world.

Whatever your view, large institution "impact" investment can be good.
Take the Goldman Sachs Urban Investment Group. Sourcing capital mostly
from institutions and high-net-worth individuals, the fund invests $5 bil-
lion in a variety of urban development and revitalization projects: affordable
housing construction, job creation, quality education, health care facilities,
small businesses.

More accessible to individual investors are the growing number of
impact investment exchange-traded funds (ETFs). State Street, a large financial services firm, offers exchange-traded funds like the SPDR Gender
Diversity ETF, based on the (correct!) idea that companies with greater
"gender intelligence" are more successful in business and in advancing both
women and men. Morgan Stanley Capital International has several environmental and social ETFs, including low-carbon and sustainability index
funds.

The entry of mainstream financial companies into SRI has led to the rapid growth of impact investment, from $132 billion in 2010 to $224 billion in 2014. Getting a big cocktail party HUG from this New Wave Impact Investing (NWII) remains a challenging, however, despite its mostly alternative investment ancestry. And for many of us old guard SRI types, these funds look more like the carefully towseled looks of bad boy and girl models than the alternative, high-impact, more-akin-to-hippy looking investments that came before them.

Maybe it's because many NWII funds are too aggressive about profit. Or maybe it just seems too easy for them, what with their huge, established client bases, seemingly unlimited business development funds, and pools of incredibly talented employees. Or it may be just jealousy, watching them ride the SRI wave my friends and colleagues worked for decades to create.

Unfair? Maybe. But while I applaud the NWIIs and their leaders and look forward to their positive impact, I won't yet cheerlead for institutions that still finance so much nasty. We can't let them "arbitrage" the big load of bad they invest in with the still very little bit of good they do too. When they meet the standards of high-impact investment saint Shari Berenbach, the universally loved, now departed former director at the Calvert Foundation, then we'll talk.

It's Your Turn

It may seem like I'm a bit down on the overall impact of SRI. At certain times of the day I am.

It's not because SRI hasn't been successful, or because it hasn't addressed all the issues we sustainability freaks hold dear. It's because millions of sustainability believers have yet to vote with their money what is in their hearts and minds: to do the right thing!

Cliché? Yes, and I know it. But that's the nut of it, and what more does SRI have to do to convince you? Dollar by dollar, SRI professionals have already dedicated their lives to amassing and amazing $6.7 trillion in SRI assets. They have doggedly pursued critical corporate sustainability activist campaigns, pioneered alternative high-impact investing, and are now sharpening the impact investment spear. All this while proving SRI can be competitively profitable.

Supply has done enough. We need more demand. We need You.

So, let's get you off the proverbial couch and invest.

What you learned in this chapter

- Sustainable and responsible investment (SRI) has had many names over the course of its 259-year history, from ethical investment to social investment.

- Modern SRI began in earnest in the late 1970s, dominated by a few issues like tobacco and South Africa. These issues provided a platform for numerous other social, environmental, and economic issues to enter SRI portfolios, from climate change, coal, and oil divestment, to alternative investments.

- New Wave Impact Investment emerged recently, to focus on proactive investments.

- High-impact investments (once known as alternative investments) offer the most SRI HUGs (huge uncomplicated gratification) but are the most difficult for average investors to find and invest in. HUG investments connect investors directly to their sustainability passions and are very popular as a result.

- Negative- and positive-screened funds, best-of-sector approaches, and shareholder activism have dominated SRI since the mid-1980s.

- Dollar by dollar, *supply* has done amazing work in attracting over $6.7 trillion in SRI assets. Now it's your turn to set the SRI industry alight with energy and assets!

CHAPTER THREE

Your Economic You and How You Invest

INHERITED FROM FAMILY, handed down from past lives, accumulated through life experience and absorbed from energy around us — however we choose to describe it, we all have an **Economic Being** that controls and conditions our saving and spending habits. Understanding your own economic being is critical to managing your financial future and to setting happy sustainability and investment goals.

From Darkness to Light

I learned the lessons of **Economic Being** some fifteen years ago, when I had had about enough of the financial insecurity that plagued my soul and haunted my every Starbucks coffee. For the sake of my health, and that of my family who suffered disproportionally from my irrational reactions to money, I had to change. The day I freaked out about buying my five-year-old boy a bag of chips was the day I decided money fears and worries had to go.

My first approach was to pull out my hard-assed hockey guy — I started ignoring financial worries, mentally strong-arming them into a corner. This worked about as well as you can imagine. I continued to make, spend, and invest, but I hardly managed my money worries. Fortunately, my wife Tonia had all things financial well in hand.

Later, when our family was going through a bit of financial turbulence, I lost it again when my kids, being kids, slabbed the peanut butter and jam on their toast like the stuff came from a bottomless well instead of seven-dollar jars that would have to be replaced. This made me realize that burying my fears was a poor strategy. Instead of denying my thoughts and feelings (yeah! I said it boys, feelings), I decided to think about why money made me uncomfortable, unhappy even, and how I could have a healthier attitude toward it — and wealth.

After some time, I found that the many of the feelings I had were *inherited*. I started calling this my **Economic DNA**. You know, how your mom and dad, even your grandparents, spent, saved, or invested money and how that rubs off on to you.

I started to think about my grandmother. Nanny lived a long life, through two world wars, the Depression, a long retirement on a small, fixed income, and too many years without a Super Bowl for the Giants. She never spared to treat or spoil us, but she definitively knew how to spread the jam on thin.

Waste not, want not; a penny saved is a penny earned. The financial wisdom of our elders doesn't go unnoticed. We soak it up as naturally as we absorb their organizational habits, political preferences, and sports teams.

Other feelings, I discovered, came directly from *my state of personal development* — where I had progressed in my physiological and spiritual life journey. Mid-life crisis sports cars or three-thousand-dollar handbags are emblematic of this. I started to call this my **Economic Ego**.

Still other feelings came from more practical sources and worries, like how to pay all our bills, save for our kids' futures AND think of one day having a happy retirement. The way I went about managing all this stuff, I labelled my **Economic Logic.**

You might think Economic Logic would be the easiest of the three to understand and deal with. But this is the most troublesome bit of our Economic Being. Sure, it's helpful to have sound Economic Logic, and we all feel good making a practical economic decision. But Economic Logic is boring. It's dull. It also always seems to be getting in the way of things we like to do. Economic Logic often makes us feel roped into a discipline of budgets, of spending wisely. Who really likes that?

From a healthy life perspective, Economic Logic is totally inadequate as a foundational principle, even if it is something financial planners will coax us into believing. Logic is hardly the thing that moves us. Logic, or what passes as logic, often gets in the way of understanding what we want as consumers and investors. Worse, because few of us are all that logical about money anyway, Economic Logic often makes us feel unhappy, and we deny it as a matter of course.

Fortunately, because of my career as a financial professional and in the economics arts of sustainability, I had some tools to investigate these companions: my Economic DNA, Ego, and Logic. What I learned was that my financial fears were not fully founded upon any rational reasons, and any benefit I derived from them was far outweighed by the worry they caused and the affects they had on my relationships, my health, and, ironically, my material wealth.

Everyone's economic being is different, and I won't go into the torturous tale of how I tackled my unique combination of these fellows, except to say that it made me the financial animal I was, and am. You may need to confront these guys at some point, or you may not. If it's something that interests you, go to my website and learn more about it. The rest of the book, note and beware, deals mostly with Logic, but I don't want you to forget the other aspects of your Economic Being. For how you *feel* about money can unnecessarily get in the way of wise and sustainable investments. It also can help guide you. So when you are engaged in financial and investment "thinkery," reflect on these three fellows, DNA, Ego, and Logic; knowing them better will help you come to terms with much of how you see your financial world.

Tales of Two Cohorts

Now, I wouldn't go so far to say your own nanny affected your Economic Being, although inevitably she did one way or another. But I will say with certainty that your age and your lived experiences have influenced your spending and investment habits. They have also conditioned your desire for a more sustainable world.

There are other important reasons to consider your age in financial planning and investment, but this is the dry kibble of investment, technical stuff that hardly explains what you will invest in and why. To understand this, a little generational navel gazing is in order.

A Note to Baby Boomers: You all got accustomed to being the center of attention, and I am sorry you don't have your own section in *ILYGAD*. That doesn't mean the tools in the book don't apply to you. And besides, we know you are the first Youth Generation, so you can play along with the Gen X crowd all you want!

Generation X and Millennials — Most to Gain, Most to Lose

The two generations with the immediate investment power to change the world are Gen Xers and Millennials. There is no definitive start or end to these or any generation, but the consensus view is that Gen Xers were born in the early/mid 1960s to the late 1970s, and Millennials from the late 1970s to early 2000s.

These dates are debatable, as are the Big Events that influenced, encouraged, tainted, guided, or otherwise shaped the values and outlooks for both generations. But dating and characterizing generations is a handy way of identifying the things that affected our values and our Economic Beings.

Many Big Events are singular moments, like 9/11 or the 2008 stock market meltdown. Others are longer lived, such as the long and ponderous collective realization of the impending peril of climate change or the sneaky, invidious social and economic disruptions wrought by technological change. Both the Eureka! and the slow-to-boil-frog-in-water types of realizations have substantial conscious and subconscious effects on how we see the world and how we behave as spenders and investors.

> *Open your arms to change, but don't let go of your values.*
>
> — Dalai Lama

Granted, Big Events are sifted through myriad filters — what your education tells you, how your friends and colleagues see things, or your spiritual beliefs. But there are clear *generational values* shaping events. Some are subtle, sharpening your existing worldview, while others are dramatic. Fast or slow, both cause you to act on your beliefs.

If you believe in, or have sympathy toward, ending poverty, the fire in a Bangladesh textile sweat shop killing 112, and the not-long-after collapse of another killing 1,134, made you buy clothes differently or make new types of investment decisions. Such Big Events may not cause you to change your values, but individually or in aggregate, they often help close the gap between what you believe you ought to do for sustainability and what you actually do.

> *In matters of style, swim with the current; in matters of principle, stand like a rock.*
>
> — Thomas Jefferson

It doesn't take too long to identify influential events shaping our sustainability values and our economic and financial decision making. The Internet is chock full of such lists. We may not agree on all the key events or the degree to which they defined an age, but some simply jump to mind, like 9/11 or the Exxon Valdez and Deep Water Horizon oil spills.

Not all events impact everyone the same way either, but it's hard not to see how Big Events serve as references points for our emotions and desires related to sustainability — or the social, economic, and environmental values we hold dear.

Generation X — Economically Battered Recyclers

Gen Xers are older, have lived through many diverse Big Events, and have seen a lot of political, social, and environmental change. The figure below shows that many of our "sustainability" values were influenced around key political and social events, especially multiple recessions, the tumultuous end of the Berlin Wall, and the downing of the Twin Towers. We had our resonant environmental moments too, but like the Exxon Valdez oil spill in Alaska, these were often more local than systemic. We learned to recycle, where Millennials must confront the life-as-we-know-it impending doom of climate change.

It's not that we Gen Xers haven't met global environmental issues head on. Many *ILYGAD* Gen Xers pointed to ozone, for example. That was a global environmental challenge our generation stared down and won. Right? Yes, but it's small fry when you think about. It's fix pretty much amounted to banning hair spray and underarm deodorant. It certainly

Big Events Influencing Gen Xers

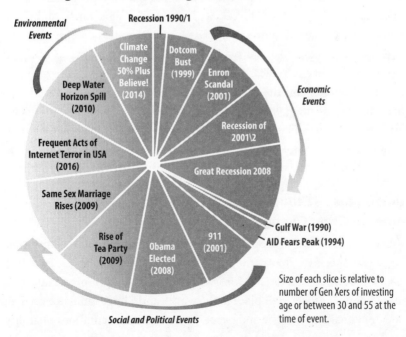

Size of each slice is relative to number of Gen Xers of investing age or between 30 and 55 at the time of event.

Social and Political Events

helped that we could see satellite photos of the "hole" growing and then receding, and that there were only a few economic actors affected. Climate change, by contrast, threatens the very nature of how we live and not just a few intractable, some would say vile, vested interests.

Ozone may not count as a Gen X Big Event, but it was a lived "sustainability" experience that helped shape our sustainability edges — which I must admit seemed a bit eroded by time, kids, careers, aging parents, aging ourselves, and so many other events large and small.

We Gen Xers are also more "set" in our social and financial ways. How many life-altering economic downturns have we seen? How many "fortunes" big and small have we seen flare up or down in stock market flames? This is good for our investment outlook, as we have seen the market come back multiple times. We have also seen enough corporate malfeasance (do you ever get tired of that word to describe willfully horrid corporate misdoings?) to know that good companies that act less terribly do better financially. We saw Nike rebound from horrible child labor scandals in the mid-1990s to become the sustainability icon it is today.

Then there have been multiple moments of political elation and depression: Obama then Trump — wow! — and perhaps more importantly, the intractable Tea Party opposition to anything on the progressive liberal agenda. Yet despite these forces, we have seen great advances in human rights around issues of same-sex marriage, LGBT, and, of course, race.

Most of us have lost the psychological plasticity of our youth, and with it, our ability to radically change our behavior (along with good vision, tight bellies, and the capacity to chill). We have a lot of that "been there done that" mentality. We change our behavior less easily, just as external-to-our-immediate-lives types of change have less influence on us as we age.[5] Yet enough of us relate quite strongly to these "sustainability-enabling" events that investing more sustainably is a real, deeply felt option.

Millennials — Economically Battered in Times of Great Change

Millennials have seen proportionally more environmental events than Gen Xers. This is not to say they are less influenced by social and political events. Not at all. Terrorism, for example, has had a gripping impact on how Millennials view their place in the world, and a huge influence on their views of equality, of justice and peace, and of environmental sustainability.

I would also argue that for most Gen Xers, environmental sustainability started with, and is still pretty much about, recycling. For Millennials, it's more about the impending and catastrophic doom of systemic climate change.

If the world is to not to collide with environmental global calamity, then we must necessarily transition to a low-carbon economy. This will happen by design or disaster, and Millennials will have to live through the change. The facade of sustainable global growth economics is melting down into the collective Millennial consciousness, making its mark in coal divestment campaigns, rooftop solar panels, and other, albeit not-yet-game-changing economic behaviors.

From a social perspective, Millennials' main influences have steered them toward greater acceptance and integration. Race, gender, and sexual orientation are hot issues and have seen the most and mostly positive change. Yet it is on these issues that the U.S. has had to learn and relearn painful and often tragic lessons. And even though women make up 40% of the workforce and the country will very soon not be majority white, there are relatively few ways to invest in the advancement of these critical social and economic equality issues.[6]

Politically, Millennials have demonstrated the will to disrupt, but living under the specter of terrorism on domestic soil has tainted their views, notably of globalization. This seems unlikely to affect the course of global economic development but may cause some to invest more at home than abroad.

Two other economic events bear heavily on Millennials, one found in the figure on page 34 and one not.

The first is the Great Recession. The unhappy coalescence of Wall Street avarice and poor regulation that caused the American banking system to nearly collapse was economically traumatic for Millennials. Even though it seems to have had little impact on Millennials' long-term economic prospects, this Big Event hit when most Millennials were just gaining economic independence, and it had a profound effect on how they spend, save, and invest.

If the Great Recession was a bomb that suddenly exploded, the second Big Event is one of endless water torture: student debt. Who could imagine the very thing that is supposed to bring you advantage becoming a millstone to your economic progress? Now at a staggering $1.3 trillion, or

Big Events Influencing Millennials

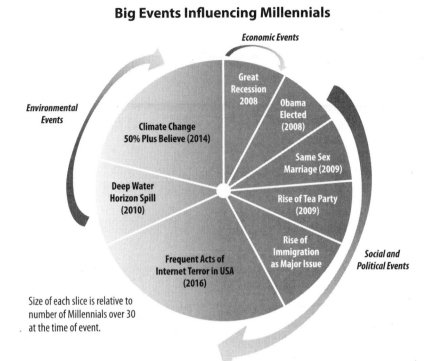

Size of each slice is relative to
number of Millennials over 30
at the time of event.

just less than 10% of the American annual gross domestic product, student debt has a simple effect on most families: It's the difference between saving and not saving. Education, it seems, has become nothing more than an economic life jacket in a growing flood of bad news: enough to keep you afloat, but the water is still rising.

Debt that high is incredible and threatens income and social equality in the future — issues highly relevant to sustainability investors. At the personal level, student loans are an indescribable irritant for too many Millennials and are at the front of the Millennial financial worldview impact queue… maybe even ahead of the Great Recession (which is proving to be more like a badly stubbed economic toe than a true drag on their financial prospects).

Generational Events Affect Financial & Sustainability Investment Planning

Understanding the generational events shaping our values and their effects on financial decision making is imprecise. I admit it.

Why even try to mush it all into a simple packet?

As much as we may want to deny, like most animals, our instincts herd us to common behaviors defined as "conventional." Big Events change how we interact with the economy and shape our Economic Beings.

Because lived experiences matter so much for our financial habits and sustainability values, the next two chapters look more deeply into the characteristics of Gen Xers and Millennials.

What you learned in this chapter

- Your economic being — the financial lessons handed down in families through the generations, your present mental and spiritual state of mind, and the nature of your financial management skills — deeply influence how you direct your finances and investments.

- Gen Xers and Millennials control immense financial assets in this "do or die" moment for sustainable global production and consumption.

- Gen Xers have been shaped by many economic, social, and political "Big Events," are closer to retirement, and more set in their ways. We are still more "recyclers" than systemic agents of change, but there is hope!

- Millennials have been traumatized by two major economic factors — the Great Recession and student debt — as they started their lives of independence, and they understand that climate change will profoundly affect the quality of their lives if not remedied.

Chapter Four

Gen X Investment Readiness and Context

T HE SECOND most entertaining thing demographers get to do is to name generations, and one of the most controversial is to put dates to them.

It might also be true that being exact in this respect is more of an interesting exercise than a game of true importance. A year or two years one way or the other is not going to affect most of the generalizations made about generations (which, by the way, is the first most entertaining thing demographers get to do).

Thus we can say with as much uncertainty as certainty that those of Generation X, the post-Boomer generation, were born exactly somewhere between 1960 and the late 1970s, or thereabouts. That settled, we can also say that there are some 80 million or so Gen Xers in America.

Gen X — Shaped in Our Youth

By generational standards Gen X is large, second only to the Boomers, and all that can be said about it has been said many times before. It's a generation that never fought a major war. It enjoyed free, quality public education. Children of the Boomers, we publicly questioned, even dared to protest for and against, Big Things that Count: war, the environment, atomic weapons, health care, and poverty, among other "sustainability" issues.

But unlike some of our hippy-dippy parents, we turned the great "what is the world coming to" question into the navel-gazing art of a very personal "existential preoccupation," leading to an all-encompassing, almost permanent state of social, financial, and sexual angst.

Middle- and upper-class kids of this generation experienced something novel that would shape our futures: mothers working full-time outside the home. Nothing novel for lower-income kids but entirely so for the rest.

We were "latchkey kids," with all the social and economic implication that went with it.

Perhaps because of this, we seemed to become independent more quickly than kids in earlier generations. Independence before the Internet led us to be more autodidactic. More than just learning things, we also learned to lead, or at least learned that we could lead if we chose to do so. In some respects, this was great. But it had some down sides, as we are also known as the "I can do it all / take care of it all myself" generation, when clearly, there are many things we can't manage to do ourselves.

This sentiment, along with an unspoken sense of entitlement, an ethos that we could be whatever we wanted to be, had a great effect on how we shaped our lives. It didn't help that divorce became common. For the first time in history, parents were fallible, unreliable. Our inclination to respect authority declined, as independence was either forced or gained earlier in life than ever.

More money coming into Gen X families assuaged our angst but also created lifestyle expectations we carried into adulthood, expectations we struggle to meet and continue to measure against the success of Mom and Dad. Freudian silly, but *a* material benchmark nonetheless.

Being highly educated only added fuel to the fires of our career and material expectations. We wanted to be something different, bigger, bolder, better. Our leadership and creativity shook the very foundations of entertainment, technology, and business. One after another, MTV, cable television, and the Internet dramatically expanded our exposure to people, events, and ideas beyond our immediate local experience. From a two- to a four-dimensional existence, Black and Latino music opened our eyes to the deeply rooted cultural experiences of others living in the midst, of a white dominated culture, and in the vast world around us. We found out that we were myopic, a discovery that scared some and excited others. National Geographic TV, travel shows, business programs, cable news ... the world was our ever-expanding oyster, personally and commercially.

Small and large business models changed almost yearly, as single-send fax machines morphed into automated multi-destination faxes, email, group email, the Internet, and then the eCloud. Who can forget the anxiously hopeful mating call of the fax machine lost in the crackling emptiness of ... then the miraculous beep, beep .... How life-altering was that?

Gen Xers grew up in the post-integration era. Exposed to diverse cultural experiences, we are somewhat more accepting of diversity, even embracing it. We didn't drive the civil rights movement, but we were first on the integrated public school buses. Inter-racial barriers were breaking down as we matured, even as many remain to cast shadows on how we treat each other to this day.

We grew to have a generational mistrust of organizations and politicians, questioning once inviolate institutions. A generation of cynics, we saw public and private institutions and their leaders as a mass of incompetent and conspiratorial asses. Nixon's Watergate, Three Mile Island, Bhopal, the Iranian hostage crisis, Iran–Contra, and the Clinton–Lewinsky debacles are the Post-it notes of our lived history.

Curiously, and unlike the Boomers before us, the media struggled to define Gen X, portraying us (as Time magazine did) as unfocused twenty-somethings, the *Friends* generation, self-involved and aimless but fun — this in a time when HIV affected over one million Americans and many millions more in other countries. According to the annals of the day, we were apathetic "slackers" who simply didn't want to become adults. Bleak, cynical, and disaffected, we faced crazy-fast change in technology, medicine, cultural openness, recessions, and the splintering of "family values."

How soon we confuse the stuff of change with the condition of youth. In 1997, *Time* reconsidered Gen X. Instead of layabouts, we became the Astoundingly Accomplishment Generation. We founded unimaginable technology start-ups and small businesses, while exponentially expanding scientific horizons in genetics and biotech. We created new forms of art, music, and literature. Our optimism finally surfaced and the once-deplored Generation X became the "Great Generation." We braved traumatic social and economic soul searching, and through hard work and optimism reversed our dismal reputation.

Gen X is now known as strongly individualistic, independent, and skeptical of authority, with dash of antiestablishment spicing. Self-starting, self-sufficient, pragmatic, results-driven, but still — ultimately, and perhaps surprisingly to ourselves — quite conventional. Mortgage, kids, corporate job.

Gen X changed the way the world operated but unfortunately without substantially altering the overall balance of negative social and environmental impacts. We see how we want the world to be, but we just can't get past ourselves and our attachments to make the necessary lifestyle changes.

Many Gen Xers do want a sustainable world but are not sure how to go about doing it in our lives, despite our incredible capacity to create, invent, and change. Like a colleague of mine once told me, "I go to Home Depot to get one or two things I need and end up buying half the store — environment, locally owned stores, and workers' rights in China be damned." And he is a professor for sustainable development!

We Gen Xers have made many major contributions to sustainability nonetheless, ones not recognized often enough. We were the first generation to question the value of time, and, unlike generations before us, developed a vague feeling that too much work, too much chasing money for material advancement, did not a healthy and sustainable life make. New agey lifestyle vogue resulted, but we have still largely failed to change our ways, to the detriment of the planet.

Gen X and Economics

Many of us Gen Xers remember Black Monday, or November 19, 1987, the day the New York Stock Exchange Dow Jones Industrial Average fell 508 points or 22.6% (this compared to the much slower March 2008 to February 2009 38% meltdown). Soon after, in the early 1990s, just as Gen Xers were hitting the workforce, a dark eight-month-long recession struck. Eight years later, the Dot.com Boom burst as a precursor to another eight-month recession, just as Gen Xers were buying our first homes, starting to save, and beginning families. And when our thoughts finally began to look forward, Bam! The Great Recession of 2008.

Generation X has been hit by multiple, traumatizing economic disasters. Skeptical about the stability of our economic futures, we were also treated to a buffet of corporate malfeasance (see, you don't get tired of that word, do you!!) from the folks that gave us the Savings and Loans Crisis in the 1980s, Nike and child labor in the 1990s, the lying and cheating of Enron and MCI/WorldCom at the turn of the century, and myriad other bad things done by companies that salted our economic cynicism with great douses of distrust.

While Gen Xers have largely realized our dreams of surpassing our Boomer parents' lifestyles, many suffered years of low incomes. This had a big impact on household formation and savings rates. Many of us lived together in group houses. (That's how my wife and I saved for our first home — thanks Darrell, Patrick, and Duncan!)

It took a while for us to get on our feet. But we did, and by 2005 the average Gen Xer had finally surpassed the average Boomer income level. This is the lesser point to recognize. For us, as for our Boomers predecessors, growing material affluence was the norm, more so than for any other past generation.

There have been many explanations for our supposed economic savvy. Among them is job mobility. Freer from convention and highly creative, Gen Xers were first criticized for our lack of career focus and a perceived crass disloyalty to our employers. Turns out, we were merely creating a new labor mobility model that turned to be good for (some) workers and the economy in general, as we started doing more of what we loved.

Gen Xers also pioneered lifestyle advances in work, from flexible work arrangements to in-house child care, continuing education, personal health, addressing overwork, and adult-care responsibilities. Women become more assertive, and while they quite unfairly earn less than men to this day, have still accumulated great wealth along the way. Indeed, women emerged in the 1990s as a client category for investment advisers. Many believe that the economic advance of Gen X is less a result of our inherent qualities than simply having more women in the workforce.[7]

> So many people spend their health gaining wealth, and then
> have to spend their wealth to regain their health.
> — Jackie Mason

Despite our work ethic and inheritances from Boomer parents, our vision of a life of balance and creativity driven by careers of passion has largely and sadly fizzled in execution. Today we work just as hard, maybe harder than our parents

It cannot help that we have material expectations beyond that of any other generation, even possibly that of Millennials. While we are decent at saving, we likely haven't saved enough to maintain our desired lifestyle into retirement, yet this is the goal of almost all Gen Xers.

Gen X is a big bold generation that really has changed the world. Our expectations are high, and we worked hard only to consume too much, with great personal and sustainability opportunity costs. Traumatized by a stream of great big Bad Economic Events, plus our loose spending habits, our investment portfolios are not what they might have been, and certainly need help, both to match our retirement and savings needs and our hopes for a more sustainable future for our kids and grandkids.

What you learned in this chapter

- Gen Xers questioned conventional lifestyle but have largely lived a more amped-up work and consumption life than our Boomer parents.
- While not as plugged into change, Gen Xers were responsible for introducing massive cultural, technological, and business transformation, ushering in a period of incredible wealth creation.
- Gen Xers have lived through many Big Events political and social; they know climate change but remain recyclers at heart.
- Along with Boomers, Gen Xers stand to influence a great deal of SRI.

CHAPTER FIVE

Millennials Investment Readiness and Context

MILLENNIALS, you are a 70-millionish-strong generation born between the late 1970s and the early 2000s that is just now coming into middle age.[8] Your generation has had many names — Generation Y, Generation Me, the Peter Pan or Boomerang Generation, for constantly moving back into your parents' place after hitting economic barriers that constrain your preferred, some would say exaggerated, lifestyles.

Cynical? Yes, a bit. But like we Gen Xers before you, you have a forever-avoiding-grown-up-things like work, marriage, and a true career brand. Feel free to doubt this characterization, but don't doubt one fact: Millennials will be the most important generation ever in the history of the human species.

Why? It's not *only* because you are one of the largest generations the United States has ever seen. Nor because over 30% or so of you have a four-year bachelor's degree, making you a highly educated generation compared to all those before you.[9] Nor is it because you are the most racially and ethnically diverse U.S. generation. And it is not because you are about 25% of the global workforce today, and will be 75% by 2050.[10] Finally, it's not because you live in an almost perpetual state of connectivity, intuitively understanding technology and how it is shaping the global economy.

These characteristics only frame the possible. What will make Millennials great (or not) will be your ability to grasp, and then systemically act on, the planet's looming sustainability disaster. The financial decisions you make will not only be critical for your families but for the entire world: How you consume and produce will determine whether the world becomes sustainable by design or by disaster.

The world is crumpling and heating as we drive madly toward the edge. Generational parkour is required to avoid this mess. Fortunately, generational awareness of our unsustainable demands on the planet is arriving just as you are taking over.[11] Hate to put this on you, but it can neither be avoided nor understated.

The Fate of the World in your Hands

Now, while generalizations about an entire generation is something of a fool's gambit, I hope some insights can be gained by thinking about the stereotypes of your exceptionally important generation. Besides, when has engaging in fool's play stopped the debate about generations, Millennial or otherwise?

So, let us to generalize.

Millennials have been called all sorts of not-so-nice things: lazy, narcissistic, coddled, entitled, even the Generation that Got the Ribbon just for Participating.[12] This, many say, has made you delusional, with unrealistic expectations in life, work, and money. Instant gratification is your thing, according to some. Amazon Prime? Not fast enough. Everything must be now; no, not now, yesterday.

> *When asked to describe who they were [Millennials], one UK Guardian newspaper reader said: "You want me to sum up the main issues facing an entire generation in an entire country? That sounds less scientific than a fucking horoscope, you mad bastards."*[13]

Middle-class Millennials are indubitably the most nurtured of generations. Perhaps overly so, but it did give you a good deal of confidence and optimism, along with great dollops of angst *and* self-esteem.

You can also be so frustratingly unstructured and nonlinear ... maddening to Gen Xers, incomprehensibly infuriating to Boomers. It's just that you Millennials are highly motivated by autonomy, earned or not. You are not clock-watching pencil-pushers either. Nor are you lazy; you understand you will have to work *all the time*. But in return you want to chill, hang out, or take a break when you really "need" it.[14]

Not called Generation Me for nothing, but maybe not for the right reasons. Mills *can* seem self-absorbed with a strong sense of entitlement. But it's not really about all that. Every generation since the Age of Enlightenment has sought to create a different, better life than the generation you followed. Most succeeded, to varying degrees and in different ways. But most also built on the foundations of the previous, Boomers and

Gen X perhaps more so than others. Remember hippies becoming yuppies? But to us it seems you Millennials want to skip over the many, many steps we Gen Xers and the Boomers took to achieve higher levels of responsibility, authority, and income.

> *"Generation Y was raised with a different perspective…. Their Boomer parents taught them that their opinions are important. So, they have an expectation to have a stake in outcomes."*
> — Jamie Gutfreund of the Intelligence Group[15]

This rubs us Gen Xers the wrong way, but we need to remember that many Millennials graduated from university or high school into one of two terrible economic recessions (2001 and 2008). You have also been experimental rats for incredible and extraordinarily rapid technological change during your early life. You spent your formative years living under the pall of terrorism and bitter divisive political partisanship that seems to have intractably divided your elders and the U.S. more generally.[16]

Despite these really horrid life-shaping events, what is so strikingly about you is that, while past generations had new visions of what "life" ought to be, a notable many of you all are just "doing" life differently.

The poster child Millennial wants to live richly. But richly is finally defined as much by enjoyment as money. Life is not *just* hard work that leads to wealth. Flexibility that blurs the line between work and life time is what makes one rich.

Ambitious? That too. But you all don't want to be the 8 am to 6 pm workaholics Gen Xers decried and then became. Gen Xers may have talked the talk, but most of us fell in line. You Millennials don't really seem to want to punch that clock, just as you don't always respect experience, title, office, and age. That's all *nada*. Who you are as a person and how you treat others is all that counts. Refreshing, isn't it!

To understand Millennials, we must look at what facilitates your attitudes. Yours is the first fully "digital generation." If you remember ":\doc…." you are not a Millennial! Computers and tech for Gen X wasn't embedded in who we are. But if you want to guess the age of someone, try to take their phone away and see what happens!

Gen X: Where is my phone?

Gen Y: Don't touch my fucking phone!

Maybe you are a bit delusional, but your marriage with tech and the Internet makes all things seem possible. Post a couple of falling-through-the-ice-on-the-local-pond adventures on YouTube: Boom! Fame! Boom! Fortune! Gen Xers did the exact same thing when young. What did we get? Frozen wet, a cold, and a scolding from Mom.

You were raised on tech, laptops, cell phones, and tablets. Tech changes rapidly: You change rapidly. Tech for you is not just tech. Tech is your operating system. Change is a condition, not an experience, and you hardly notice it. There are no upgrades, just change. This makes you adaptable in a way most Gen Xers can't even grasp.

Interconnectedness makes "down the street" and "around the world" all the same. You share and collaborate as a second nature. Incessant connectivity gives you more than just information, also motivation, admiration, even admonition. It's a full plate of emotions, and from the outside, you seem solitary and collective at the same time.

To the Mills, massive and constant information, biased or otherwise, is your daily grist. Boomers and Gen X still admire the talking heads of CNN or Fox. Not so much Millennials. You listen to social media pundits, pro and amateur, independent voices, alternative media, and more. News and information is democratized and travels freely across continents. Acts of terrorism, natural disasters, celebrity dramas, and political crises can be very personal, and deeply affect your social and economic consciousness in ways Walter Cronkite, Barbara Walters, Wolf Blitzer, or Bill O'Reilly (ewww) never could.

Your information dynamic doesn't just shape just your worldview, it's beginning to shape *the* worldview. Just look at political surveys during the 2016 presidential election and you will see something much more than an entitled generation wondering about its own prospects. It seems like you Millennials disliked uber-Boomer Hillary Clinton almost as much as you hated the racist, bigoted, misogynistic lying Trump. Yet a significant number understood Trump's alter "smash-the-system" ego, and found it appealing enough to vote for him despite (hopefully) having to bite their tongues, cross their fingers, hold their noses, and gag on their breakfasts before pulling the lever. Many more of you simply adored Bernie Sanders, whose stunning lack of policy detail but similar smash-the-system intentions were also incredibly compelling to your wired-for-change mentality.

Millennials are less concerned about structure and often less interested in what other folks think about you. Technology conspired to have you electronically interact from an early age in a way different from all other generations. 9-11 and the constant specter of homeland terrorism and gun violence, on a magnitude only seen in war-torn countries, also makes you different in profound ways. With all this it's no wonder that, while Gen Xers *talked* about living our values, a notable number of Millennials are actually living them.

Gen Xers seem pretty much the same as Boomers, with a touch more awareness of sustainability issues, and for the most part, we have not lived fundamentally different lives from our parents. Millennials, at least the later ones, do. You are not just loosening structures as Gen Xers did, you seem to be rewriting the code for how to live.

This is not to say all is grand in Millennial Land, or that you *all* live life differently. Enough are becoming small-plot farmers, gigging the economy, working part-time on purpose, freelancing, designing different living arrangements, delaying responsibility, etc., to make the rest of us pay attention to alternative ways of living, many with a sustainability orientation.

This should give us all a lot of hope!

How this translates into a clear purpose-driven life, as many Millennial pundits are wont to proclaim, is not entirely clear. Pretty much everybody wants some purpose in life. I am not sure I know what purpose means when it comes to Millennials, though I do know many observers mistake it for a desire to "save the world." Sadly, this is probably not generally true. Rather, Millennials see purpose in life as having a more balanced lifestyle, with more focus on living than work.

We can't equate this to wanting a more sustainable world. Yet your greater openness to new ideas, your youth-centric and civic-minded culture, and your level of connectedness all give you exceptionally strong sustainability sensitivities. Your community extends far beyond the backyards that limited my youth, and many Millennials feel deep empathy towards connections around the world.

Many of the "great social questions" that drive older folk to froth and fury are almost non-issues to Millennials. Gay, lesbian, bisexual, and transgender is not politics but possibilities. New ideas and ways of living don't scare you: That's what life is all about.[17] Millennials are also naturally passionate about community and environmental issues. How can you not be? They are interconnected in more ways than any other previous generation.

Yet to say Millennials have some well-laid plan for making the world sustainable would be the stuff of nonsense. Rather, you want a life well lived and to avoid wasting precious time on things Gen Xers and Boomers did in earnest, often with unsatisfying and inconsequential outcomes. Not sustainable per se, but a good place to start.

Millennial Economics

Millennials were once branded as the twenty-somethings always moving back with their parents. Educated, entitled, and fussy, you would rather live in the basement than take a job you didn't want or think was deserving of you.

This portrait is not quite right.

As a group, you didn't seem to be as in much of a hurry to start independent lives, but then again, most of you came into the work force as the global economy stalled in 2001 or melted down in 2008. It didn't help that the Boomers, only just starting to retire, and Gen Xers had all the good jobs.

In fact, the "we-would-rather-live-at-home-than-get-on-with-life" characterization is a bit of Millennial folklore. Oft-cited statistics of Mills living at home *included* those in college, many of whom were living on campus but kept their parents' address, so the basement-sponging meme is actually the result of higher college attendance![18] Millennials *are* indeed forming households and having children later than any other generation. But like generations before you, who swore to do life differently, the number of Millennials doing just that is enough to notably move demographers' generalization needle.

This attitude seems even-handed, even dispassionate. Take your generational view to formal marriage, which has two distinct parts: emotional and economic. Many Mills are delaying formal marriage, even avoiding common law marriage, and not because you see it as a bad thing; far from it.

Rather Mills are more economically calculating. Many want "sex without hassles" and caretaking duties, and many more simply want the economic benefits of shacking up and companionship as a test of their partner's character.[19] After trial by fire, far more women are choosing to go it alone, with or without kids, trusting themselves over a partner.

Making the formal marriage mistake can be costly both financially and emotionally. One fact arises consistently: More than half of all partnerships,

Millennial or otherwise, end in a financial divorce. This is a generation-defining issue with untold implications on how Millennials can and should do their financial planning and investments. Men fear alimony and child support; women fear financial dependence.[20]

Set within the context of too many Millennials having gone unemployed far too long, and the really depressing pay levels of many entry-level jobs, it's easy to understand late starts and alternative lifestyles. The timing of your "coming of age" couldn't have been worse either, what with thirty years of income stagnation capped by back-to-back economic disasters. The average household wealth doubled between 1983 and 2010, but not for Millennials. Until recently, their wealth was 7% less than their parents' at the same age.[21]

> *Up until very recently, I didn't know that it was only in the 1980s that regular people started using credit cards to get themselves into thousands of pounds of debt. I didn't know that it used to be free to go to university. I didn't know that couples used to be able to live off one person's income while the other partner (albeit a woman, usually) stayed at home to look after the kids. I was born into a world where all grown-ups work long hours, share houses and sofas they haven't paid for and carry on like this is just how the world works. Millennials Are Idiots.*
>
> — Cited by Paris Lees[22]

Pouring salt on the wounds of this economic context, Millennials are also shaped by dramatic levels of student debt, which began to rise precipitously early in the past decade. Today, student debt is over $1.3 trillion in the United States, mostly owed by Millennials. Long-to-recover housing prices are one more wrench in the economic soup of torture.

The fullness of the financial nasty endured by Millennials early in their adulthood, combined with their upbringing and lifestyle vision, leads to a complex story involving values, lifestyle choices, and economic prospects. This is a generation with high, perhaps unrealistic, lifestyle expectations, which leave them with higher-than-average levels of dissatisfaction with earnings.

None other than Janet Yellen, governor of the U.S. Fed, confessed to Congress that Millennial money behavior was something of a mystery, saying, "We're just beginning to understand how the Millennials are behaving. They're certainly waiting longer to buy houses and to get married. They have a lot of student debt. They seem quite worried about housing as an investment. They've had a tough time in the job market. Exactly as the economy strengthens, I expect more of them to form households of their own and buy homes. But we've yet to really see how this is going to affect that generation.[23]

Millennials and Income

The average income of Millennial couples is dramatically lower that the national average, and their disposable income is just a bit more than the incomes of average couples thirty years ago. In 2013, Millennial college grads were earning slightly more than Gen Xers did at the same age ($45,500 in 2013, versus $43,663 in 1995).[24]

Mills may be closing the generational income gap, but with an average of $17,000 in debt, it probably doesn't feel like it. That's over 180% more than the average American of the same age in 1995. It not just a feeling. A Millennial interviewed by the *Guardian* said, "Everything I've made in terms of a pay rise has gone into living and saving. My lifestyle has remained exactly the same. Any dent in employment or income would mean I'd have to go back to sharing [living arrangements] again." Moving up "requires a huge savings effort and a bit of time with baked beans on toast and glamour-free holidays to get your foot in the door."[25]

Economic trauma has had a heavy impact on your financial outlook. Stagnant incomes and fewer jobs give you Mills the feeling you may not be able to make up lost ground. Feelings are important to saving and investing, as we will see later. More tangibly, economic context and desired lifestyle conspired to cause Mills to start saving and investing later in life than other generations. Many Mill *ILYGAD* interviewees, like Rick from Georgia, have only just started to invest, and only then because he joined economic forces to live with his girlfriend; this is the first time he has been able to save.

Millennials feel debt is holding them back. About half of Millennials in a Wells Fargo survey said that more than half of their income goes toward paying off debt, and the same number report living paycheck to paycheck. Many don't or can't save for retirement. Top reasons for not saving: not enough income (84%) and more immediate priorities, like paying debt

(77%).[26] Of this debt, credit cards claim 16%, mortgages 15%, student loans 12%, auto 9%, and medical debt 5%. That's a whopping 57% of income just for debt repayment![27] Some 22% of college-grad Millennials are in such bad shape that they have had to use alternative sources of finance— even the nefarious payday lender, the evil incarnate of the financial sector with fees and rates that can top 150% annually.[28]

No wonder Mills did not seem to be growing up and doing the things adults from previous generations did at certain points in their lives. Lifestyle and late out of the blocks. We need to remember that Boomers and Gen Xers turned out to be exceptional generations for material possessions and set a high bar for Millennials, who are far from lazy and whose economic performance might not be an aberration but a regression back to the historical mean.

Say what you want about intergenerational competition, but perhaps it's not such a bad thing. The whole McMansion culture is overrated and bad for sustainability. Given the plight of Millennials, economist and former consultant to the UK Treasury Diane Coyle wondered whether "we can continue growing the economy in the same way we once have."[29] Many of you ask us, why would we want to?

Experiencing and Saving

Debt, dim employment, and poor income prospects constrain the economic advance of Millennials. Their purpose-driven, life–balance approach to life does not help. Many want to live the good life now and have a penchant for instant gratification, both of which conspire to create a whole new lifestyle term: landmark experiences. This is travel with friends, going to music festivals, enjoying sporting events, attending out-of-town weddings, etc. — regular and *not* inexpensive activities. One survey had an equal number of Millennials saving for vacations as retirement. The rest … put it on the plastic.

Some would call this profligate, reckless financial short-sightedness; some might just say, "Life is short, why not?" Either way, many things young Boomers and Gen Xers had as financial objectives — a first home, a cottage, a boat, a motor home, etc. — are things most Mills just can't see ever affording. But expensive fun things to do are attainable and fit with their Internet-driven gratification impulses. If you can't afford a house, a really nice hotel on the beach helps to make life worth looking forward to.

Despite, or perhaps because of, their economic trials and tribulations, and contrary to their brand, Millennials want to save. Almost paradoxically, some 56% of you report saving 5% of your income over the past few years, not the recommended 10% — but given your debt, damn good nonetheless.

This seems to be a rising trend. About 47% of Millennials had a savings plan in 2014, and more than 60% had emergency funds.[30] Despite this success, 14% of Millennials reported saving nada in 2015, which is 6% more than reported the year before.

> *"The percentage of my income that I save is the only thing I can control," says Adams, summing up the attitude of many of today's young people. "If they're not going to count on Social Security, they understand that they need to save more to reach their goals."*[31]

Thank the gods you save. This, and the fact that enough Millennials are less bought in to the "system" to have created doubt about the conventional way of life, give great hope. Your worldview is arguably better aligned with sustainability ends than the two generations before you. Being savers and alternative lifestyle proponents may make you natural sustainable and responsible investors and offer the world a fighting chance of saving us from ourselves.

What you learned in this chapter

- The fate of the world is in your hands, Millennials. Your saving, spending, and investment habits will decide if global production and consumption will influence systemic sustainability.

- Millennials are just coming of age economically, after suffering through two Big Event recessions in 2001 and 2008. Slowed down by gigantic student loans, this generation is want to save and invest.

- Said to be purpose-driven, Millennials seem to want a good life balance: to live first, work second. This is not exactly a sustainability purpose, but enough Millennials are seeking alternative lifestyles to provide inspiring examples of what is possible and fulfilling.

Part Two

Financial Planning for Investing

CHAPTER SIX

The Who, What, and How of Financial Planning for Investing

S o: Boomer, Gen X, or Millennial (even you, Boomers!), do you know who you are and what you want to do now? In the future?

Think about it. I am sure you know. I am also sure you know why I am asking. Don't go all existential now. I am talking the basics. What do you want to do year in and year out in the near future? What do you see for yourself in retirement? Your family? Kids? (gulp) Grandkids?

But also think about what you want the world to look like. The communities you inhabit, the parks and wild places you want to keep pristine. What are the things you care about, want to preserve, want to see changed?

Think big, large, and long. What do you care about? Then think about what you want your personal and financial legacy to be, and how it could contribute to sustainability, however you may define it.

There is little precedent to guide you in this type of financial, retirement, and estate planning. That's because most financial advisers care mostly about your financial goals and, more ominously, *The Number*: the exact amount you will need in retirement to give you the lifestyle you desire. (They will say merit or deserve, but that is a BS selling ticket.) On the other hand, new agey-type advice tends toward, "have a vision and it will come true."

By now I assume you know that I am somewhere in between, perhaps a bit more toward *The Number*! But somewhere in between these poles is a realistic dynamic fit that will help you define your needs, your life today and in the future, and contribute to your vision of how the world ought to work.

People can obsess over *The Number* or run from it as fast as they can. Despite my lightly veiled cynicism, it is a useful indicator, even in a world where monetizing everything is having a devastating effect on the values we hold dear. I suspect we all also know in our hearts that a single number does not a livable, wonderful life make, for you, your family, your community, others the world round, or critters large and small.

Only you can make that kind of life. And you want to do this because you care about more than just yourself and your family. But in the back of your mind there is a wee blinking light, a warning signal that scares the crap out of you. It is the "Yes, I do care, but I don't want to go broke caring for the world either" warning light. Some would call it your 1.5-million-year-old neuropsychological blinker that reminds you of scarcity and that your next meal is far from guaranteed.

Fair enough, that's a lot of DNA to overcome, and you should *heed the warning*. It's a good thing. Why? Because it's not easy to invest for your own future and that of coming generations if you're constantly broke.

You Can't Get From Here To There Without a Plan

So, what is the first step to profitable and sustainable investment? Simple: Start financial planning now.

Ha, you say! What about all the new age stuff in Chapter Three, defying my Economic Logic to be happy and all that! Yes! That stands. But now we are going to put all that new age stuff to work, to help you overcome the nastier bits of your Economic DNA, Logic, and Ego, so you can be truly happy (about your investments anyway).

We also have some savings and "unconsuming" things to address. For unlike the Boomers, we Gen Xers and Millennials have proven less willing or able to save today for benefits tomorrow. We use far too much of our money (and credit) to buy things we don't need, things that take up physical and emotional space in our lives and don't ultimately make us happier, all the while frittering away precious investment resources.

Constant streams of corporate promotions and increasingly sly marketing tempt our conscious and sub-conscious alike. Siren calls from the deep to spend and be happy. Resistance is not futile if you have a goal, a plan, and the means to execute it. If you are to be content now and in retirement, and if you are to help save from world from consuming itself to death, save for investments you must.

> *A budget is telling your money where to go instead of wondering where it went.*
>
> — Dave Ramsey

But I don't have to tell you that now, do I? Or do I? I was, to be honest, a bit surprised in the *Invest like You Give a Damn* (*ILYGAD*) interviews by how little control most interviewees admitted having over their budgeting and financial resources. We all know a financial plan is a good thing, and I am always shocked when people, well, don't. Don't plan, that is. I am disproportionally shocked when clearly bright folks don't plan. But most of us don't have a plan. For the few of us that do, we don't follow it very well, or even at all. I know that sin!

Still, many of us have "overblown" opinions of our financial decision making and planning capabilities. Some 74% of Americans surveyed had a "great deal of confidence in themselves" as financial planners, yet the average American had saved less than $35k for retirement![32]

Almost all the folks I talked to for *ILYGAD* admitted to near total failure when it came to getting organized, planning, or monitoring their investments. It seems the "organize" part of that chain of events was the hardest part, "Where are those damn documents" being the most common refrain.

Some of my interviewees thought they had good excuses. Most didn't. Many claimed having the "401(k) sign-up-and-forget-about-it syndrome." Fair enough, and for some, this seems a fine way to invest; and maybe it is. But this approach hardly excuses you from financial planning — spending and saving — to maximize your financial future. This is important because your investments are not about how you plan to live in the future but how you and the rest of us on the planet will be able to live in the future.

The distinction demands active attention. It will take some time too, but maybe not as much time as you are groaning about in your head as you read (another project to do???). As I will show you, once organized, being financially fit takes about the same amount of time each year as you might take to buy a new dishwasher or set of tires (both of which, by the way, will likely wear out long before you retire).

Your Financial Front?

As with anything in life, planning is as much about good process as it is anything else. A list of "to dos" I can give you. But unless you are an obsessive-compulsive organizer and have no one else in this world you are responsible to or for, it's unlikely that the planning process will not require some planning itself.

The first step in the process is choosing someone to manage your finances and investments. That person must know your household's financial habits and traits. They are not the existential "Economic Being" we discussed in Chapter Three. Okay, there is a bit of that. But the focus here is on how your Economic Being shows up in day-to-day financial decisions. This is the Financial Front Man or Woman of your Economic Being. (Read Chapter Three if you have no idea what in hell I am talking about.)

What we need to know here is less about what *caused* your Economic Being to become what it is and more about how it shapes the decisions that get you to take money, or not, out of your purse, wallet, backpack, or bank account. That is all about your Financial Front Man or Woman, or the persona you feel as you make financial decisions big or small.

Are you a saver or a spender? Are you oblivious to flows of money through your household? Are you a compulsive bargain hunter? Feel itchy to invest in Malaysian gold mining outfits or prefer U.S. treasuries?

Not sure? Here are four categories, which can help situate You and, if appropriate, your Significant Other (SO), on a continuum to better understand your financial ground game.

Spender? Answer this: Do you find a bargain hard to resist? Do you like the thrill of the purchase, be it for yourself or someone else? Do you spend when you know you shouldn't, especially if you a) know it's beyond your budget and b) are not sure how you will pay for it? No judgement, just answer the questions. Honestly.

> *A bargain is something you can't use at a price you can't resist.*
> — Franklin Jones

Saver? Is savings an end for you? Do you feel anxious spending money and relieved to have not spent it? Do your friends call you out for being cheap (aka conveniently taking a bathroom break when it's your turn to buy a round)? Is going to a ball game or eating at a good restaurant an expense or relaxing fun? Be honest, no judgement; just something you need to know.

Debtor? Not all debt is bad; we know this. A mortgage is a good way to have a great place to live, and hopefully enjoy a little home value equity growth. In this case, debt is like forced savings. But some don't mind paying lots of interest to enjoy things now rather than later.

Do you see debt as an investment? Can you calculate the cost and the return of using debt (both the things it buys and the other intangible benefits like the gratification of sending your kid on a student exchange you can't pay for with cash)?

If you can live with debt, you have Debtor attributes. Please don't confuse this type of Debtor with the "I want things now, debt be damned" type, which we deal with later.

Investor? Do you see some financial and/or valuable intangible return in everything you buy? Or do you see risk everywhere: risk of not getting a return on a great bargain or on a great investment?

Do you hate losing out on a possible return? Do you calculate the odds of receiving the return on every financial decision you make? Does this apply to how you spend money, time, and donations?

If so you are an investor!

These are the most common types of Financial Fronts. Each has different psychological imperatives that need to be addressed, placated, manipulated, and excited to get the plan you need and then to implement it. If you want a financial plan you like and stand a good chance of following, your planner (be it you, your significant other, or an investment professional) needs to consider and apply your Financial Front knowledge for each phase of your financial life (i.e., year in and year out, into the near future, early retirement, and late retirement).

It's not rocket science, but it does require some insights and strategies. That's because whoever your planner is, they will have to know more about you than just *The Number.* (remember that mythical savings number you need to retire on?) They will need to be an educator, decision maker, and honest broker.

Knowing your needs and interests, short and longterm, will help diminish some of the unhelpful noise and nonsense that can surround financial decision making (or non-decision making — as the case may be!), to help interpret and shape achievable financial objectives that make you happy!

These Financial Front types are generalized, and you probably have a bit of each in you. One or two will dominate, and it's good to know which excites and stresses your emotions the most and the least in your financial planning, investment outlook, and decision-making process.

You can figure out how your Financial Front looks by plotting your types on the graph below. Each of the background gray lines represents 2 of 10 possible points, where 10 is the most intense feeling and 0 the least.

Grab a pencil. Meditate and then let your emotions guide you ouija board-like as you plot!

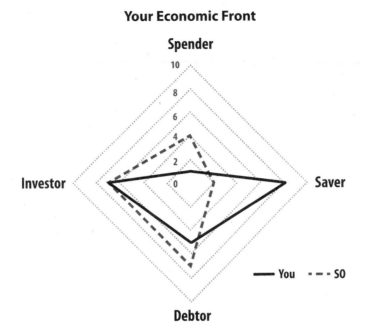

Your Economic Front

Understanding and accepting your significant other's (SOs) type is also very, very, very important. Did I say *very* important? You absolutely must do all the exercises in this book together with your SO. Do not fail your partnership. Do not let your husband say, "Go ahead, honey; you do it." This is the shortest route to disaster, guaranteed.

Plotting the Financial Front together is imperative. Do it non-judgmentally and I promise you will discover important things about both yourself and your SO (and maybe not all financial) that will help you meet your financial and investment goals. Remember to kiss or hold hands during the discussion that ensues! At the end of the discussion, take a selfie of yourselves to celebrate... so cute. (Send me a copy if you want, and I'll put it on *ILYGAD*'s Facebook page).

The Big Things of Financial Planning

With Financial Front sentiment out of the way as far as it ever can be, we can proceed to the next step in financial planning for investment success and saving the world.

This is the part of the chapter you thought you were going to get. You know, the "X" number of secret bullet points to power lift your investment portfolio to unimaginable heights so you can skip happily through life and retirement! Sorry — a few bullet points make for fast reading but are generally useless in financial planning, not to mention an insult to your intelligence. We both know things are not that simple.

I do have a list, but you don't really need to follow *everything*. It's like Captain Barbossa said of the Pirate's Code in the first (*and best*) *Pirates of the Caribbean* movie: "Code? Well… it's more like a guideline"

Also, like any list of this type, my list is not comprehensive. No list of this sort can be, and don't let any adviser tell you otherwise. The nature of prognostication, financial planning, investment, and personalities simply don't permit definitive. If you persist in thinking so, I have some property in Florida to sell you.

Also, these lists — mine or those of others — are, as the Good Captain said, just guidelines. There is simply too much to financial planning to cover all your needs in a book primarily focused investment. But I believe my list is broadstrokes good, and will give you big-picture ideas of what you need to do to get the most money to invest, be happy, and save the world. Plus, if you are like most *ILYGAD* interviewees, you will change and add to the list at will.

1. **Your Financial Core** — Reflect on your current and future earning potential, be realistic, set goals you can meet. It sucks to be realistic, as it can constrain the power of what is possible over what is present. But you need to have a realistic core to your plan before you can jump into your wild financial dream goals.

    We will get to all that crazy presently. In the meantime, the basics will do.

    Based on what you know, calculate for each year of a five- or ten-year period what income you think you can generate, starting with this year. Be as detailed as you want, or go order of magnitude, whatever makes you happy. Appendix One has a list you can use to get started.

    Now do expenses. What does life cost? You can stick to the normal recurring items for now, e.g., housing, food, transport, insurance, education, etc. Or go into minutiae, if that is your thing. Make your estimates realistic, based on extending your current life style into the future and incorporating any change you can anticipate.

It's not about having it all. It's about having what you value most.

— Jean Chatzky

2. **Your Dreams** — The next step is to dream up some goals and then translate them into monetary terms. This is the fun stuff and it's simple (ha!). Take the time you need to dream up a wish list of things you want to *do*, *buy*, or *support* in the future. Ask yourself, where do you want to live in five and ten years? What lifestyle changes do you want for you and/or your family? Do you want to upsize or downsize to a new home? Thinking of buying a small hobby farm? Add a cottage in the back for Mom and Dad? Travel?

Whatever you want, budget for it and see what it looks like on paper. Think beyond the Core. Consider the expense implications but also the personal returns. You may want to limit it to one or two items you want to spend money on, donate to, or invest in this week, this year, and in the next five, ten, fifteen, etc. years. Or you can plan for a wholesale lifestyle change. If you don't visualize and plan for it, achieving it will be much harder.

3. **What is Important?** — Here is where the proverbial rubber and road meet. Separate out each individual dream item and rank them as financial priorities; and please, please do this with your SO! Find out where your Financial Core and Financial Dreams collide or collude. This is where you can decide, based on your Financial Core, what you can live with and without and/or identify the changes you need to get on with meeting your dreams.[33] Shane Yonston of Impact Investors and a First Affirmative Financial Network affiliate suggests that instead of priorities, you might consider "needs, wants, and wishes" instead. Whatever categories you do choose, be realistic about their implications on your current and potential future financial context.

4. **Figure It All Out** — Work off the facts established in steps 1–3 to determine what you will have left over from expenses to invest (i.e., beyond regular expenses, not forgetting taxes), including a rainy-day fund (3 to 6 months of no income). Try to make it a monthly sum, if not annual.

The result of step 4 is……….… a big-strokes household budget for the next ten years! Yep, you did it. Don't get too carried away though, it's just a budget vision. One that will work well enough for the investment planning in the coming chapters, but is still pretty simple, more like a guide: Arrrgh!

> **A Budget:** *An estimate of costs, revenues, and resources over a specified period, reflecting a reading of future financial conditions and goals. One of the most important administrative tools, a budget serves also as a (1) plan of action for achieving quantified objectives, (2) standard for measuring performance, and (3) device for coping with foreseeable adverse situations.* businessdictionary.com

Or

> *Process of allocating money from your weak, skank ass job in order to buy food, pay rent, car payments and insurance and still have enough to buy party supplies.* urbandictionary.com

Division of Financial Management Tasks

One housekeeping process that cannot be avoided is the question of who will be responsible for implementing your financial plans and, ultimately, your investments.

That is, who will make sure your plan doesn't just sit on the shelf? Just as trains need conductors, ticket collectors, and snack bar attendants, your financial plan needs responsible, hands-on-board organizers for accounting and, most importantly, making sure the plan runs on time.

Even if you are alone (i.e., no significant other — SO), you should do this. You need to do it even more if you have an SO. You need to do this even if you want to outsource all or part of the work to a financial planner, accountant, or other service provider. If you want to outsource, check out the bonus chapter at the end of the book. It provides a detailed look at how to choose a financial planner, a process I recommend even if you think you or your SO will be the one doing all the work.

Either way you go, and in the interest of sanity, you are going to have to list all the financial management tasks required by your household. This includes bill and receipt management (e.g., noting receipt of bills, verifying amounts, paying them on time, and keeping a record of them).

Now set up a schedule of financial check-ins. Yep. Meetings. You have to do this or you will be unorganized and rudderless, unless of course you are

Cyber Borg; then feel free to skip the rest of this chapter. I recommend a monthly get-together, but quarterly can work too. Keep the meetings quick and to the point, unless you like to talk about finances, then let it fly where it flies. You can find an example agenda in Appendix Two.

Do this meeting with yourself if you don't have an SO. Seriously, you will like it and benefit from it. Invite a friend if you want company and/or input on your decisions.

At the first meeting, divide all financial management responsibilities between yourself and your SO and/or financial planner according to interest and capacity (or willingness). Don't forget to include investment management and oversight, something we look at in more detail later. If you or your SO don't want to do any or all of your household financial management and you can afford it, outsource the damn stuff.

If you decide only one of you (if in a partnership) wants to be involved in financial management, the regular financial meetings to discuss activities and progress are even more important. There is *nothing* worse, nothing, than you or your SO urgently needing to know what is going on financially in your household and not knowing what to do or where to look for information. Transparency and communication are just good financial management; and both are a two-way responsibility. By the way, I hear they're good for loving relationships as well.

Of course, you don't have to love your financial planner if you delegate the work out, but you do have to keep them accountable to your interests. In fact, liking them too much may be counterproductive for an accountable relationship. How many times have I heard people say, I have an accountant or financial planner, but I never hear from them. That's because they, like you, are busy. And financial planners, like you, like money. So if they can save time by not talking with you, they will. They need to be held accountable.

A friend of mine, Felicity, lost her husband later in life and had to take over the management of her finances, including her investment portfolio. Not easy. But with the help of her daughter, she went through all the steps listed above and learned to manage her finances very well. In the process, she developed a good relationship with her investment adviser, David, who had had a long relationship with her late husband. When David was about to retire, he recommended that Felicity work with Peter, another adviser at his firm, whose average client portfolio was four or five times her own modest $500,000.

Felicity was worried she would not receive the attention she had grown accustomed to with David. So we devised a plan to make sure the new guy stayed on point. We came up with five tricky and very serious investment questions for Peter, and asked him one a month for five months. He got the message that Felicity was on top of things, and soon she was enjoying the same high-level professional relationship with Peter as she had with David. Now she even gets movie tickets and other small perks sent to her every few months, as well as quarterly calls!

The moral of this story, DYI or outsourced: You have to be proactive to manage your affairs well. Regular check-ins with your adviser, yourself and/or your SO are key.

Getting Your Financial Papers Together

Once you've settled the whole who-does-what dance, you need to get all your household financial documents together: accounts, loans, investments, insurance policies, etc., and then put them in a safe place, preferably in their own file folder with papers filed in chronological order (hard or electronic copies) .... Or is that too anal? Maybe, but it works.

TIP: Time to budget for a fireproof safe?

Make sure your SO knows where all the papers are. If you have hard copies, put them in a safe place, preferably somewhere handy in case you need to dash out with them for some reason. You may want to think about a fireproof/waterproof safe. (You can put thumb-drive copies of your electronic files in here, as well as annoying-to-replace documents such as passports, birth certificates, visas, etc.) Save electronic copies in the cloud as well, or, for the more paranoid among us like myself, on an encrypted thumb drive.

Do I have to say share your password(s) and/or combination(s) with your SO? If your kids are grown, it's probably a good thing to share the information with one of them as well. If you don't have an SO or kids you trust (ha!), tell your next of kin, best friend, or whoever you have chosen as your power of attorney and/or the executor of your you-know-what (aka last will and testament). They will need to know where to look for your stuff if Bad Things happen. If you don't have a will, executor, or power of attorney lined up, get that done.

Do it now. Stop reading. What are you waiting for? Go.

What you learned or initiated because of this chapter

- What are your core income and expenses are.

- What is your prioritized "dream" income and expense statement is.

- Why and how to have household financial management meetings.

- What is your household financial management division of labor is.

- You now have your financial documents & passwords in a fireproof and accessible place.

- Your last will and testament, power of attorney, and executor are all organized.

Now feel free to open a bottle of champagne, eat an organic apple, and/ or dance a jig in celebration.

What Do You Need to Retire On?

A STUDY BY GOBankingRates.com found that one in three Americans has nothing saved for retirement. Women are 27% more likely than men to have no retirement savings. The average U.S. household 401(k) account had less than $120,000, and the median was around just $31,000.

No wonder people are in the workforce longer. But then again, life is short, so why golf? It's bad for the environment anyway.

More people are staying healthier longer, taking up fun or low-stress work in stay-active jobs. I saw a story about a woman in Arizona who taught kindergarten until she was into her mid-seventies and then thought to get a real estate license! Me, I want to tend a bar where all the crazy artists and political activists hang out. What do you want to do?

Don't be scared, is what I am saying. The median active age of Americans not struggling with a health issue is around eighty-five. "Retirement," said Ross Slater of Toronto, now in his fifties and looking great, "is when I can't work anymore at something I love. It's going to be a Great Long Slowdown — GLSD — not a final retirement."

Still, for all the freedom that retirement or the GLSD allows, you need to plan. While you are working, your primary goal should be to build wealth. If you work after you retire from full-time work, or shift to part-time work or a career that pays less, your goal ought to be to maintain your wealth.

Many also think wealth is all about *The Number*. You know, the number that the retirement calculator spits out based on some superficial-yet-telling variables. *The Number* is both important, and, as I imply in various parts of the book, not as important as many make it out to be. It is just one indicator of how you choose to organize your life, assets, income, and expense management now and in the future, and not a tail to wag your financial dog.

Sigh....

Now that you are back from checking out *The Number* (again) can we continue?

I truly hope you liked the result. If not, take heart, it's not the end of the world, even if most financial planners suggest as much by the look in their disapproving eyes. As my mom used to say, "Phooey!" How can a number define you, now or in the future? We all have a choice about how we manage our affairs and life, and it's certainly worth more than a number.

Why the cynicism?

Western industrial society is rigged against happiness and sustainability from the get-go. From kindergarten on, we are scared to death by a system (yes, I said it and it feels so good!!) that conditions us to be so afraid of scarcity that we often fail to notice abundance.

Numbers play a big role in scaring us.

The only way to get a great job is to get great grades. Then it's how many extracurricular courses you take to augment your grades. Then it's how much you score on your SAT. Next, the amount you need to make to live the lifestyle you "deserve." Then it's about how much you don't have. Before you know it, *The Number* is staring you straight in the face.

At each step of our economic life, the entire economy and almost every level of government tells us to spend more, or that we don't have enough saved. The financial industry is actively complicit in this and strikes the fear of the gods into us by telling us our lifestyle (which is really just the lifestyle their corporate buddies in other sectors tell us is ours) is at risk if we don't save massive amounts for the life we deserve (which they will happily manage for a fee).

Spend more, save more. What about life? It's not healthy... cue the airsickness bag.

Inevitably, sustainability investment is about numbers too, but it's equally about not about succumbing to numbers. Sustainability is often about the things we can't just put a number on. The value of a pristine lake? Of a safe and vibrant community? Paradoxically, the MasterCard advertisement brilliantly gets this right: Some things *are* priceless.

The Number is not the end game. It's kind of important, but not what is *really* important.

So, what about it?

Conventional wisdom suggests you need an annual income of around 70 to 80% of your current annual income for a secure retirement. This means you will need to save roughly 15 to 20% of your current income (if you start early!).

If that makes sense to you, well, we are done. Thanks for reading this far, skip to Part Three.

Of course, it's not that simple, because as you age, your costs will decline, then possibly increase again. At first you will spend lots travelling, doing projects, visiting, maybe even helping your kids out financially; then you'll start reading more and sitting on the porch as you slow down; then you get frail and then, well, you die. We all do.

My Buddha has sharp elbows, so I say what needs be said: Death is sad, but it's a natural thing. The only thing worse than death itself is being unprepared spiritually or monetarily for it. Death is unavoidable, but preparing for it is not. I can't guide you spiritually, but financially we can do something. And as we talked about before, being financially prepared means knowing how you want to live now, all the way into your meditative years!

How you invest is critical to this vision.

How Much???

In the previous chapter, you visualized the type of life you want now and in retirement. You also calculated your income and expenses, now and into the future. You should have also organized your papers and information flow, including who will manage what.

So how do you get from now to tomorrow and to thirty years from now?

Let's start with the bad news.

One of the two most common retirement planning mistakes Gen Xers make is not saving enough. The other is spending too much! Remember the median 401(k) of $31,000? That may not be you, but if you are like me and in your fifties, it may be "yikes" time.

Millennials can relax a bit more; you have more time and flexibility to get to retirement, save for a home or a sustainable business project, etc. Want to pay off your home quickly? Take a year or two off? These things can be planned for and are not a great big deal in the scheme of things. You can save and plan for being "unconventional" without affecting your retirement goals much — assuming certain income and expense conditions, of course. You may not know exactly what you want to do, but simply knowing you want to do something outside the great humdrum (with commensurate expenses needs and savings goals) between now and the Great Long Slow Down is not enough.

What do I need to be *responsible* to my goals and be sustainable? you might well ask.

A widely accepted rule of thumb is that you can withdraw 4% of your retirement nest egg to live from in your first years of retirement (adjusted for inflation, but don't worry about how that works for now).

That might sound good until you crunch the numbers. 4% of $200,000 is a mere $8,000.[34] Even if you add an average annual Social Security benefit of about $16,000, you're all of $8,000 above the poverty line of about $15,500 per person. Even if you are not a financial geek, you can see that all that lies between you and poverty is your investment portfolio. If you live with a significant other (SO), you can add another Social Security check to the mix, and top out at $41,000 pretax. Not bad, but still not much compared to most, and not enough for most of us, especially the youthful ones.[35]

If we accept a 4% return rate, you would need to have a portfolio of $930,000, combined with Social Security, for two to top out at pretax income of $70,000, or the amount experts say maximizes your happiness. If you are lucky enough to have a pension plan from work, or can stash a bunch of cash away from downscaling your home or selling a second home or property, or have alternative income from rental properties or what not, then you need not have such a large investment portfolio.

If you are young, the world is your oyster. If you start saving only $363 a month, at age 25, and assume a 7% rate of return (the stock market average is about that over the long term), you would have the $930,000 *Happy Number* by the age of 65! Think about it; that's only $12 a day.

Try as I might, I just can pass up on the oh-so-cliché "Just don't drink your daily Starbucks" advice. But it's so true! Don't drink your Starbucks and you are almost halfway to the twelve dollars a day you need to save for a happy retirement.

We make so many little decisions every day that we perceive, psychologically at least, as financially insignificant. The Starbucks example reminds me of my friend Alex. Alex is a hardworking assistant to a state governor. His wife Lulu doesn't work outside the home, and his salary is the sole source of income for the family. Alex's father worked all his life to start and run a successful custom pump-making factory and taught Alex the value of saving and investing. Lulu knows the value of money too and is careful at home — but she has the Starbucks bug, once a day, sometimes twice.

Alex, the gentleman he is, did a bit of research and decided if he bought a modest but good expresso maker, Starbucks coffee beans, and some Starbucks mugs he could replicate the experience for Lulu at half the cost of going to Starbucks. He even got a Starbucks apron and offered to make the coffee when he could. Now, I'm not sure about you, but the savings would be just a bonus to seeing my SO in a Starbucks apron making me coffee most mornings. Ahh! The joys of saving!

Yes! The Number!!!!

It's all so simple, right? So simple, in fact, there is not much more to say about it. You are an adult. Make wise spending choices now, or suffer the consequences later. It's not differential calculus. Don't buy a McMansion. Don't buy a Porsche. Eat healthy. Don't run up the credit cards. Live comfortably and sustainably.

Sermon over. But the question remains: What will you need, given your current and anticipated economic context to save and invest? What is *The Number?*

Cue the (in)famous retirement calculator... [36]

Retirement calculators are online applications in which you pop in some income, life, and inflation expectations and Bam! out pops *The Number,* or the theoretical amount you need to have upon retirement to meet your chosen lifestyle expectations.

Please be cautious. Most of these calculators can scare the crap out of you (and I am sure they are supposed to, as they are offered free by financial planning companies, mutual funds, etc., to get your business).

Many of these calculators are limited because they are one-dimensional. Some can also be deceptively simple, as they are hardly sophisticated enough to do more than provide an order of magnitude guestimate of your future financial needs. Put in a regular savings amount today, under certain assumptions, and learn what your assets will be worth at retirement (or whenever you want to start using your savings).

But calculators don't include much about real-life events that get in the way of or help with your investment goals. These events will happen, and we can't be sure how or when. Major real estate events like downscaling or selling other valuable assets may or may not be on your schedule when you do your calculation. Don't forget inheritances, or the fact that you can save once the kids are gone. Then there are the negative events I am sure you worry about: health issues, job losses, market downturns, etc. A couple of calculators do try to incorporate these types of events into their algorithms, offering multiple income stream options, date specific asset sales, etc., and are worth checking, even if they are a bit complicated to use. See Appendix Three for examples.

Life events affect the calculators' straight-line savings curve. Don't fear the word curve, it's not as puzzling as you think; indeed, it is so simple it took me a month in Economics 101 to learn that a curve can be a straight diagonal line! Calculator asset-appreciation curves are like that, algorithmically straight, though we know life is hardly like that at all. Our ability to save and invest warps positive and negative over time; or, unlike the calculators, actually curves! Your ability to save is usually higher when you are young and lower when you are middle-aged, especially if you have kids. (They can get expensive around 12 or 13 and even more so for a few years after that.)

Flat-line savings assumptions, I can tell you from experience, don't really work. If you are like many Millennials these days, your income curve may also look (quite deliberately) like waves on the shore: some years high, some years low, as you take time out of "conventional" life patterns to explore or mess around. As Ken Jacobs of Sustainable World Financial Advisers and a First Affirmative Financial Network adviser out of Golden Colorado reminds us, this is the moment to recall that "one size financial planning does not fit all! One client will have kids, others won't; one is single, another is married; one wants to retire at 60, another will work much longer; one will pay off her house at 55, another, likely never will. We need to be careful with rules of thumb and examples. With or without the help of a financial planner, people must be prepared to adjust each piece of the financial planning puzzle to their own circumstances."

Calculators are still instructive. The one I like to use is from Bloomberg. It shows that if you invest 11% of a $70,000 pretax income starting at age 25 for ten years ($641 monthly) in a fund that tracks the Dow Jones Industrial Average, and then contributed nothing more for 30 years, your portfolio would be worth over $930,000, assuming a 5% return (or a conservative 2% less than the long-term stock market average of 7%).

An average 5% annual yield on that amount will give you a $37,200 income (pretax). If you add $466 more a month to this portfolio between the ages of 55 and 65, you get another $70,436, topping out at a tidy, you guessed it ... $1M for an estimated average $40,000 pretax annual income. (Again: Figures in current dollars and include only your investment portfolio and no other assets, e.g., real estate.)

Think of it. If you and your SO between you make only $70,000 — less than two combined average Millennial starting salaries of $47,000 — all you need to save is 5.5% of your annual income each to retire with over half of your pretax income! Now that's not just *The Number*, it's the Happy Number!

Wait a minute, Marc! You calculated poorly, surely it's less! No I didn't. Remember you will likely be in lower tax brackets when you retire, so you get to keep more of this income than if you were working! This is the rough equivalent of $70,000 annually!

If you are Millennial, think about saving 11% of your annual income for five years before starting to save for retirement. This would net you around $24,000 or so, just enough in many cities for a down payment on a modest apartment or starter home, a stepping stone to bigger assets or rental income. If you can do this, you should be able to continue to save the same amount without affecting your savings-led lifestyle.

A Word about Social Security

Some of you might have noticed that I included Social Security in my retirement outlook. Is that a smart thing to do, asked *ILYGAD* interviewee Jesse: "I mean after all, who really believes it will be around when I hang up my playing boots?"

This is a good point. The current estimate for when the Social Security fund will run out of funding is around 2035. That's 28 years from now, so for many of us Gen Xers this is less a concern than it will be for the Mills. This estimate assumes no changes to the way money is collected and distributed. A more likely scenario is that sometime before 2035, changes will be made to up the retirement benefit eligibility age, or decrease the amount beneficiaries will get. Some believe, for example, that the current Full Retirement Age of 67 will be increased to 69 or 70 to resolve the system's potential insolvency.

A lot will happen between now and the time you retire. So be smart about Social Security. Read up on it. Decide among the several options available for when you can begin taking it. Delay it, and your checks may be bigger. Take it early, and they could be smaller, only more of them. There are also some other smart strategies to consider as well. A good financial adviser can help maximize the outcomes of your choices.

Most of all, if you don't believe it will be there to help you, save more.

What you learned in this chapter

- The average American simply does not save enough to retire on. Scared yet?
- You will need to save 10 to 20%t of your current income to retire with 70% of that income (depending on market conditions and when you start to save, of course).
- A $70,000-a-year household income is the happy number for most; what is it for you?
- To have $70,000 a year during retirement requires saving $641 per month from age 25 to age 35, and then $366 in savings per month from age 55 to 65 to become a millionaire and retire with an estimated $40,000 to $50,000 annual income (pretax, current dollars).
- You can plan for unconventional income streams and still meet investment goals.

Put your feet up, relax a bit. You deserve it, this was a stressful chapter.

CHAPTER EIGHT

Saving for Retirement and the Grim Reaper

S AVINGS REQUIRES DISCIPLINE. Right? Yuck. But you need savings to invest, and if you don't try to save, you can't invest, so why are you reading?

Okay, yes, we are mostly all bad to various degrees about anything that requires discipline, particularly if some slightly more gratifying alternative is nearby. That's why I recommend that you make *automatic* monthly investments of the amount you found as your goal in the previous chapter.

Do this and you will not miss the lost income, not at all. You will simply adjust your spending. This strategy has been proven to work time and again for all types of people (unless you are a super Spender type; then you may need to think about a spending/credit restriction plan!). If things are tight on a month-to-month basis, contribute the minimum you can afford. As little as $150 a month can help, and will make you feel good to boot. (And if you did this from age 25 to 65, you would get almost a quarter million dollars in savings — assuming historic stock market averages.)

> *Money is a terrible master but an excellent servant.*
> — P.T. Barnum, businessman and showman

What helps even more is to save and invest a significant portion of expected or unexpected lump sums that come your way. Take half of every bonus, the inheritance from long-lost Aunty Joy, the sales of an asset, and invest them. Blow the rest on adventure, experience, the next big Kickstart movie exposing a bad economic thing going on....

Lumpy income streams can be very good for asset building. A friend of mine, Bijan, was trying to decide about whether to continue as a consultant with irregular income or take a full-time job he was being offered. At thirty-nine, he was beginning to worry about asset accumulation for retirement. "If you take a job," I asked him, "do think you can save a chunk of your salary every month, say 20%? If you can, you are gold. If you can't, you may want to consider staying a consultant, where the checks are bigger, if less frequent. This will allow you to make the occasional big stocking of your investment cupboard." For Bijan, it was not either/or but a question of how to meet his family's needs and still save in an appropriate way.

First, know that the best way to build wealth is not just through saving money. It's about saving money *and* investing well. So before you prepare for retirement, it goes without saying that you need to be able to save for retirement. The best way to do this is to start by assessing your expenses and debts.

If you are smart and disciplined about debt, you know it can leverage lots of good things. If you can, only use it to buy a car and/or a home. For the rest, do what Grandma did: save. Old fashioned? Yes, but it's a strategy that will likely make you richer and the world more sustainable. Why? Because if we all waited a bit to spend, we would likely consume less and save the difference!

Waiting and planning can also help you stop compulsive-impulsive buying, which is the equivalent of crack cocaine for the economy and speeding us to environmental ruin. Waiting also dramatically increases the marginal return to your pleasure. (Some of us remember the old catalogue-shopping days when purchases took weeks to arrive. No same-day delivery, but, oh, what joy when the packet finally arrived!)

Okay, that's not so convincing in the face of so much pressure to buy, buy, buy, and gratify, gratify, gratify, but don't let companies tell you otherwise — saving is healthier for you and the planet. Instant gratification, by contrast, is like the last popular Beyoncé song; you know the one. See, you don't, but it was great, the best ever, right up until the next most popular song by someone else knocked her off the chart or you had heard enough of Beyoncé to make you cover your ears and scream in pain when she came on the radio. Nothing personal, Beyoncé; you rock.

Debt, Not Often Your Friend

If you have expensive credit card debt, seriously think about debt consolidation. But don't just do that, snip up your cards too.

I mean it.

If you don't need expensive credit, don't use it. Pay it off with a home equity loan and snip that card up. (Or why not try the classic putting-the-credit-card-on-ice trick, or as I call it, the frozen senate of financial second thought?) You and the world will be better off.

If your debts are more serious, then there are programs (many run by nonprofit organizations) where you can find various forms of debt counsel and relief, everything from debt renegotiation to outright forgiveness.

Don't be proud. Call now. If you need one of these services, do not fall prey to the bad guys of debt relief, you know, the bastards that promise the world and only end up taking your car or house. There are even some "nonprofit" fronts doing this evil trick.

Beyond expensive debt, most of us have some form of what you might call necessary debt for homes and cars. The average American has about $111,000 in home debt. If you are locked into a low rate, you might not want to hurry to pay that off first, but if you can afford it, weekly or occasional lump sum payments will save a ton on interest.

The key is to prioritize debt payments by cost, and above all stop using expensive debt unless you are desperate. Just don't do it! Because the faster you rid yourself of debt the more you can invest, and that is good!

Now, I would never tell you how to live, but if you follow those basics you are not only likely to be financially wise but also sustainability wise. Less stuff makes for a better, less expensive life, helps you retire well and maybe even younger, and is better for a world chewing up resources at four times the natural replacement rate.

I could go on, but you get the pointy parts of my observation. Sustainable living requires thought and discipline. Joe in San Francisco once told me when he was separating from his significant other, "I never knew how much money I really made until the divorce. I was making too much to really bother keeping track of all my expenses. I got sloppy with spending too much and not saving at all. I guess I should have been on top of it and had more purpose in my financial life." His advice now: "Live well; live simply; invest; and share what you don't need with purpose."

I Have Mentioned Death. Now Taxes.

Obviously, a full-blown review of taxes is not something I want to do here. But we all know that managing taxes is important, and doing it well can have a very positive impact on your financial welfare, both before and during retirement.

For most of us, finding out more about taxes is an exercise in fingernail pulling only a masochist would purposely look for: Tax knowledge is truly as horrible as it is boring (except perhaps for Mark in Toronto, who loves to juice an income tax return). It can also be so terrifyingly complex that you are never sure to have gotten it right, even if it is done for you by someone else.

A great tax accountant can do wonders in legally minimizing your taxes and, as important, laying out a tax plan for your future. The cost of good tax advice may hurt today, but often repays itself many times over in the future. This is particularly true if, like many, you have irregular or several sources of income and/or are thinking of a little extended time off at some point in life.

If you do go to an adviser, and want to sound somewhat smart, read this list to them:

- I want to know about my tax loss carry-forwards!
- Is an Alternative Minimum Tax ("AMT") a legal and correct option for me to consider?(I would add ethical option as well.)

Tax-Deferred Income

The most common tax-deferred investment is an individual retirement account (IRA) and deferred annuities. Deferring taxes means you pay them later, usually in retirement when your income is lower and you should thus pay fewer taxes. Money in your tax-deferred accounts grows tax-free, including interest, dividends, capital gains, etc. You also benefit because the money you invest is taken off your income before calculating your taxes, which can lower your tax bill.

The most common tax-deferred vehicles include Traditional and Roth 401(k), 403(b) and 457 Plans, IRA Deductible and Nondeductible, Roth IRA and 525 College Savings Plans. Remember to also check out spousal IRAs.

The current maximum allowable annual individual deferral for 2015–17 for 401(k) is $18,000, and for a SIMPLE 401(k) plan is $12,500. Under certain conditions you can catch up on your maximum allowable limits not made in past years.

Contact the Internal Revenue Authority or your financial adviser for more detailed information. You might need it!

- What about charitable giving and income tax optimization?
- How about transferring income to others in my family?
- Is my home or second home an option for tax deductions?

If you want to sound even smarter, ask about income timing distribution from taxable retirement accounts. Are there advantages to waiting a few years to withdraw money, or is it better to spend more now?

Remember that the general rule of thumb for withdrawing taxable assets is to allow tax-deferred assets to grow first. This still holds but may not fit you and your lifestyle. Depending on your current income and expected retirement income, you could ultimately pay more tax on tax-deferred savings.

Tactically managing your taxes, especially in early retirement, can yield good returns. For example, moving money out of tax-deferred assets at low marginal personal income rates or converting portions of the balance to a Roth fund (like a 401(k) except you pay the tax now, not at the time the funds are withdraw; also called a Roth IRA) can give you better control over the amount of taxes you will pay over the long term. It also can provide some added income and tax flexibility today and in retirement.

These are just *some* considerations; there are many others, and good tax advice and/or study is required to nail all the points that will be relevant to your situation.

What you learned in this chapter

- Saving makes you happier and healthier, and the planet more sustainable!
- Save monthly in addition to your 401(k), using an automatic withdrawal plan.
- Save most of any planned or unexpected large asset sales.
- Save 50% of unexpected lump sums; blow the rest!
- Be debt wise: Pay off expensive debt, but maybe not inexpensive debt.
- Beware of debt consolidation services.
- Have a good tax plan.

Celebrate something today, who knows when the end....

CHAPTER NINE

Gen X Investment

Gen X and Investment: It's All About Retirement

THE YOUNGEST GEN XERS are in their early forties. Yikes! Not that over forty is old; it's not. But some turbulent waters lie ahead ... andropause sporty car urges, menopause emotions, empty nesting, etc. Each one alone can wreak actual and psychological havoc upon even the best-laid plans (but especially those of couples). My advice: Set aside some funds for therapy.

Moving past the existential angst of middle age, investment for Gen Xers is all about retirement. By now, most who will buy a home have done so. Many will have low to no student loans. If you have kids, well, that can be expensive.

But from now on until the Great Long Slowdown (aka retirement or semi- retirement), save and invest you must, because it's now or never. I'll say it again, Gen X is all about retirement.

Having cleared my throat of all the Gen X fun in Chapter Four, we must "buckle down," as my Father used to say, and delve into things conventional.

For direction in this, I look to my mother-in-law for guidance. Rita has travelled the world on a relatively modest retirement fund, despite losing her beloved husband Alvaro, who passed at sixty-six from an unexpected illness. That happens all too often and can have devastating implications for financial planning and retirement.

Not for Al and Rita — they planned well.

Al and Rita emigrated from Hong Kong in the spring of 1968 after troubling riots broke out in the then-British territory. The riots were said to have been instigated by *Little Red Book*-touting, pro-Communist Chinese and anti-British protestors. Chaos reached a peak in July of that year, when hundreds of demonstrators crossed into Hong Kong from China to clash with the Hong Kong Police, leaving some dead and many more injured. Violence, protests, shouting in the streets, and Communist-style graffiti — "Blood for Blood," "Stew the White-Skinned Pig," "Fry the Yellow Running Dogs" — terrified the local population.

Who wouldn't be afraid? With relatives in Vancouver, my in-laws bolted, arriving on the West Coast of Canada in late 1968. Al and Rita had the benefit of family, but their Goan (Portuguese Indian) descent colored their early years. Both had worked at the Hong Kong Shanghai Bank (now HSBC) in Hong Kong, Al as a senior executive and Rita as an administrator. They were used to privileges the very White Canada greeting them simply did not afford the middle class. And, as you can imagine, it wasn't easy for people of color to get work in Canada at that time.

After episodes involving vacuum cleaners that didn't work quite so automatically as the "ladies" magazines promised, Al and Rita settled into a middle-class life in Vancouver. Over the years Al, working as a financial professional at Merrill Lynch, and Rita, as a teacher's assistant, managed to save an incredible amount of money while putting three kids through school and university. They didn't always have much cash, but they knew what they wanted before and during retirement. Paid their mortgage first, insurance second, savings third, and then the rest.

When Al suddenly died, it took Rita some time to recover, but in memory of her husband, she has lived life very well since. With the help of Tonia and her two brothers, Leo and Patrick, Rita organized her finances to meet the way she wanted to live. Lots of travel adventure, a lovely home and a nice car, and money enough to help the kids and grandkids. Straightforward financial saving and planning, but the vision came first. It was a strong vision, one that sustains her financial planning to this very day.

So it must be with us Gen Xers. Financial planning, and yes, I will say it: discipline. I am not saying you need to sacrifice everything today or that being frugal is the goal. Unless of course saving money gets you going; then by all means, get your freak on.

If saving doesn't ring your bell, you can still live fully in the present but with financial wisdom for the future. I mean fully, because you only get one kick at the proverbial life can. (For Millennials bothering to read this bit, I am referring to Kick the Can, a game gangs of Gen X youths once played outside on late summer nights ... hordes of friends running pell-mell across neighborhoods, hiding from and seeking others, and if you were lucky, kissing your sweetheart for the first time behind the rhododendron bushes…. Ahh, but I digress.)

Being fully present, sucking every morsel out of life, requires financial peace of mind. That means understanding who you are and what you want. I won't go again into all the things that make "You" your own special *Economic Being* (your Economic Ego, DNA, and Logic — See Chapter Three), but what I will say is that with a bit of determination you can minimize day-to-day financial worries, or at least feel more comfortable with them while having a successful retirement vision like Rita and Al.

The financial planning process for Gen Xers is different than it is for Millennials. Why? Well to start with, we are older, the best part of which is that we normally invest less emotional energy into… well, pretty much anything, even things that seem bad or negative. Gen Xers didn't coin the phrases "Life is too short" or "Been there, done that" or "I'm too old for this shit," but they often apply to our view of things.

> *"Money, it turned out, was exactly like sex, you thought of nothing else if you didn't have it and thought of other things if you did."*
>
> — James Baldwin

But for many of us, this advantage is offset by the limited time we can give to… well, again, anything. Sure, I could tell you to devote an average of just two hours a month to financial planning and investments, and that would make you richer. You might even do it, because if ever there was something that can help you maximize your investment returns, attention is it. Investment is like a garden in that respect: It likes nurturing.

But face it, if you don't already devote this minimum amount of time, you're not going to just because you are reading this book. Gen Xers are at the peak of life distractions. We are a time bank with capital allocation pressures beyond measure. Never-ending demands of career, ever more complex social and family lives, kids, dogs, neighbors, community volunteering, full-time scared from political and economic cable news, terrorism, choosing universities … and let's not forget the angst about how to enjoy your whole eight minutes of personal time each week. This is not a sandwich on a plate but one where all the ingredients have been thrown up in the air for you to eat before they hit the ground.

While all this may feel true, it's no excuse for not planning and managing now. Fortunately, we Gen Xers are independent and strong-willed, we are the HD — Home Depot — Generation. So let's apply the power of DYI and look at some of the common issues related to Gen X needs, to allow you to live well now, have a great retirement later, and help a make the planet better, for always.

Financing Your Investment

Gen Xers have been good at investing in their 401(k) accounts, not because we necessarily wanted to but because defined pension plans pretty much started going the way of the proverbial dodo in the 1980s.

That meant we had to independently decide how much to contribute to our plans and/or our investment portfolios. We also made the reasonable assumption that Social Security, like one of the five to ten species the planet loses daily, might not be around to help us out in retirement. We are on our own.

Fortunately, what we will need is relatively simple to calculate in order of magnitude terms. Why? Mostly because we can pretty much predict the cash flow needs of the typical retirement. A classic retirement and retirement plan has an expense curve that looks a bit like a double-humped ski hill. At the beginning of retirement, you are on top of the hill looking down. You are fit and full of that just-retired vigor. Your retirement expenses are the highest they will be as you begin down the slope. As you slow down, usually in your late seventies or early eighties, your costs so go down as you swish toward what my porch-sitting expert Great Grandpa Herb did for thirty-five years of retirement: slowing right down!

But as you move toward your last years, your expenses may start to rise (yep, I said it — my Buddhist inclinations cause me to look that one right in the eye). You will get frail, fall ill, and eventually join the chorus in the sky (or however you see the end). This is an age when you could require more help and attention. Costs can increase, and so up the expense curve you go. But expenses are often less than when you are jaunting about Cambodia, Thailand, or even just visiting relatives in Toledo.

How much you need in the final years depends on the nature of your frailty and the quality of care you need. (Make sure you tell the kids or friends in charge what you want!) You will likely also want to consider what you want to leave behind and to whom, including your favorite causes and such.

But this is an idealized ending, one probably made more for financial planners selling annuities than it is for you. You may be aging, but envisioning something different is not a function of age, last I heard.

My advice: Be crazy. Continue working part-time in retirement. Take jobs you've always wanted. If they don't work out, quit. (If you have never quit a job, it's a great feeling, highly recommended.) I want to be a bartender or, if my daughter opens her restaurant, her gruff nice maître d'. Don't give up, or in to age. You are a sustainability warrior. Keep fighting. That said, you can be conservative crazy.... If you are worried about money, there are options to avoid living in penury.

The Big Retirement Moves

Living on a fixed income coming from an investment portfolio that's not going to get much bigger in your retirement, or more commonly starts to shrink, is not something we are used to. An increasing income balance is what we are used to seeing (hopefully) through the course of our lives. A smaller amount every month can be quite scary. I'll return to this theme at the end of this chapter, but for now the single most important thing you can do to manage your investments is to address your expenses as you near, or enter, retirement.

We all know how to address the little expenses in life. Right? The drip, drip, drip of unnecessary consumption is bad for your pocket book and bad for your investment portfolio. Most people also have large, expensive assets that cause financial stress and lost savings opportunity costs. Here I refer to assets that you may not need but keep because they mean something to you.

Now, the first thing most financial planners will tell you is that sentiments have no business in finance and financial planning. Bull.

We buy and keep all sorts of things we don't need simply because we want them. It's common, for example, that people refuse to sell stocks they inherited from their dad, large houses the kids grew up in, cottages that defined summer, or all sorts of other valuable assets because of the memories they cannot let go of. Unfortunately, these assets can quite often be a financial drag, and/or the money from their sale could help improve your investment portfolio and comfort in retirement.

Why am I saying this? Some of the largest cuts to your income or, conversely, your biggest expenses, are often driven by feelings — or more euphemistically, by lifestyle choices. As my urban sociology prof used to like to point out, people are far from the uber-rational *Homo economicus*. He would cite the all-too-common example of how people will buy a house — usually the single most important asset of their lives — based on the color of the front door. Okay, a bit tongue in cheek, but you get the point.

Here's a real example.

Many people have a second home or a time share. Often these assets cost a lot to maintain, and maybe they don't use it that much. Then sell it. Right? Ha! A good friend, Tom, in lives in Toronto, Canada (and is somehow a misdirected Ottawa Senators fan — hockey, that is). Tom and his family co-own a cottage in Northern Ontario, and he would rather see my Toronto Maple Leafs win the Stanley Cup than sell the cottage even if it was costing him an arm and a leg. Keeping the cottage is not a financial decision, so it literally has no value unless he is forced to sell for one reason or another.

It's the same for our home in Mexico. Given globalization, it's unlikely my Mexican-Canadian kids will live in this rambling crazy sustainable delight we call home. Yet it is the foundation of our lives, and we want to leave it as a legacy to them. But rather than burden them with the house, our plan is to leave the kids with seven years' worth of funds dedicated to maintaining the place after we are no longer using it. According to Waldorf education lore — the kids go to a Waldorf school here in Mexico — life evolves in seven seven-year periods, so that should give them enough time to decide what to do with the place.

If you see this in the future for yourself, then plan for it. If not, and things like a cottage, second or third car, motor home, etc. are costing too much, sell 'em. [37]

Similarly, things like weddings, family reunions, and family trips can be five-digit expenses that make huge dents in a savings or retirement budget. If you want to spend on them, go ahead, but plan for them and save extra, particularly if they hit in retirement.

I hate to bring up my Senators-loving buddy Tom again, but damn, he and his partner plan so well. Tom works for a major Canadian university and likes to joke he has "one of the last full defined benefit pension plan jobs in Canada." His life partner also has a job at the same university. Despite the promise of 70% of their salary in retirement, they saved a fair amount. Why? To pay for the crazy five-digit stuff. They plan to blow it on experiences — travel, weddings, etc. — with their family!

Pension Plans

In terms of pension funds, Gen X was the transition generation as companies in the US and Canada shifted from **defined benefit plans** to **defined contribution plans**.

Workers, of course, preferred the former as they provided defined incomes in retirement. Businesses prefer the latter, as it frees them from future liabilities.

For the Gen Xers, at least those in the middle class, the shift to contribution plans meant they were responsible for managing their own investments. In practice, this mostly means checking a few preference boxes on an investment questionnaire. Most plans are transferable if you change jobs, and in some cases you can opt out and manage your own funds. Whatever your asset base is at the end of your working career, will define what you earn in retirement.

Most people will simply defer the taxes via IRA and **401(k) accounts** until they must take the required minimum distribution at age 70½. Then they get hit with the tax torpedo, where all IRA deferred income becomes income, as does Social Security. This can bump you to the next bracket for higher Medicare (Part B) premiums. As tax levels are at historic lows it might be wise to make some **Roth** conversions, where you take a tax hit today to avoid bigger ones in the future.

There are other expenses, some you can anticipate, others you can't. When planning for retirement, you must assess your kids' needs (if you have them), aging parents (if you still have them), and the yippee-have-fun experience things as well.

If you are in shoes like mine, which are not unlike most mid-Gen Xers, you might have had your kids later in life. This means university for them while you are in your late fifties! Ack. Because I am Canadian this is a much less scary than it is for Americans. For education costs, I have only five bits of advice: Save, teach your kids the value of money, save, teach your kids the value of money, and let your kids pay as much of their post-secondary education tabs as they can through work and loans. This builds character. And for most middle- and even upper-middle-income Americans, the cost of a good school can be retirement fund busting. Help them to a point, but don't lay your retirement savings plan aside for them. It's up to you what you do, but do what you do without sentiment, knowing it could be either getting kids through university or being poor in retirement. It may be that teaching the kids to manage their own financial affairs is a better investment than simply paying for things. The kids will be fine and will have lots of time to pay off their debts.

There are some creative options if you don't have the cash now but insist on helping them. Sell your second home or downsize your current home. If you skipped the bit about being sentimental with your finances, go back, find, and read it, because what comes next might sound harsh: If you must sell something to help the kids now, take a picture of it and then sell it. With the cash, you can help your kids, increase your income, decrease financial (life) stress, save ten Indian villages, invest in a wild organic food start-up, and perhaps much more. If you are certain your house's value will increase, you could think about taking a small second mortgage to help the kids, but be careful about any "sure" thing.

The folks at Boston College have a great website on personal finance, and they talk about the downsizing option. They figure that, even with a mortgage that is paid off, housing can swallow up as much as 30% of your retirement income to maintain. They did the math and found that moving from a $250,000 home to one worth $150,000 can yield $75,000 (including moving and real estate fees). That $75,000 could equal $3,000 or more income every year, or $250 a month in a retirement account, not to mention lower expenses on a smaller home that could add the same amount again to your income. The question is: What do you want to pay for, new gutters or a trip to Europe?

You must look this one in the eye. Fooling yourself or being afraid of the eventualities is just bad for everyone. Be brave and set dates such as; I will downsize at this age; sell the cottage next year; move to a retirement home in ten years; or, etc. You might even consider giving some of your money to your kids or favorite cause as you start to spend less in retirement, rather than wait until The End. It's always nice to see the fruits of your labor while you are alive.

> *TIP — if you want to give money to the kids before you die,*
> *don't necessarily give away your assets. Rather give a portion*
> *of income generated on assets. Give for a specific purpose*

within your means and without making them dependent on
you for money.

Speaking of the fruits of your labor, be as generous as you can to causes that help support more and better sustainability. If you don't have a charitable giving item in your budget now or for retirement, put it in, for like anything else in life, if you don't make it a goal it likely won't happen.

Retirement and the Emotional Shift

It's becoming increasingly popular to talk about the emotional aspect of financial and investment considerations. This is a good thing, and its importance cannot be understated, especially for Gen Xers, who often identify self with work. Also, it will be a shock as work income dwindles or is no more and the balance of our investment accounts start to go steadily DOWN and not UP, as we hopefully have become used to for the past few decades.

Financial decision-making when emotional only mixes and muddies the planning waters. It can also have dramatic impacts on the discipline most of us require to meet our investment goals. Don't underestimate the effect of leaving your social network on the job either, as the amount of time you must fill in retirement could be as vast and cold as a windswept Oklahoma ranch in winter. You will most likely come to meet a whole new You and SO as well, and who wants to do that while coming to terms with a new financial reality in retirement?

For this I have only two pieces of advice. The first is obvious. Find a financial adviser, a counsellor, or a therapist. It can be a friend, a stranger in a coffee shop, or your pet beagle. I've found "who" doesn't really matter if you can talk without being judged (yeah! guys, you too). If you've done your financial homework before retirement, and follow my second bit of advice below, you probably don't need their advice anyhow.

The second piece of advice is akin to the old credit card on ice trick.

Remember back when you had to have your credit card to make a purchase? I used to tell folks with spending problems to freeze their cards in a glass of water to give them a few moments of sober reflection before spending on credit. This was an effective slow-down-and-think mechanism (especially before microwaves).

You can use the same trick with any financial decision by putting yourself on ice. Okay not literally (unless you live in Minnesota; then you have the option to do so between September and late June). Rather, never make a rash emotional decision on big-ticket items. Whatever you do, make sure you run through the impact scenarios on your finances, because in retirement, money tends to go only one way. Meditation works, but if that is not your thing, talk to the beagle.

Wrapping It Up

Gen Xers have had a good economic run, despite hitting the walls of numerous Big Bad Economic Events. Emerging work–life balance, distrust of the establishment, constant threats to economic well-being, and some sympathy toward the environment is a curious mix, one that has led many Gen Xers to approach financial planning and investment in their own ways.

Many of you may have started this chapter thinking it would be about investment only to find it was more about financial planning. But I say again, without good financial planning, what is there to invest? Good income and expense decisions give you more investment funding; more funding gives you more investment options; and more options serve your financial welfare and maximize your sustainability impact! Easy math.

But if there is only one thing you take from this chapter it should be that feelings count. Indeed, life is all about how one feels and lives and loves. But in finance, you must plan and have some discipline to create the context that supports how you want to feel and live. Not so easy math.

And if you want to contribute to the sustainability of the planet, planning is even more critical, as it adds another layer of emotion to the game. There is a lot more I could have blathered on about Gen X consumption habits, etc. But really, if you want to get guilted for your consumption habits, there are plenty of other places to go for that. Let's stipulate that we are all honestly struggling to break out of that part of our Economic DNA and Ego that causes us to over-consume. You know what to do on that score.

My goal, and hopefully yours too, is to pile up the bucks so we can invest wisely with the force of your assets behind our sustainability investment decisions, both before and in retirement.

Gen Xers may be the last generation to enjoy what is considered a conventional retirement (which is really something relatively new to the world anyway). How you invest and live in your retirement is an enormous opportunity for you to take on sustainability challenges. You will have the time, the knowledge, the experience, and, hopefully, the money to help right egregious environmental, social, and economic injustices.

Save, live, love, and invest sustainable.

What you learned in this chapter

- Let emotions guide your vision, but let logic drive your financial and investment planning.
- Plan to have two hours a month for financial planning and investment management.
- Plan for three retirements: the first where you are active and healthy, the second when you are healthy but less active, and the third when you are frail and need help.
- Assess big expensive-to-maintain assets, deciding if you should keep them or sell them, and if the latter think about choosing a date for selling in the future, or plan for expenses in retirement.
- Put all big-ticket expenses that could affect investment and savings goals on "ice" for a while for sober second thoughts.
- Plan and save specifically for big-ticket expenses beyond your regular investment savings.
- Don't use assets or cash you need for retirement savings to pay for kids' education if you can't afford it; they will be fine without it, and you won't be eating Purina for lunch in retirement.
- Consider giving kids or sustainability causes part of your income as you start to spend less later in your retirement.
- Take a photo of your favorite tree to remind you why the hell you are reading this book.

Chapter Ten

Millennial Investment

W HILE THE MILLENNIALS' ECONOMIC CONTEXT might seem a bit bleak, it's not that bad. Among you, you currently control some $3 trillion in investment and other liquid assets (not including your real estate!) and by 2020, will own over $7 trillion.

As the *Guardian* newspaper — known for its sustainability perspective — noted, the asset transfer from Boomers and Gen X to Millennials will transform the $30-trillion universe of Americans' investable assets.[38] The impact will be a ton of well-educated Millennials with about $120,000 of inherited, investable assets each, and many with much, much more.[39]

A lot of thirty-somethings are currently putting retirement savings aside. Just over half of college-educated Mills contribute to a retirement account such as a 401(k) or IRA, with an average balance of $7,450.[40] Seems the 2008 Great Recession taught Millennials to at least *try* to save. Most Millennials who are not saving yet report wanting to before the age of thirty-five.

What are Mills doing with their savings, besides landmark events? Not much, apparently; very little Millennial money is actively managed, and I don't mean the buying and selling of stocks. A shocking number of Millennials, including many interviewed for *ILYGAD*, leave their "investment" money in certificates of deposit (CDs) or, worse, in a bank savings account! Most don't even know how much interest they are earning, or that the principal value of their savings is being munched away at by service fees and inflation.

While this is hardly a way to maximize the return on your savings, there are some good and bad sides to having cash. On the bad side, you are losing money, *not* just not maximizing returns. On the good side, your stash gives you some cash to start investing to support sustainability efforts.

In or Out (of the Market)?

When it comes to investing, Mills are gun shy. Their confidence in the stock market was shaken terribly by the 2008 near-global financial meltdown. Factor in what behavioral economists call the Millennials' need for "anxiety adjusted returns," or the best possible returns relative to the stress and anxiety endured, and your generation is not the easiest marks for stock promoters.[41] Watching terrible, stress-inducing news or reading jargon-filled investment reports hardly excites either.

> *"If you save three percent [of your income], retirement will be a lot like college. You'll eat a lot of ramen noodles, but you won't look as cute doing it."*[42]
>
> — Greg Davies

Financial analyst David Greg found that only 59% of Millennials think the stock market is the best place to invest. This compares to 66% of all Boomers. Greg thought the Mills' hesitancy to invest would erode over time as the memory of the Great Recession faded. Nope. In 2014, less than half of Millennials of investing age still thought the stock market the best place to invest. This said, 40% of college-educated Millennials do have a variety of securities (stocks, bonds, mutual funds, etc.), investments found mostly in their defined-contribution 401(ks).

This is higher, surprise, surprise, than 37% for the U.S. population. About two-thirds of those Mills investing in the market have retirement accounts via former or current employers (e.g., 401(k), IRA Thrift Savings Plans). About a third of college Mills also have IRA accounts *not* linked to their place of employment. Of those with employment-based plans, some 71% chose how their savings are invested. This is important for sustainability investment. More on this later.[43]

Some Financial Planning Guidance

The first and best advice for Mills is to visualize the type of life you want, now and in retirement. Only then can you figure out what you want to do with your money today, tomorrow, and thirty years from now. Unlike Gen Xers, you have more time, and thus greater flexibility.

Want to pay off your home quickly? Take a year or two off? Not a problem: You can save for these things and not affect your retirement goals in a big way — assuming certain income and expense conditions, of course.

This type of visioning helps with expenses and savings goals for the great life you want to live between now and the Great Slow Down (retirement or semi-retirement). But what do you need?

In Chapter Six, we discussed *The Number*, or the amount you can or want to save for retirement. Through the Bloomberg Calculator we found that if you invested in a fund that tracks the Dow Jones Industrial Average and contributed just 11% of a $70,000 annual pretax income starting at age 25 for ten years (or $641 monthly), *and then contributed nothing more for 30 years*, your portfolio would be worth over $930,000 (assuming a 5% return, or 2% less than the long-term stock market average of 7%). If you added $466 more a month to this portfolio between the ages of 55 and 65, you would receive another $70,436, topping out at a tidy…you guessed it… $1M (current dollars, again). This would give you an estimated $40,000 a year, pretax. Add your Social Security check (assuming they still exist) and you would have an annual income of around $56,000, or the median annual American household income.

If you and your significant other (if you have one) make $70,000 between you, or less than two combined average Millennial starting salaries of $47,000, all you would have to save is 5.5% of your annual income each for ten years to retire quite well, thank you very much!

Saving this amount can be challenging. Especially if you are saving for a home as well. Many would counsel saving for real estate prior to savings for your investment fund. My advice: Do both. Put as much as you can into tax-deferred IRAs while saving for a home or property, if only to establish the investment savings habit, and take advantage of available tax savings. Imagine — if you invested 15% of your income for five years, you could have an estimated $58,000 for the down payment on an apartment or house or some other larger asset.

These are modest amounts assuming you have reliable income around the Millennial average. But achieving this target still requires some discipline.

My wife's cousin, Ryan, had discipline by the boatload. As soon as he graduated from school, he began to save with one goal in mind: buying an apartment. He would do all sorts of things for cash, including buying seasons tickets for the local football and hockey teams and reselling the seats to friends at a modest profit.

After several years of saving and, yes, living with his mom and dad, Ryan had scraped together enough to buy a one-bedroom apartment in the outrageously expensive downtown of Vancouver, Canada, at the tender age of twenty-seven!

That's the trick: discipline, and Ryan had it by the boatload. You don't? I can help with two words: automatic withdrawal. You don't have to contribute a large amount, you just need to save consistently.

Needless to say, middle income-earning Millennials must be thoughtful about their financial choices. Use affordable transportation. Buy a modest first home. Be creative about your vacations, etc. Get someone else to pay for the fancy wedding! Deal with credit wisely, and pay expensive loans first.

These are basics financial rules that are not only likely to make you *financially* wise but *sustainability* wise as well. Less stuff equals a less-expensive (better?) lifestyle, which is good for a world burning up from over-consumption.

Investing and Millennials

When you turn to specific investment needs, you ought to go through the financial and SRI asset allocation exercise (see Part Three). Numerous surveys have found that Millennials tend to have conservative portfolios for their age. One survey found that 30% of Millennials have a quarter or less of their investments in stocks or mutual funds. This is shocking and speaks to two things.

First, many Millennials don't believe they have enough savings to make stock market investments. Rick of Georgia keeps his "investments" in a savings account. His reasoning is that the amount is too small to invest. This doesn't have to be the case, as you can begin to buy some funds starting with as little as fifty to a thousand dollars. Domini, Calvert, and Pax World, all popular social investment funds, have minimums as low as $1,500, $1,000 and $1,000 respectively, some with subsequent investments as low as $250.

Second, the observation suggests that Millennials don't know a lot about inflation. Bank accounts are the brick and mortar equivalent of a mattress as both cost you lost income to inflation. If banks didn't provide security, they might even be worse, as mattresses don't charge monthly fees. Savings account interest rates don't often go above the inflation rate, so it makes zero sense leaving money in such accounts, unless you need it to be quickly available.

Liquidity for a Millennial can be important given they don't always follow the conventional path. Taking time off for adventure is common:

extended touring, volunteering long term for important causes, investing in a community farming adventure, etc. These experiences should be congratulated. Do it, they will make the world a better place. Taking time out will not hurt your retirement savings goals much either.

If you are on a more conventional path (or even if you are not), you will likely be saving for a home or real estate of some kind. Commendable! But this may mean you want to have quick and low-cost access to your savings. If so, money market funds are a good place to park cash for the short term. Money market funds are *somewhat* better than a bank account in terms of return. If you don't already have one, you can open one in any online investment or trading site, most for free. Many sites will even throw in a few free transactions, often the first five to ten. There is a good chance your bank has an investment arm you can access. Some credit unions also often have access to money market funds.

If you own units in a **mutual fund** from a company with a family of funds, you can sometimes move your money between funds with little or no cost. This means you can put your money in a higher potential returning fund, say a large capital equity fund, and then shift it to the money market fund later if you need to increase your liquidity. Be careful to investigate fund fee costs (see Appendix Five on fees). Also be careful not to withdraw tax-deferred savings from an IRA, as that will cause taxes to kick in.

If your money is *not* in a tax-deferred retirement account, you can take cash out for a fee modest enough to not hurt too much if you *really* need it but high enough to curb the Imp of Unnecessary Consumption that might be whispering in your ear of the empty delights of buying more stuff.

Putting Money in the Market

Many Millennials are stock shy. I know I have always been that way. My wife, on the other hand, has always been eager to take advantage of the ups of the stock market. And she has been right most of the time. When we were young she bought small cap stocks with higher potential upside. No risk, no reward, she would say. Problem is, higher risk also means higher potential for bad investments. But her approach allowed us to invest in some great companies and funds.

We invested in our own community credit union's preferred shares at a guaranteed 7% return. We purchased some other credit union preferred shares (like equity shares but usually pay a dividend, have no voting rights, and sometimes other qualifications affecting liquidity and risk). We also invested in labor-friendly venture capital funds. More recently, we have been in and out of some smaller solar investments and a couple of financial companies. Our adventure into large and medium cap options didn't turn out so well, but did give us a tremendous lesson in that exotic investment beast!

> *"I don't want to be invested in just one company or one sector. At the same time, I also don't want to put all this work into actually managing my money," says Cristina Cordova, a 26-year-old Stanford grad who invests through Wealthfront and also pushed the start-up where she works to offer a 401(k). Of the few good things that came out of the Great Recession, creating a thrifty generation that appreciates the value of a buck and the need to save may be one of them.*[44]

Risk is relative, and whether you invest aggressively or fearfully is a matter for you to decide. You need to find the balance that works for you. The rule of thumb is the younger you are the more aggressive you can be, particularly if you buy large cap stocks and plan to hold long term. Most Millennials ought to be *at least 60% in equities,* even more if want to maximize potential returns. The balance can be in bonds and a bit of cash.

If you are still nervous and confused about stock markets, it's all good. Pretty much all you really need to know is that that the average annual return of the Standard and Poor index from 1950 to date is about 7%. Knowing this should change your mind about one of two things.

First, if you, or your financial adviser, wants to actively manage your investments, you might want to reconsider. You can likely get the same return if you stick your money in an index fund and forget about it.

Second, if you worry about the stock market and interest rates going up or down, don't, because they will, and unless you are the chair of the Federal Reserve Bank, there is nothing you can do about it. For most of us, stock market and interest rate gossip only channels indigestion and/or bad decisions.

The buy-quality-stocks-and-bonds approach is a good approach for risk-averse (and lazy) investors, especially if you purchase funds. If you want large company securities, the "buy and forget" strategy provides good return prospects and very little work once investments are made.

Polly in New Jersey, for example, is a self-described buy and forget 'em type of investor. "I don't buy and sell anything. I just prefer not to at this time in my life. Really there is no time…. What I would like to do is to monitor more closely family finances and investments. That be useful."

This is good advice for most Millennials, but only if you plan to stay in the stock market. A study by the mutual fund giant Fidelity found a whole lot of their 401(k) fund holders jumped out of the market after the 2008 meltdown. Sold it all. By 2015, a third of them had *not* gotten back into the market. By the end of 2015, the accounts of those who had cashed out and reinvested later had risen by 27.2%. Those who had Stayed Calm and Invested on? Their accounts rose 160%![45]

Most of what I have described is known as **passive investment**. An active approach is where you buy and trade on a regular basis. This is rarely advisable for most non-investment professionals; heck, even for professionals! Study after study has shown actively managed accounts cost more to maintain and often have worse results than comparable index funds.

Most people are not interested in actively trading individual companies or funds, or even using an active manager. If you feel the urge, go ahead. Just know that there are two types of risks.

The first are market risks, some of which I have described above. These are risks that no one without insider information can avoid. The second are what I call *Dodo Risks*, or the entirely avoidable risks that come from our own silly impetuousness.

For example, have you ever gotten the call? You know, the one where your friend tells you to buy a penny stock because his friend's second cousin Rocky or Bunny has some inside information no one else has? Think micro-sized tech companies offering the next huge selling gadget, or mining outfits in the Himalayas on the brink of a huge gold find.

Unless you are the water delivery person who happened to be refilling the meeting room water machine during a board meeting where they decide to accept Facebook's offer to buy them out, by the time you hear whatever made the stock hot (if it's true at all), the price will already be losing steam. Short advice, don't invest.

Investment and Emotions

Millennials will benefit from the length of time they can be in the market. But the tendency to want to divest at the slightest bad stock news, or to believe Rocky and Bunny, underscores the many other behavioral implications of investing.

Many of you will be reluctant to enter the market. Some of you will feel this way because you don't believe you have enough money to invest. Others might not want to invest because they feel they don't know enough about investing. Others (all?) feel they are just too busy or otherwise occupied in life to want to become familiar with investing.

For those who do invest, many will need a virtual seat belt (at least at first) to feel comfortable with the ride because, as the saying goes, the only thing you can predict about the market is that it will go Up and it will go Down. Psychologically strapping in requires a bit of homework so that you stick to your chosen investment strategy and, more importantly, don't panic when the market or your portfolio dives.

These negative sentiments are barriers to investing comfortably. Listen to your intuition, but confirm with facts.

On the other side of the equation are those among us who are just too optimistic about the market or a stock. What we need to remind ourselves is a sure bet does not exist. A very smart friend of mine once started following an investment advisery newsletter that boasted of a 100% record for *shorting* stocks. Did you just hear the alarm bells? 100%! If you didn't hear the bells, stop reading, there is nothing more in this book for you: Go to Vegas and have fun, and the pain of losing your money will be over quicker.

There are plenty of sentiments that can affect your desire and ability to invest or manage your investments. There are two tricks to being happy with your portfolio management. The first: Manage your own funds, do all the exercises in this book, and make a good plan. Pay one or two financial planners to review it. Then revise and get going. The second: Pay a financial adviser to manage your money after a thorough check of their credentials, working style, and performance.

A Note on HUG Sustainable Investment for Millennials

The beauty of being Millennial is that you have time. And just as you can miss a year or two of income or savings and still retire in abundance, you can also afford to take a risk or two in your portfolio. This means making a couple of high-impact investments for some really big HUGs, or investments with Huge Uncomplicated Gratification!

HUGs are there for the taking. Mostly with venture capital risk levels, these highly sustainable investments are becoming increasingly popular and available. Invest in a friend's organic micro-brewery; provide capital for a cooperative housing project; put money in a fund investing in micro-finance institutions in Africa.

Jesse of Geneva holds two HUGs. One is shares in Oiko credit, a worldwide cooperative promoting sustainable development through loans, capital, and capacity-building support to businesses in developing countries. The fund invests in microfinance institutions, cooperatives, fair-trade organizations, small-to-medium enterprises, and renewable energy projects. Oiko credit has over $1,209 million in assets working with over 800 partners worldwide.

"I don't have big money in Oiko," Jesse explains, "but I have worked in the industry, even served on the Oiko Board of Directors. I like Oiko for its investments, but I also like it because it has a whole infrastructure set up; it has scale of impact." Individual investors can buy a depository receipt for as little as $200, which typically pays out a 2% annual dividend (not guaranteed).

Jesse's rationale for taking below-market returns: "Publicly traded companies are bound to short-term thinking, and that will define their actions, which almost by definition is not well aligned with the sustainability challenges of today. Sustainable must have something more to do with a *lasting* value proposition, which creates in the ecosystem it is a part of, a healthy and harmonious mutually reinforcement type of development."

Most of your sustainable investments should aim for competitive market returns. More on that in Part Three. However, if you plan well, even on a modest income, you can get these kinds of HUGs with the confidence your Great Long Slowdown (aka retirement) will not be any worse off financially for having made them. Win or lose, you get an impressive sustainability impact return you would have never gotten otherwise.

What you learned in this chapter

- Millennials are decent savers and, after inheriting from their Gen X and Boomer parents, will control many more trillions of dollars and have the market influence to push sustainable investment to the next level.
- A bit shy of stock markets, Millennials keep too much cash under the "mattress."

- Many Millennials are saving for the unconventional, such as extended downtime from work, funky real estate purchases, and important life events, all possible if planned for and managed.

- Putting even just a small amount — $150 — in a retirement investment account every month can add up if you start young!

- Millennials are young and can afford to invest in sustainability HUGs without jeopardizing their financial security.

- Rejoice in the flexibility of youth; do some yoga; it doesn't last long....

Part Three

Sustainable Investment

Chapter Eleven

Investment Basics

R ISK IS A BIG, BAD WORD for many people, particularly when it comes to investment. But risk you must, for without risk most will not meet *The Happy Number* retirement goal. Savings accounts will not get you there, so into the market you go (once you've done your financial planning, of course, including considerations such as savings for a home, your children's college, emergency funds, etc!).

This may scare you, but as investor Robert Arnott once famously said, "In investing, what is comfortable is rarely profitable." That's why previous chapters discussed financial sensitivities a bit more than most investment books. If you've not read Parts One and Two, go back and do it now! It's important.

Why?

To invest comfortably, you need to know where your risk-return zone is. Knowing this will help your feelings about financial risk guide, and not impede, investment decision making best for you.

If your risk tolerance is too low to invest in the securities needed to meet your *Happy Number*, then you are going to have to figure ways to step out of your comfort zone. Conversely, if you have no nose for smelling out risk, or don't care about it, then you may be taking on more risk than you need.

Basic Investment Types, Risks, and Returns

Each investment type has an element of risk, some parts of which are definable, other not so much. This is true of the three types of investments most investors consider.

The first is **equities**. Equites are stocks, or any other security representing an ownership interest in a company.

Common stocks are the most *common* type of equity. They are shares of a company, each of which is worth the total market value of all company shares divided by the total number of shares of the company outstanding. A single share in a company with a total market value of $200 is worth $2, 10 shares $20. Common stocks are securities that represents ownership in a corporation. Those owning common stock have the right to vote on the election of a company's board of directors and corporate policy. If a company is liquidated (chopped up and sold), its common shareholders get paid for their shares after bondholders, preferred shareholders, and other debtholders. A preferred stock is like a common stock but has a different form of ownership, namely, a higher claim on assets and earnings. It also usually has dividends that are paid before those of common stock shareholders (but usually without voting rights). In this way, preferred stock has both debt and common shares features.

Equity investing refers to the buying, holding, and selling of company stocks. Most stocks are listed on a regulated stock market. Returns from shares come as capital gains (i.e., share prices rise as a company's overall market value rises) and dividends, cash, or stock that a company determines to distribute to its shareholders (usually quarterly). Common share ownership gives you a vote at company annual meetings, or, as noted in

Common and Preferred Stocks

A *common stock* is a security that represents ownership in a corporation. Holders of common stocks exercise control by electing a board of directors and voting on corporate policy. In the event of company liquidation, common shareholders have rights to a company's assets only after bondholders, preferred shareholders, and other debtholders are paid in full.

A **preferred stock** is a class of ownership in a corporation that has a higher claim on assets and earnings than common stock. Preferred shares generally have a dividend that must be paid out before dividends to common shareholders, but the shares usually do not carry voting rights.

Preferred stock combines features of debt, in that it pays fixed dividends, and equity and has the potential to appreciate in price. The details of each preferred stock vary.

Source: investopedia.com

Chapter Three, you can give your vote to a third party, such as a financial adviser or the managers of a fund that you invest in.

Equities come in all shapes and sizes. For now, it's important to know only the basics. There are common shares and preferred shares (explained in box). There are large, mid, and small "cap" stocks. These refer to the total market capitalization of the company (the price per share multiplied by the number of shares available for purchase; this is explained further in the next section). Investors also refer to value or growth stocks. Value stocks are judged to be trading at a price-to-earnings ratio below average and are deemed to be undervalued because their prospects for growth are not reflected in the stock valuation. Growth stocks trade above the average price-to-earnings ratio because they are deemed to have greater prospects for growth. Put another way, their earnings growth is relatively high.

The second most common investments are **corporate and government bonds**. These are debt securities issued by companies or governments and sold to investors. A company's ability to generate income to repay **bonds** (interest and principle) is the only guarantee an investor gets with this type of security. This guarantee is more than you get on most equities, but you don't get any ownership rights. In the event of corporate difficulties, bond holders get paid first.

A Word or Two about Stock Selection

Sad to say, even most professionals don't do stock selection well. Sometimes they win; sometimes they don't. In fact, their stock selections often underperform those of chimpanzees. What?

You might not remember Burton Malkiel's book *A Random Walk Down Wall Street*, but you may recall his theory that "a blindfolded monkey throwing darts at a newspaper's financial pages could select a portfolio that would do just as well as one carefully selected by experts." *The Wall Street Journal* took up the challenge and found that professional stock pickers did only slightly better than random darts thrown at pages of the *Journal*, and only a hair better than the Dow Jones Industrial Average.

Knowing this you may feel inclined to get your darts out of the case and roll with the chimps. Or maybe (better) not. Either way, stock selection is not a stroll through the zoo.

Like equities, investors can buy and sell bonds. This causes the value of the bonds to fluctuate as market and issuer conditions change. Because bonds have an interest payout that is known in advance, they are typically less risky than equities. Less risk means they also tend to have lower returns. Be careful to note bond ratings, from really good triple A to junk level. Need more of a definition?

Putting more into short-term bonds is less risky as interest rates can rise, but you get paid less interest in return. Long-term bonds have higher interest rates for the same company; however, they require tying up your capital longer, which implies interest rate risk. Who knows where rates will go? Many portfolios hold both short- and long-term bonds as a result: short for buying opportunities if rates rise and long to capture higher returns.

Cash and equivalents are the third type of investment. Cash is that stuff you keep under your mattress, in a coffee can on top of the fridge, in your savings account, or in your money market fund.

Cash equivalents include any other short-term investments that you can cash out quickly, say within three months. This would include **U.S. treasury bills** and short-term **certificates of deposits**. The key thing to know about cash is that it is liquid — available on short notice to buy things with! Cash should not be confused with credit cards that many *seem* to work like cash but alas must be repaid, usually on short notice; hence the coffee can over the fridge.

Cash equivalent investments are good short-term parking lots, but not great investments. Bank accounts are the worst. Incredibly, savings accounts and money market funds hold 30% of all individual investors' funds in the United States: bad, bad, bad! History tells us you will lose about 1.7% a year on your cash as inflation chips away at it![46] So unless there is a good reason for holding cash like this, don't do it.

Each type of investment has a generalizable risk level and return potential, and each tends to behave differently over time as economic and market conditions change.[47] Rule of thumb: Equities have more risk, bonds less, and cash the least. For return potential, the inverse is normally true; equities have the best return potential, followed by bonds, then cash. I say *normally*, because the value of any type of investment will vary depending on when you sell it (or in the case of cash, spend it).

Since the early 1950s, the Standard and Poor 500 of large company equities average inflation adjusted return was just over 7.0%. The Barclays

U.S. Aggregate Bond Index, which measures the performance of U.S. investment grade bonds (e.g., U.S Treasuries, government bond issues, corporate bonds), has averaged around 8.4% since 1980.[48]

Of course, any company stock can go bust, and they do go bust from time to time; even some of the so-called value stocks. Remember the great market meltdown of 2008–09. I do. I vividly remember the moment I figured things were really going south fast. It was March 2008. I was in a traffic jam in Mumbai, India, with plenty of time to read the innumerable billboards alongside the highway. On one I saw a picture of a gleaming, oversized New York blue glass skyscraper apartment building with improbable hanging gardens on random floors. Beautiful. The advert was for an investment fund with a "guaranteed return of 20%." Later we came to know this was one of those infamous almost-took-the-global-economy-down, collateralized-debt-obligations funds full of rotten residential mortgages. That very moment, sweating in a Mumbai taxi, I knew the market was screwed. Within two weeks I was 90% cash. Talk about timing, right?!

Not so fast, it's A Happy Story only so far. It gets sad, sadly. For in the crush of work, life, and fear of the unknown, I did not reinvest our cash until 2012. This cost me a loss of about 4% and an opportunity cost of about 28%. Market timing, it turns out, is as much about understanding the market as it is understanding your capacity to make investment decisions. To this day, I am unsure which is the bigger challenge of the two.

One moral we can find in this story is that if you buy and hold quality stocks, the risk that you are taking on is *often* more related to market movements than the performance of the company. This makes holding onto stocks through all the market crazy a better means to decent returns. Understanding risk in the market is challenging to say the least. Trying to predict the future of a given stock … well, many think this is just a fool's gambit.

What is Financial Asset Allocation?

Buying the right mix of investments is a way to avoid having to guess at future market conditions and the performance of a given security. Investors use many strategies to get the mix right. Among the most common, successful, and simple to use, in my judgment, is **asset allocation**.

Asset allocation is a serious subject. It is so serious, if you Google "Asset Allocation Humor" you get a big Zero. Nada; rien; nichts. It's either that serious or investment folk have no humor. (If you ask Google for *investment humor*, on the other hand, you get some gems, including this one, from investment professional Charlie Munger: "It is remarkable how much long-term advantage people like us have gotten by trying to be consistently not stupid, instead of trying to be very intelligent.")

So, what is this humorless thing, asset allocation?

According to *Investopedia*, asset allocation is an investment practice that balances risk and reward by dividing your portfolio according to your investment goals, risk tolerance, and investment horizon or how much you want to make, how afraid or unafraid you are of the market, and how long it will be before you need the money you are investing. Asset allocation in practice means how much equity, bonds, or cash as a percentage of your total capital you hold in your portfolio.

As you know, there are many classes of stocks and bonds, and the performance of each varies consistently under specific economic and market conditions. Some tend to go up in one type of market, while others tend to go down. Growth economies are good for equities, those of smaller companies in particular. Bonds are often better in sluggish economies, when equities' value growth can stall, even contract.

This means each security has different risks. But conversely, each also provides a means to portfolio diversification that can round off the ups and downs of your portfolio as a whole.

Asset allocation strategies can be quite complex and employ all sorts of securities. Or they can be simple. In *ILYGAD* I use only the very basic allocation categories of cash, fixed income (i.e., bonds), and equities, which I also divide into three risk classes: low, average, and high.

Assessing equity risk can be complicated. Such assessments include individual stocks of many types and shapes and can include equity funds, each with different risk and return profiles.

Company size is one measure of risk, typically defined by market capitalization or the company sale value of outstanding shares. Micro companies have less than $300 million in value, small less than $2 billion, medium $10 billion, large $100 billion, and mega more than $100 billion. Larger and more established companies tend to have less risk, while smaller ones normally have better growth potential but higher risk. Value stocks are generally in well-established companies and usually have lower risk ratings. These are all just general risk classifications, and again, there is no guaranteed way to assess corporate risk.

Geography can also be used in allocations for both equities and bonds. Common categories include U.S. domestic, global, international, emerging markets, regional, frontier, etc. Developing country markets are normally higher risk, but again, the highest potential return as well.

These are the basic terms and asset classes. Other professionals use other terms, so it can be confusing. While conventional asset allocation guides are generally applicable, the allocation you decide on must be right for you. It must fit your goals, risk outlook, and investment horizon: There is no magic formula for the critical allocation jigsaw. Because I can provide only the minimum here, I urge you to read up on asset allocation.

Applying Financial Asset Allocation

Financial asset allocation done to your satisfaction and standards can reduce volatility in your portfolio through diversification. Choosing the right assets allows you to dilute risk across asset types, which can improve your portfolio's earning potential. The right allocation can also avoid constant tending of your portfolio to meet the vagaries of the market.

The general rule of asset allocation is that you take more risk when you are young, then get more conservative as you get older. When you are young, time is on your side, so you can also ride out market downturns looking for those juicy long-term average returns.

> As we age, we usually have (1) more wealth to protect, (2) less time to recoup severe losses, (3) greater need for income, and (4) perhaps an increased nervousness as markets jump around.
>
> — John Bogle, Founder of the Vanguard Group

As you get older, less risk is conventionally called for. This means lower-risk and value stocks, especially those paying good dividends. The figure below shows a fairly conventional asset allocation by levels of risk tolerance, which also roughly corresponds to typical age-based allocations.

Note: When you think about your own portfolio, remember to figure in other non-market assets of value in your asset allocation calculation, including your home, other real estate, antiques, art, boats, jewelry, etc.

If you are risk averse or older, income-generating, high-quality bonds should take a larger share of your portfolio. They are less risky and can provide good income. Wisdom also has it that as you age you should give up

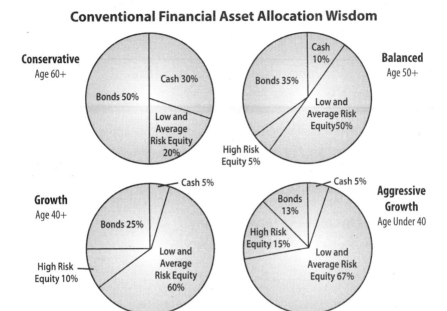

Conventional Financial Asset Allocation Wisdom

Conservative Age 60+
Cash 30%
Bonds 50%
Low and Average Risk Equity 20%

Balanced Age 50+
Cash 10%
Bonds 35%
Low and Average Risk Equity 50%
High Risk Equity 5%

Growth Age 40+
Cash 5%
Bonds 25%
High Risk Equity 10%
Low and Average Risk Equity 60%

Aggressive Growth Age Under 40
Cash 5%
Bonds 13%
High Risk Equity 15%
Low and Average Risk Equity 67%

on most equity risk, for more constant and steady income streams. This guideline is changing a bit but still conventionally applies.

What does asset allocation look like in practice? Take my example. I am fifty-four, have three teenagers, and don't see myself fully retiring until around seventy. My portfolio is aggressive for my age with 70% equities, 20% bonds, and 10% cash. I don't have a company pension and am in line for only basic Social Security, so I want to be a bit more aggressive.

On the other hand, we have some real estate investments that are not particularly risky. This allows me to be a bit more edgy with equity. When I include real estate in my portfolio, my equities drop to around 20% of our overall asset base, so my portfolio stance as a percentage of my household balance sheet is not particularly aggressive.

A commonly held rule of thumb is that the proportion of bonds in your holdings should be around the same as your age, although it could be less if you plan to work a bit longer than the typical retirement age, as I do. This guide works well for average mid- to late-Gen Xers if most equities are dividend-paying large cap companies.

For Millennials under thirty-five, you should hold mostly equities with various levels of risk suiting your risk-return appetite. Some suggest a balance of 20% large cap with lower risk and return potential, and 15% to 25%

mid to small capital companies with more risk and potential growth. You should keep some cash in your portfolio for quick access, particularly for investment-buying opportunities and/or non-security asset purchases.

Both Gen Xers and Millennials should consider geographic diversification. Some international equity and income exposure can provide risk coverage, as not all regional markets move to the same rhythms. A stake in emerging markets might be good for the long term, but only if you have the stomach for it, and only well-known securities!

Cross-industrial sector diversification is also important, as not all sectors respond to market and economic conditions equally. Basic consumer goods and health care companies often do better in slower economies, while technology is often better in a rising economy.

Poor sector diversification can cause problems. Once I got carried away buying two rail stocks (I hate truck transport emissions) when I needed only one. Shortly after buying: POW! transportation tanked like a 1960s bad guy being hit by Batman — Millennials, don't even try to understand this one — leaving me to wonder why I didn't buy Costco or some other stock rather then two stocks in the same sector.

If I have misled you into thinking that there are absolute asset allocations by age, forgive me. There aren't. The guidelines noted above are only intended to give you a sense of what conventional investment allocation looks like for younger and older investors.

Well done, asset allocation is important as you age and your investment context changes. Good allocation is also good for the mental health of Millennials, as "setting and forgetting" can tame some of your market-induced crazy. It's good for Gen Xers health too, as winding down equity risk in favor of income securities keeps our hearts beating at a decent rhythm.

In Appendix Three you can find a list of asset allocation calculators. One I like is on the Smart Asset website.[49] CNN Money has another simple-to-use allocator.[50]

Rebalancing Your Financial Asset Allocation

You absolutely must remember to rebalance your allocations as your holdings gain and lose value and upset your desired allocation.

Think of tires on a car. Every now and then they need rebalancing. So too will your portfolio as the market inevitably pushes some investments up in value, and others down.

Your portfolio will also need realigning to remain in sync with your evolving risk tolerance, income position, and future needs. That's the polite way of saying as you get older. When you are in your thirties and forties you can check alignment every three to five years, or after a major stock market event. Over fifty? Like that full physical you promised your significant other you'd do: Every year.

Rebalancing can require selling a portion of your investments, sometimes a scary portion, even if they have been good performers for you. Say your Google and Facebook stocks went up 100%; terrific, right?! Yes, but then these two stocks might dramatically increase the proportion of average risk equities in your portfolio. A rebalancing could be in order to keep your overall portfolio age-risk-investment allocation plan in place. You may want to sell some of Google and buy other asset types, or sell both and buy several new equities or bonds, depending on why you are rebalancing.

If this sounds like too much work or you are not going to trade on your own, you can also find packaged funds, or combinations of funds, that fit your asset-allocation needs. Not surprisingly, some of these funds are even called *asset allocation funds*! Others are called *balanced funds*. These funds hold more or less fixed proportions of asset classes — equity, income, and cash — in allocations meant to attract investors with particular risk and return profiles.

Critics of some of these types of funds argue that standard allocation solutions can never fit an individual investor's needs.

I agree and disagree.

I agree because all investors have unique profiles and needs. But I disagree because of convenience. Few investors are interested in or have the capacity to invest in funds and/or securities on their own. In the end, it may be better to have good, relatively inexpensive, if imperfect allocation than none at all. For example, I don't like to research bonds and bond funds. Don't know why, but I don't. I am an equity guy, I guess. So instead of fingernail-pulling research, I simply assessed and bought the best, heavy into-bond funds I could find. Simple easy, and I got a whole portfolio of corporate bonds working for me in one afternoon!

Market Timing

This brings us to market timing. This paragraph will be a short. Rule of thumb: Don't do it. Timing the market is just too hard.

Some investment professionals have explicit market-timing strategies. That is, they try to buy when a stock has its lowest or sell it when it reaches peak value. The buy or sell decision is determined by an investor's prediction of share price movements and can be based on any number of analytics, from technical stock analysis to tea leaf reading.

I jest? For most of us — and judging by their record, for timing strategists too, as they are as often right as they are wrong.

> "We ignore outlooks and forecasts…" We're lousy at it and we admit it …" Everyone else is lousy too, but most people won't admit it."
>
> — Martin Whitman

Market timing is vexing for anyone, pro or amateur. The best advice is not to do it. I know. Knowledge often comes from bad experiences, and if you have ever been an active investor, you know this lesson. A decade or two ago, we bought a bunch of Nortel, a former Canadian high-flyer large cap tech stock at what turned out to be 75% of the way to its peak price. Following our strategy, we sold half of the stock at a reasonable profit — but then, instead of selling the rest, we got greedy and waited for more! Sure enough, the price kept climbing. And we waited. Then it started sinking. This can't be for real, we said as it sank below our buying price. We tried to dollar-cost average for a win, buying more stocks as the price declined. Moral of this story: We never sold, and Nortel went the way of the Dodo simply because it sold wires and switch boxes and didn't keep up with wireless innovation. (I keep the stock valued at $0.0001 in our portfolio as a reminder about timing.)

> Those who have knowledge don't predict. Those who predict don't have knowledge.
>
> — Lao Tzu

Unfortunately, there are many such sad investment stories to learn from, and unfortunately, logic does not always make an investor decide on the best course. Take the very good friend of Jason from DC, who freaked out in the 2008–09 market meltdown and sold off almost all his holdings. Jason's best efforts to convince his friend that the market would return did nothing to sway him, and his friend wound up losing more than half his pre-crash portfolio by selling. Had he waited, he would have ridden a market that saw an over-100% appreciation by 2013.

Getting Help from an Adviser

> *If investing is entertaining, if you're having fun, you're proba-*
> *bly not making any money. Good investing is boring.*
>
> — George Soros

If you are the type who has the knowledge, time, and interest and can withstand the vicissitudes of the market without breaking into shingles at the least negative news, trade away. Even if you are not of this type, you still need to get involved in your portfolio management. Just not directly. Get help from an adviser.

The advice you get in this or any other book, from one adviser or another, should be simple and straightforward. For the average middle- to upper-income earner, investment can and should be simple. Develop an asset allocation plan suited to your risk tolerance. Buy and sell investments matching your long-term needs, with more holding than selling. Do this yourself or with your adviser. More than this you can do. But your investment risk might go up.

Boring advice? You bet. But it may not be all that dull, once you know that even with very low levels of risk tolerance, some very stimulating sustainability investments are waiting just for you.

What you learned in this chapter

- There are three main categories of investment: equities (with various categories of investment risk), fixed income, and cash.
- You need to develop an asset allocation plan to best meet your
  - investment goals — how much you want to make on your investments,
  - risk tolerance — how afraid or unafraid you are of putting money in the market,
  - investment horizon — how long it will be before you need the money you are investing.
- In practice, asset allocation means how much equity, bonds, or cash you hold in your portfolio, as a percentage of your total capital.
- You shouldn't time the markets, rather trust long-term, patient investment.
- If you don't feel good about managing your finances, don't. Seek an adviser.
- Celebrate making it through this chapter by doing something completely void of definitions or numbers!

CHAPTER TWELVE

Sustainable and Responsible Investment

IT MAY COME AS A SURPRISE to you that there are some basic rules for putting together a sustainability portfolio you can absolutely love (or at least, not completely dislike!).

Choosing the basic sustainability criteria to guide your portfolio is relatively easy. That's because only you know the social, environmental, or economic sustainability that is important to you, and no one can tell you different!

That's the good news. The bad?

Assessing sustainability investment performance requires homework. There are guidelines, but the problem is, as with almost any aspect of investment, sustainability investment selection remains as much an art as a science. But unlike corporate financial performance, there is much less readily available sustainability performance data for the average investor. What is available, as you will see, can be a whole lot more subjective than definitive.

This chapter will help you sort it all out through a series of exercises. The underlying concepts I use are similar to those in financial asset allocation planning, except once done you will have undertaken a sustainable and responsible investment (SRI) asset allocation matched with your financial allocation.

This is going to be fun!

Turning Your Sustainability On

The first thing you need to do is list your sustainability passions, biases, pet peeves, nasties, and goodies.

Using your own words, write whatever comes to mind. We can match your thoughts to the terms used by the SRI industry later. What do you care about?

When I first did this exercise for my 2017 portfolio reallocation, the words that spilled out: energy, food, human rights, misleading advertising, and advertising that promotes sustainability. Figuring this part out isn't rocket science. I wish it were, because maybe then I might sell many more books. But really, I can't complicate things, so just get at it: What are the things you want to see change in the world? Or alternatively, what are the things you want to see less of, things *you* think are really messing up the place?

The list can be as short or as long as you want. No rules.

Don't let your biases get in the way either. Use them as guidelines, not barriers. Your utopian sustainability vision for the world is valid and will be devastated if you don't use it to guide your choices. I like to start with the positives. Others start with what makes their blood boil.

Either way, choose issues that grab you, engage you, make you passionate. As you may have guessed, mad can lead you to things you will never invest in (negative-screened investments). Happy themes will have you wanting investments that proactively impact your sustainability interests (positively screened investments).

Need ideas? Go to Appendix Four and you will find a list of social, environmental, and economic SRI categories used by SRI professionals. They include most of the common screens, negative and positive, discussed in Chapter Two. The list is helpful, not only because of the ideas it may offer you, but also for framing your thoughts using standard SRI terms. This can come in helpful when are exploring your SRI investment options or talking to an SRI financial adviser.

I have found that listing more general interests can also help guide me. Marta from Mexico, for example, is a tech and gadget gal. She knows tech can play a big part in changing the world for the better. She is always on the lookout for companies with interesting tech innovation providing sustainability solutions. Passionate about this, she is highly motivated to find companies she wants to invest in.

One company she likes for this reason is Ford Motor Company. Ford, she found, is using food waste to make bioplastics for car parts. The way Marta sees it, there is too much waste in food processing. "These things can't be eaten, they are not economical to compost, so it goes to the landfill," she told me. "Bioplastics are recyclable and a great way to avoid using petrochemicals!"

Applied in a best-of-sector approach (or as I call it, the "hold your nose and invest" approach), Ford might come out as an investment option for many of us. Even if you don't like holding your nose, I guarantee you this: Your Ford food bumper will give you plenty of cocktail party bragging rights.

Investing in concepts, products, or services that grab your interest *and* you care about is nothing but good. You will want to stay on top of the trends, gaining knowledge to feed your capacity to assess the companies involved. The ultra-famous investor Warren Buffet uses this approach, telling us to invest in things we know, like, and understand.

Don't like cars, but think transportation is a problem for sustainability? Try some other transportation stock. That's me. Every day when I drive one of my two combustion engine cars, I get sad, then mad, then depressed. I am the problem. But in Mexico, where oil and natural gas fuels electricity production, and where there is literally no electric car infrastructure, buying electric is just as bad as putting gas in the tank and certainly less practical. So unless my city morphs itself into a futuristic all-things-walkable utopia with great public transportation, a car it is.

> *If you don't study any companies, you have the same success buying stocks as you do in a poker game if you bet without looking at your cards.*
>
> — Peter Lynch

Now if you *do* like cars and *can* buy an electric or a hybrid, you can be like Sampriti, *ILYGAD* interviewee who has fueled up with gas just twice in two years! Think about leaders in electric: Tesla, Nissan, and Toyota, for instance, all have proven long-term commitments to hybrid or electric. Or you can explore up-and-coming hydrogen (BMW).

Or jump cars altogether and go to freight. This what I did. I decided to vent my hate of combustion on rail, because if there is anything less troublesome than the sixteen million transport trucks in America, I am not sure what it is. Nothing personal, truck drivers, but your industry is hard, very hard on the climate. In mid-September 2015, I took advantage of a downward market swing and bought two rail car manufacturing stocks, which according to several research outfits had all the right buy signals. Then demand for coal plunged (yeah!). It turns out, transporting coal was a bigger part of rail car sales than I imagined! Ha! I should have gotten the coal signals better. Sad losses for some time, but rebounding nicely as I write.

Ironically, even though these stocks underperform my other less exciting sustainability stocks, I am still more revved up about rail than anything else. As the economy sorts itself out this year, rail will be back and these mid-cap value stocks will return.

Similarly, you may really dislike an industry, say the financial or chemical industry; completely understandable from a sustainability perspective. But from an investment allocation perspective, it may be important to include stocks from one or both sectors in your portfolio, if only for risk diversification purposes.

Or it may be that a mutual fund you own, or are looking at to buy, could include stocks from these sectors. There are many ways to structure your portfolio to balance the absence of one sector or another. In the end, you might have to face the fact some sustainability choices have overwhelmingly negative financial implication for your financial allocation strategy. Holding your nose works, and investing in something that is not perfect may result, at least until something better comes along!

Sustainable and Responsible Investment (SRI) Allocator

I have developed a simple tool to help you find your best sustainable and responsible asset allocation while respecting your financial allocation needs. It has five steps. Do the exercise to become familiar with SRI investment selection, or do it to shape your SRI portfolio. You can also do it as a part of Chapter Fifteen, which provides a more comprehensive plan to get you off the couch and investing.

Step One — Defining Your SRI Passions

Take the list of SRI issues that make you mad, happy, or both. (If you still haven't done this list, go back to the instructions above and do it!) Make sure you love it, and then finalize it. You can go to Appendix Four for example lists of SRI categories and issues.

Step Two — Distributing SRI Impact Points by SRI Category

Now imagine you have 100 *Sustainable and Responsible (SRI) Impact Points* to distribute among your listed SRI passions. The more passionate you are about an issue, the more points you give it and the potential impact you may have on a given issue.

To get going, we start with broad SRI categories and issues. The table below is an abbreviated list that gives you a sense of how this step works. (The SRI Impact Points do not add up to 100 in this table because it's not a complete list.) I put in two of my own points allocations as examples. Environment is a big issue for me, specifically carbon, so it gets 20 Impact Points. For similar reasons, I also decided to allocate 15 Points to help spell the end to fossil fuels.

Human rights are an issue for my soul. I've seen enough human rights abuses in developed and developing countries to boil my sustainability furnace for a thousand lifetimes. Everyone deserves the same high level of human rights. Treating each other poorly for reasons of class, race, gender, age, religion, or how you identify yourself is a fundamental cause underlying our very unsustainable world. From an economic perspective, it just makes sense to extend and respect human rights in business. Companies treating their workforces and stakeholders well have been shown to perform consistently better than those that do not.

This is true for all people, but particularly for women in business. With few exceptions, companies willfully or unintentionally insult women in innumerable ways, unjustly holding them back, putting them down, and paying them less, to the detriment of business performance and civilization

SRI Impact Allocation 1			
SRI Category	Impact Points Category	SRI Issue	Impact Points Issue
Environment	35	Carbon	20
		Biodiversity	0
		Fossil Fuels	15
		Climate Change	Etc.
		Etc...	Etc.
Equality	10		
		Women	
		Human Rights	
		Etc...	Etc.
Community Development	-	-	-
Peace	-	-	-
Health	-	-	-
Pornography	-	-	-
Governance	-	-	-
Etc....	-	-	-

generally. Based on this, women get five of my Impact Points and human rights five too. (Remember, all my SRI Impact Points should add up to 100, but because I am showing just a slice of my portfolio, only 45 are shown.)

Once you've identified your categories and gone through the necessary iterations to get the proportions by category and issue, you already have the broad outline of your desired SRI allocation. (The total should add up to 100 SRI Impact Points.) Shout Yeah! Dance around a bit, and celebrate your being two-fifths of the way there!

Step Three — Allocating SRI Impact Level

After you divvied up your *Impact Points*, you need to apportion points at the *SRI Impact* Level you want for each issue. This step provides the basis for selecting investments, which will define your SRI asset allocation while meeting your financial asset allocation needs.

Let's walk through a couple of examples to see how this works in practice.

Do you want carbon out of the air? Me too. That's why it got 20 of my 100 Impacts Points. But how big of an impact do I want? A very big one or to just avoid the very bad things type of impact?

In the table below, you see five levels of impact. These levels are subjective, but you will get how they work once you start to compare SRI opportunities. You will also likely change allocations as you find investment opportunities you like but which upend your initial allocations. That's okay, it's an iterative and learning process.

SRI Impact Allocation 2							
		Impact Points					
Category	Issue	Total Points	Low	Below Average	Average	Above Average	High
Environment	Carbon	20			15	5	
	Fossil Fuels	15			15		
Equality		10					
	Women	5		5			
	Human Rights	5	5				

Step Four — Selecting SRI Investment by SRI Asset Allocation

Once you have your desired SRI Impact Points allocated, you need to match your allocation with investment vehicles.

To show you how this step works in action, I found five securities that match up (more or less) with the allocation table we just completed above. There are many sources you can use to find these SRI investments, including the Sustainable and Responsible Investment Forum (USA) and Morningstar investment information service (see box below). In Canada, you can go to the Responsible Investment Association.

For carbon, I found Tesla (of Elon Musk fame). Tesla is a mid-cap company listed on the NASDAQ stock exchange. It has a focus on personal transport but also does batteries and some solar power (via ownership of SolarCity). I am not naive when it comes to getting rid of personal transportation vehicles, which, in my mind, severely impair the prospects for urban sustainability, but I dislike carbon emissions from combustion engines even more. I judge Tesla's sustainability rating as Above Average as a result.

I gave the **Guggenheim Solar Exchange-Traded Fund** a High SRI impact allocation as it invests throughout the solar sector in all sorts of great

SRI Impact Allocation 3							
		Impact Points					
Category	Issue	Total Points	Low	Below Average	Average	Above Average	High
Environment	Carbon	20					
	High — Tesla	15				15	
	Guggenheim Solar ETF	5					5
	Fossil Fuels	15					
	Powershares Global Clean Energy Portfolio	15				15	
Equality		10					
	Women	5					
	Pax Ellevate Global Women'sIndex Fund	5		5			
	Human Rights	5					
	Calvert Conservative Allocation Fund	5	5				

companies innovating carbonless energy sources and entire carbonless energy systems.

For Fossil Fuels, I like *Powershares.* I rated it this as Above Average SRI Impact as the companies in its portfolio produce several types of energy, some limiting carbon emissions, others with none. This is more of a transition out of fossil fuels investment, one that is more proactive than the divest-from-fossil-fuels approach, which I do not find all that satisfying.

For Equality, Women Issue, I chose the *Pax Ellevate Global Women's Index Fund.* The fund focuses on women in management and on boards

On Morningstar Sustainability Ratings: Semi-dry but important background information...

Just so you know, the SRI Impact categories used in Invest Like You Give a Damn correspond to the five globe symbols used by Morningstar to rate the sustainability of funds and stocks.

Morningstar is an investment information service providing individuals with information similar to that available to financial professionals. It has a sustainability rating system for many of the stocks and funds it covers. Morningstar data and information is clear and simple to interpret and, importantly, is independent of any fund or fund manager. Best of all, basic information is free, and some public libraries subscribe to the more detailed Morningstar data.

Morningstar uses a solid methodology to assesses how companies manage environmental, social, and governance factors relevant to their industries and relative to their peers. I recommend you read the information available on their website. You don't have to recreate their system for your own use. But understand that it is similar to those of many SRI advisories and funds. And, like many SRI firms, Morningstar bases its ratings on data provided by Sustainalytics (an independent SRI data company, that covers more than 4,500 companies globally).

Am I biased? Yes! Is Morningstar perfect? No. But I will tell you this: Their information can reduce the amount of work you need to do to complete your sustainability and financial asset allocations. Full disclosure: Sustainalytics was founded and is led by my former office mate and friend, Michael Jantzi, a globally renowned corporate sustainability analyst.

of directors. This is a very important strategy if you are interested in promoting and rewarding women's participation in the corporate world. It is clearly demonstrated that women are a highly underdeveloped competitive asset in many companies. This fund makes a very strong statement, hopefully inspiring not only investors but also women in business and the aspirations of young women and girls. Because the fund primarily focuses on women in management and board of directors positions, and doesn't go into the theme deeply (e.g., remuneration, work conditions etc.), it has a below average impact.

For Equality, Human Rights Issue, I chose the *Calvert Conservative Allocation Fund*. This is a great but low-impact fund, as it has multiple positive and negative screens, focusing on respect, promotion, and commitment to fundamental individual and community rights.

Step Five — Matching Sustainability Impact Allocation and Financial Asset Allocation

Once you have your Sustainability Impact Allocation sorted, you are going to have to categorize investments by their risk class to ensure you are getting a basket of assets called for by your financial asset allocation. This can be a bit tricky, and you will likely need a few iterations to get the mix right.

Environment, Carbon: While I love Elon Musk and all he does to power change, *Tesla* is a company with more financial risk than, say, GM or Apple, which are here-to-stay, large-cap companies. Tesla is far from a proven commodity and a bit dependent on Elon Musk. It is a medium financial risk.

Guggenheim Solar Exchange, Traded Fund is an index fund that tracks the MAC Global Solar Energy Index. It includes all sorts of companies in the solar industry, from manufacturing to financing to operating and project development. Good company diversification is offset somewhat by the relatively young clean-energy subsector. The fund, as a result, is a medium financial risk.

As mentioned, for the Fossil Fuels issue I picked *Powershares*. This index fund is based on the Wilder Hill New Energy Global Innovation Index and holds over 100 companies from around the world representing a range of energy technologies. This is a medium risk investment because, while geographically diverse, the fund has many small and some micro-cap companies in its portfolio.

SRI Impact Allocation 4							
		SRI Impact Allocation		Financial Allocation % of Portfolio			
Category	Issue	Total Points	SRI Impact Rating	Growth			Income	Cash
				Low	Medium	High		
Environment	Carbon	20						
	High — Tesla	15	Average			10		
	Guggenheim Solar ETF	5	Above Average		22			
	Fossil Fuels	15						
	Powershares Global Clean Energy Portfolio	15	Average		19			
Equality								
	Women	5						
	Pax Ellevate Global Women's Index Fund	5	Below Average		27			
	Human Rights	5						
	Calvert Income Fund	5	Low				12	10

Pax Ellevate Global Women's Index Fund focuses on women in management and on boards of directors. Developing paths for women in business is a competitive corporate asset development advantage in my mind. Because the fund invests primarily in large capital firms and is an index fund, it is rated a low risk.

For the Human Rights issue, I chose the *Calvert Income Fund*, which held over 58% of funds in U.S. corporate bonds and asset-backed securities. It has competitive returns compared to peer indices.

To be honest, this last step is a bit of a discovery process rather than a linear activity. And you will find that a perfect alignment of your financial and SRI asset allocations is not necessary for you to feel good about your portfolio. There is no rule saying you absolutely must align perfectly (unless, of course, you are a Virgo like me). If you like a given SRI issue for financial reasons, then over-allocate. I would not recommend seriously dislocating your financial risk allocation, however.

The result of this exercise is an Above Average SRI Impact Allocation, with a mix of impacts. Most impact is Above Average and High, given the energy and carbon investment selected. Lower Impacts are in the Women and Human Rights investments. The trade-off is that most of these investments are in larger companies with good potential branding of women and human rights issues in global and large national companies.

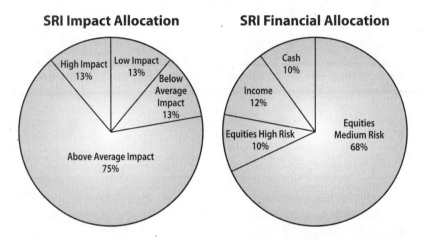

SRI Impact Allocation

High Impact 13%
Low Impact 13%
Below Average Impact 13%
Above Average Impact 75%

SRI Financial Allocation

Cash 10%
Income 12%
Equities High Risk 10%
Equities Medium Risk 68%

The resulting financial asset allocation is a balanced allocation appropriate for either a late Millennial or early Gen Xer. It has some solid growth potential with a mix of mostly medium- and low-growth equities but some higher-growth as well. It has some solid income generating from competitive funds and a bit of cash for biting into more investment opportunities as they come along.

Huge Uncomplicated Gratification (HUGs) Investments

One type of investment opportunity you will not easily find on Morningstar, or any other investment information service for that matter, is high-impact SRI opportunities.

You may recall, I refer to these investments as HUGs, or Huge Uncomplicated Gratification investments. Like the glowing tentacles of the Tree of Souls in the movie *Avatar*, HUGs viscerally connect you directly to the change you deeply care about. You may know them: They are local cooperative farms, community electrical grid enterprises, women-owned construction companies, organic breweries, mixed-income housing projects, microfinance investments in Africa, and much more.

By their very nature many but not all HUGs also have rather high financial risk. That does not make them undesirable investments — quite the opposite. Millennials with their long-term investment horizon and Gen Xers with disposable income can both consider these types of investments within a well-allocated portfolio.

Careful, though; not only do HUGs often have venture-capital –type risks, they are often highly illiquid. If you need your capital out in a hurry there can be fee penalties, or you may have to wait until the company has cash to give your money back, or both.

My wife and I went looking for HUGS in the early 1990s when we were in our mid-thirties. We decided to invest in a venture capital fund operated by the labor union movement. We put a few thousand dollars into the fund, which invested in labor-friendly, tech-type start-ups. Others, like *ILYGAD* interviewee Jen and her husband in San Francisco, invest in a restaurant-foodie-brewery company where they are customer-owners. And remember Jesse in Geneva, mentioned earlier, who has money in Oiko Credit, which invests in microfinance organizations, small-scale renewable energy, agricultural producer cooperatives, and much more in over thirteen developing countries.

Every year more deals like these are created. Many offer equity or quasi equity — as in, you get to be an owner of a project — or long-term debt certificates with fixed or variable interest.

Given the nature of these deals, many are highly attractive for their sustainability impact. There is a catch for investing, though, as most HUGs can be sold only under two conditions. The first is that the purchaser must be an accredited or sophisticated investor, a euphemism for people with so much money they can afford to lose some.

Non-accredited investors can invest too but only under specific rules of the recently enacted JOBS (Jumpstart Our Business Startups) Act. The Act allows equity crowdfunding platforms to permit non-accredited investors to privately invest in companies meeting several different offering criteria, including being offered through a Security and Exchange Commission-regulated intermediary (a broker dealer or a registered funding platform). An individual investor making less than $100,000 annually can invest up to $2,000 (or 5% of yearly income), while those making $100,000 or more per year can go up to 10%. Other investor and company criteria apply.[51]

Some lower-time cost, lower-risk options also exist. Calvert Foundation is one; it offers a Community Investment note for as low as $20. Notes invest in affordable housing projects, community economic and social development, some education, innovative local climate change solutions, and even some international fair trade and microfinance (among other great things). Notes are priced below market but have reasonable liquidity considerations.

If you want something a bit more "hands-on" in your neighborhood, you can look for community development financial institutions (CDFIs). These are registered financial institutions that aim to fill capital needs in underserved markets and populations. They can include community development corporations, community banks or credit unions, and local loan or venture capital funds. Like the Calvert Foundation, CDFI investments can offer below market returns, but the environmental and social returns typically more than compensate.

When you are in your twenties or thirties you can go for HUGs with the confidence that if they don't fully work out, or pay so well, your Great Long Slowdown (aka retirement) will not be any worse off financially, only better for the sustainability impact you might have had. If you have cash to spare, I would recommend an investment of this type. More than this, if you have time to spare, volunteer — many of these ventures benefit from responsible, active owners and promoters!

HUG investments are harder to find than, say, a Vanguard, Fidelity, or even a Domini social fund. So no matter how much of a HUG you want, you may not be able to find one. Check out Impactspace or the Global Impact Investing Network for more information on HUGs. Also check out the CDFI Coalition, which has a convenient CDFI locator tool on its website.

What you learned/did in this chapter
- Listed SRI passions to guide your portfolio SRI impact allocation.
- Allocated 100 SRI Impact Points to each of your SRI passions.
- Allocated SRI Impact Points by SRI issues by Low, Below Average, Average, Above Average, and High impact (the same system used by the free Morningstar investment information service).
- Researched securities (stocks, funds, etc.) to meet your SRI impact classification.
- Matched SRI allocation of select securities to match your financial asset allocation.

- Considered if you can get a typically higher-risk and/or lower-return HUG — Huge Uncomplicated Gratification — investment.
- Speaking of HUGS, go find someone and give/get one now!

CHAPTER THIRTEEN

Why You Don't Give a Damn About Investing Sustainably

"THERE ARE MANY REASONS," says Cheryl Smith, an executive at Trillium, a leading sustainability investment management firm out of Boston, "that sustainable and responsible investment (SRI) is not yet a retail movement and the greatest cocktail party chatter topic ever. Simply put, it's neither simple nor easy…. Simple and easy only gives you Donald Trump."

Sad but true.

The SRI industry's inability to connect, *really* connect, with people seems to be the first big reason people don't seem to give a damn.

But people do give a damn. Millions of people care about things sustainable, even if they don't use the word sustainable. It's damn hard, in fact, to find someone who *doesn't* give a damn about something sustainable.

It's equally hard to find a sustainable investment that is broadly available and super sweet attractive. As Adam Kanzer, a managing director at Domini Impact Investments, says, "People like to know what they are buying. And when they look at an index fund or best-of-sector negative fund they see only the 'Bad Things,' or the one company they don't like, maybe Coca Cola or Apple or what have you. They don't get the rest of it, the process of how we put a sustainable portfolio together, the influence we can have to improve corporate practices, and, of course, the need to structure a portfolio to provide a decent financial return. We all have our own personal high standards we'd like to see reflected, but as investors we need to deal with the real world. We invest in global companies, and none of them are perfect. We in the SRI industry sometimes make it difficult too, trying to sell a complex idea. We like to educate people about how the markets work and, in the process, sometimes we lose people in the details. The bottom line is that your investment decisions matter. We may spend too much time explaining how the sausage is made."

Information and knowledge gathering is a huge challenge to the industry, one that the investor sometimes does not fully appreciate. So even while the SRI industry might not provide perfect solutions, it does all the things investors need to feel confident about their investments. All they really need to do allocate their assets among different funds, and SRI professionals do the rest. "As opposed to managing your own investments," adds Kanzer, "we take care of the information asymmetries for you."

Many people want it to stay that way, no questions, no worries. On the other hand, some investors want big change, big impacts. Finding Coca-Cola in their portfolio may not do it for them, but investing in solar-powered underground vegetable gardens in unused factories does. But who gets to invest in these types of HUGs? Not many people. Even with the increasing popularity of so called high-impact investing and with Millennials' sustainability interests, for some, anything less is just not enough, so why bother? In many ways, Sampriti is both a typical and an atypical sustainable investor. She is typical because she cares a lot about a good many social and environmental issues and, admittedly, wants to know more about her own investment practice. Sampriti is somewhat atypical in that she works in the investment industry and has a MBA from Wharton.

"This is the *moment* to get off the couch," she says. "We are constantly being asked for charitable gifts. And there is a commonly held feeling that one should give to charitable organizations. So why don't we, myself included, not align our investments to the same ends? Why do I treat these two things as different? I follow the market; I have an MBA; why do I treat them differently, and avoid public securities that are not directly aligned with my values? When the Girl Scout comes to my house, I buy cookies I don't really like just to help the troop. It's a sales technique designed to make you feel good! And it works.

"I think we can also be as intentional about making investments.... Many of us think it's only for people who have done well. But that's not necessarily true. Most of us in our mid-forties started at the age of twenty-five or so with our first 401(k). This was typically our first major investment platform, and most of us opted for the generic Vanguard things. We looked at risk and historic return, and that's about it. Quick and easy.

"If I had had more education about SRI opportunities when I was young, I may have done something differently. But it's not just information. It has taken a while to for me to coalesce my thoughts around what really matters in life, from the grave injustices we can see all around us to routine gender bias and abuse of power and privilege and the heinous results. Life allowed me to see some sickening landscapes of environmental damage and of deep poverty. It takes time to accumulate, absorb the meaning of these images, to form a vision, and to find what we care about, the things we most treasure.

"The first is about wanting to invest in something you feel good about, and maybe, at the end of the day, even something you can love. There is so much jargon, self-justification, in SRI, like this is the way to go, the only and greatest way to marry morality to your investments. The SRI space is full of people who are very mission-oriented, and doggedly believe SRI is the only pursuit. This is amazing and important.

"But do they talk to me, in ways that connect with me?

"SRI mutual fund investments still feel a little further from 'my' purpose. It seems very passive. It may be a good way to begin with SRI, but the impact, the pure impact, that's harder to find — a 'do no harm' approach, opposed to really making change. I need to feel closer to the change I want.

"The second challenge is simpler: accessibility and connecting the product with the willing investor. SRI products just don't seem easily accessible, and it ought to be easier. The other side of that, and the third challenge, is the need to improve investors' financial literacy. We know that one dollar in early education returns millions in kids that are more involved in civics and have stronger, more pluralistic views of the world. But it's not fun to get educated on SRI!

"The last challenge is about SRI and your financial portfolio. For some, SRI makes, or seems to make, getting the right level of risk and return potential difficult. I know it's not, but we need to pay attention to our asset diversification strategy for SRI. With the myth of higher risk and lower return, we need to overcome this barrier, mythical or not.

"My work in investment, largely on Global 1000 company best practice, has led me to believe that identifying best corporate governance and compliance practice creates competitive advantage. Sure, there is social and environmental purpose in mind, but good management is just good management."

Sampriti left off saying that she doesn't want a passive approach to investment, even if for some people that is the way to go.

Polly, on the other hand, is a self-confessed, buy 'em and hold 'em girl. She lives outside New York City with her family of four. She works for a microfinance support organization that provides financial services to poor women in the South Pacific, is super smart, and has loads of hands-on experience making positive social impact. No-nonsense, straight-up, and to the point, Polly has a good handle on the challenges she and others face when wanting to make more SRIs.

"Sustainable and responsible investment? What does that mean? I was always a bit confused because it seems sustainable can be anything from environmental issues to poverty to taxes. Let's not even talk about what responsible means!

"When I think about investing with the goal of making the world a better place, I think of social impact investing. Not some mutual fund that avoids tobacco. I see investing in things with big impacts. Investing in companies that have obvious positive environmental impact: solar, wind, recycling. I just wouldn't lump other things into it.

"I know that there are funds that are beginning to focus more on this kind of impact, and that SRI is gaining in terms of awareness. But it has to fit our needs, my family's needs.

"We work with a financial adviser and are pretty hands-off about our investments. It's our second adviser. Our first, we found her via word of mouth. She was with Lehman Brothers, but she moved to Morgan Stanley Smith Barney, and when she left we got handed over to a father-son team in a Morgan Stanley office fifteen minutes away, which was convenient. They seem good, they are certified financial planners and tend to follow basic rules of thumb for investing.

"But my husband and I are boring about financial management! Or maybe better said, conventional. We do the basics, things like managing our debt, deciding what is good versus bad debt, paying our credit cards every month, paying more on our mortgage when we can, and saving for kids. But actively managing our investments? Not such a high priority.

"My husband? Definitively not interested in managing investments. I like the idea. But it's not like I have friends dying to sit around and discuss things with me. I get the feeling that my advisers are nice people; they don't really think about or focus on us. The investments they recommend are obviously based on a lot of research, but it seems boilerplate for people our age. I've asked around to other friends, and no one is excited or thrilled with their financial advisers either. They all have the same feeling, a visit or call every three years.... not enough!

"I would like to redo our investments, really dig into the portfolio to see what industries the companies we hold are in. I like to know the risk–return ratio. Our recent 401(k) performance is off and this makes me mad. Sometimes it makes me just want to stop investing. I know the conventional wisdom is to ride out the highs and the lows, but I am not sure we are living in a very conventional world anymore.

"I guess we just stick to the retirement income objective and max out our savings, and get what we get on returns.... We don't even know about Social Security — might help, maybe, might be gone too.

"So much of our financial planning depends on real estate prices and an eventual downsize of our house! But who the hell knows? We sure hope to make a bit of a profit off the house once the kids are gone. Financial planning just never seems to get to the top of the list, with so many other things to do.... I just run out of steam.

"As for social and environmental investment, we know they exist and like the idea, but neither my husband nor I really know about how they work. Neither do our advisers. I am just not sure what the options are. I mean, I should. I work for a save-the-world organization.

"Maybe I am not prioritizing this stuff. But with all the things we do: working full-time, volunteering for kids' sports teams like T-ball, paying bills and dealing with other house stuff, running errands, etc. Like it took weeks to fix up a mess when the payroll company at work screwed up some tax stuff.

"Stupid things always come up, and they push important things to the back burner. And I look at my portfolio, and it makes me feel not so good about things I think I should do, and want to do. I do have the mentality of being more active in my own personal finance and investment planning, which should be part and parcel of aligning my values to our investments. I am curious to see if others are as pathetic! Maybe that would spur me to action, and I would be more thoughtful and proactive with our investments.

"For some people, ignorance is bliss [about investment planning]. And maybe they will have to work until they are eighty-five. Maybe some people don't know and some simply don't want to know. The advice we get from our advisers: Your priority is retirement; then you save for kids; they can get financing, scholarship and loans, and you don't want to be a burden on kids. This stuff is scary!

"I am thinking about all this while being overwhelmed with so many other 'life' things happening! Now you want me to take on another project to do SRI?! With no support system or framework, a nice but unengaged financial adviser? My realtor contacts me more than my financial planner. So, if I were to make a move to more SRI, it would have to be a very good move and would require some work. And let's face it, I recently did more research on buying a new printer online than I did to find my financial planner!

"I really think if we had available and accessible resources, like a simple-to-form club or something, like other self-help movements, then that would help. You need a community in some respect to do SRI, access to resources when you get stuck and need help. It just seems there is no one there to help you ... and if not, the good intentions to do SRI never happen."

Polly is like many others considering SRI options but really needing help. I checked around and found a few SRI investment clubs, but not many. Time and knowledge are big constraints to more SRI; Polly is representative of that.

Joe, on the other hand, lives on the West Coast with his significant other. As the head of an international development consultancy office, he, like others interviewed for this book, knows a lot about sustainability. He also likes to dabble in stocks from time to time but only with his play money.

"Some of the biggest constraints to sustainable and responsible investing I have found," said Joe, "are that people don't know about investing generally. Most don't even want to make investments. It's kind of strange, really, because, for people working in bigger companies at least, the information is there and it's not hard to get help. Most just end up checking the box on the 401(k) options their friends chose. Is that choosing an investment?

"Some people choose on a whim. Take my friend, for example. He put money in the Martha Stewart brand and GE after the 2008 crash. He may have glanced at a few stock reports, maybe not, and hasn't checked the investments since.

"Maybe that's good, right? But who knows. Maybe if the returns were out of sight he would pay more attention. I might too if the sustainability impact was out of sight. Of course, there is the opposite; I remember looking at the SunEdison building awhile back, when its stock was going up rapidly and got to a billion or so each! Kidding, but it was high, over $100. And now? Now, it's worth $7, maybe, and there is some kind of class action going on. Glad I missed that.

"I want sustainability returns though, and every day when I drive into San Francisco I see things I want to change, local things I know we could make a big sustainable splash with. Just a bit of thought, effort, and capital needed. Artist cooperatives, natural food markets, things like that. But I don't; we don't. That's like SRI, I just don't have the time to invest.

"I know there are lots of SRI funds around. Even Fidelity has some, which I wonder about! I have some straight-up equity and bond funds, nothing special. But I know if I could find the right SRI fund, I would even sacrifice a half a percent a year to a social or environmental cause I liked!

"I don't even know if that's possible, or if I would have to give up return. I prefer not to, and I've seen lots of corporate social responsibility research that shows things like diversity, environmental care, etc. correlate to better stock performance, so I don't think you need to sacrifice returns.… Causality runs both ways, and I know one thing: The best managers are not into coal mining these days!

"I just think that SRI is quite sadly aimed at a small subset of the American public. I mean I just read that 43% of Americans couldn't deal with a four-hundred-dollar emergency. Most have only basic financial literacy."

Joe also said he knew that it was a myth that SRI underperforms the market. But he also knows most people are unaware of this.

That is something Adam at Domini Impact Investments deals with every day. The average retail investor simply doesn't have an "optimal" level of financial literacy. It's not because they don't want to learn. They do. People care about their investments a lot but don't have the time to learn how they work. That makes the job of the intermediaries, the financial advisers, so incredibly important. The average investor often will not read a fund's prospectus or check online about past performance; it's just not something they want to do.

"There is a bit of a Catch-22 in the investment world," explains Kanzer. "One reason you hire a mutual fund manager is that you're not a financial expert. And then you're expected to be a financial expert to protect yourself and make the right decisions. On top of that, we all have too many choices.

"That is one benefit of SRI," adds Kanzer. "It can touch people at a different level. It gets them to talk about things they care about and engages them in real conversations about personal goals. Social and environmental outcomes are also part of your investment returns, whether you know it or not. All investments have a positive or a negative impact. We are intentional about trying to create a positive impact."

The siren call of caring was always with Katherine. A management professional working on the East Coast, she is conversant with investment and sustainability. Still young, in her thirties, she can relate to both the "hard" quantitative side of investment but the human side of the equation.

Katherine and I discussed many things, including how people don't make as many friends in their thirties as they did in their twenties. A lot of people are very focused on career and don't even have time to sit down with the friends they have, let alone gather with new groups of the same age to talk about investments. Instead, we remember the times in our twenties when that was all that we did.

Of course, as we get older we have a harder time sharing our financial emotions. Money can be such a sensitive comparison issue, always prevalent, in the background of conversations, and we all seem to drift to people of the same income status.

"But it's a sensitive issue," as Katherine attests. We talked about many of our friends who would despair about their finances. One we chatted about was a public-sector administrator who had little confidence about finances, and was getting some help on her IRA from another friend with greater financial knowledge when she was around twenty-eight. The woman was open and vulnerable, and like many people felt unprepared for the future financially. At the time, she didn't have lots of money but wanted to start setting goals but really didn't know what to do with what she had. It was a big learning time and still a big concern. Both Katherine and I discussed feeling the same at around the same age.

Katherine sees the challenges of getting investors to even think about SRI. We discussed many of the challenges, and the first we agreed upon was return. People would love SRI if they could always get 8% annual return. But that's hard to achieve, even in regular investment.

The second challenge we talked about was education, and we found it's amazing how many people talk about SRI, even impact investment, but don't even go to mainstream SRI websites to get information. There must be a motivational way to make it easy to access SRI information and then understand what it's all about!

There are many barriers to successful SRI investing, and information, we agreed, is a huge one. Investment is complicated, SRI even more so. What is affordable housing, for example, and why is it important? The answer: education, education, education! To get to the mainstream, we decided, investors need to understand that investment is one language and SRI is another and that people can't pick them up just like that! It became clear, to us anyhow, that we need to learn and not just grab the first product that comes along like many do when faced with their 401(k) plan list of eligible investments. It requires time and energy to learn about SRI.

The third challenge we spoke of is related to the second: We forget that most companies we invest in are helping people to build things. This is important, but then again, many people just want to make money. Still, for many others, especially around the age of forty, this never resonated; it can feel dirty, greedy, and distasteful just to think about how our investments make money, while other people can't even invest for lack of capital. We did find hope in the not-uncommon sentiment of wanting a more communal culture, societies that help each other; the hope that the Pope, the UN, and millions of organizations doing good things give! These kinds of connections can make us all feel like our purpose is relevant and with the times, and is getting people to change their frame of thought toward good things.

The theme of incremental change. This is busting SRI. The biggest successes? Yawn. Tobacco and weapons. Cheryl Smith of Trillium knows this: "It's unfortunate but true," she says; "SRI 'wins' have been more about process than product. Yet the hope of convincing a tobacco or oil company to not be a tobacco company or oil company is a ridiculous ask. But people tend to want that! We can get Intel to be better stewards of water, or the Gap to care about human and labor rights. We can and do get incremental change. Does this excite people?"

Julie doesn't think so. In fact, after spending a lot of time living in Asia, she came home to the United States recently really wanting to invest in SRI. She had read a lot of information and found that because "I know a lot about investing and sustainability, the SRI marketing really turns me off. Totally overselling. I can't imagine how it can attract someone who doesn't know so much.... All the terminology. For a newbie, it's hard to know what it all means. Most people don't have time to figure it out either. I can only imagine how deceived someone would feel if they bought into a boring index fund only to find investments in all the companies that they think really suck at sustainability."

If lack of investment knowledge limits active personal investment interest, when it comes to SRI, what keeps people on the proverbial couch and on the SRI sidelines most? The need for a connection or a Huge Uncomplicated Gratification or HUG investment.

Take Emily. Emily is a young professional several years into her work life. She took a circuitous path to responsible investment. She studied international relations in Spain and Egypt and started working in NGOs, always chasing donations from the private sector and corporate philanthropy. This got her thinking about graduate school, specifically about political rights and voting.

When Emily got back to the States she went to law school, where she saw the impact of corporations on human rights. She went on to work in the investment industry and maintained her interest in human rights, always seeking a way to align clients with their mission.

"Mission.... It's very individual, very personal. To be an adviser with the responsibility of meeting a person's mission.... Wow! Each institution has its personality and stakeholders, what they value, etc. The role of the adviser should be to help clients clarify their missions or adapt them to what is out there and make a link to portfolio strategy.... That's difficult.

"As for myself, I guess I could say I am looking forward to, but really have not been able to do much, on the investment side. There are so many exciting opportunities for accredited investors. The public side [publicly traded securities] is more a risk-management strategy, with bland sustainable opportunities, even the thematic approaches. There are too many regulations, many good ones, protecting investors to really get the impact investments out in the public investment domain! There are some, like the Calvert Foundation, which seems to 'democratize' sustainable investment.... It's below market given the risk, but at least equal to short-term treasuries.

"I think another challenge is the gap between SRI funds that have not done well enough to motivate investors. The SRI product is often not motivating. It's a different story, a different way to think about impact, which is more incremental, not the same or as exciting as improving a watershed, recovering a stream, or providing microfinance. The impact of publicly available SRI funds is just harder to see, and the language of environmental, social, and governance risk mitigation....

"There are a number of approaches where you can get with the 'better players' who know what they are doing, how they engage; then you can understand the end results of their performance.... The story needs to be told, but also the investor needs to want to know. There are some terrific opportunities, for example, in water and energy, that fit endorphin-seeking SRI investors.

"It's about marketing, I guess. High-impact investment opportunities are not for everyone, but everyone wants them. Not everyone is satisfied or turned on by the incremental change of SRI public funds. This is tough because intuitively we all know we need more than incremental change, but we also know that many people, heck the economy as a whole, depend on companies in these funds, and to expect them to change overnight may not work out for anyone."

Deborah, a hero of mine who works at an international inclusive finance organization supporting micro-finance institutions in the developing world, would agree. Like many others in sustainability-related employment, she feels her work is already contributing. (And she is right.)

Deborah relates that her investments are "not fully aligned with my values, but when you are working in social issues all day, then go home and spend the time, what, researching SRI? Who are those superhuman, weird, amped-on-SRI people? This is no easy, do-it-yourself project. We have just to make it 'easy for advisers' to offer great SRI."

Off the couch

I have to begin the end of this chapter by quoting Adam Kanzer from Domini again, when he notes, "SRI makes so much common sense, so why isn't everyone doing it? There is a huge number of *our* people, *Mother Jones*, *The Nation*, etc... lots of them, many, many more than there are investing in Domini, Calvert Investors, Pax World, or First Affirmative Financial Network. It's a large number of hardcore sustainability types. Why aren't they investing?"

Connecting the dots is one thing. Most just can't manage to overcome the crazy of daily life to get at SRI. We see the connection but can be confused by investment generally, and even more by SRI!

You want to retire well and are worried, often worried sick, about not having enough money. It doesn't help that conventional financial advisers steer you away from SRI, often perpetuating the myth that you are going to lose money.

Mostly it's just that SRI seems too complicated, too complex. Most want to write the check and get on to other things. Most of you certainly don't want to spend your weekend reading and researching. "Buy-and-Hold Polly" for most of us is okay.

But Polly knows better and, like most of us, knows that improved financial literacy and a bit of time off the couch nurturing our investments are the only way to maximize financial and sustainability returns.

CHAPTER FOURTEEN

Who Does Give a Damn about Investing Sustainably?

THERE ARE MANY MORE CHALLENGES to making SRI than we can stipulate.

But there are many deep pleasures to be had too. Some are the joys of connecting, of doing something more than just making money, like making someone else's life better *while* making money!

Where are the specific sustainable investment pleasure points that inspired investors to invest? And how did they manage to do it given the challenges? Two words:

Vision and action.

Vision is the biggest part of making sustainable investments. People feel it their bones, passion linked to vision, for their world and the world.

And it takes action. It may take many dozens of baby steps, as Rick from Georgia says, but connecting your vision to the financial decisions you make, big or small, is such a good feeling. And Rick should know; he got his vision started being a sustainable consumer, then decided to work in sustainable industries, and then....

Well, you get the story. Like a spiritual awareness, SRI adds to the plea-sure of a fuller life. Though most of the folks interviewed for *ILYGAD* will tell you they are not pure or perfect about sustainability, it is their goal to be so. They have an almost Buddha-like approach to it. Patiently, one step after another, they will reach perfection.

Like many things in life, the vision is key but the execution makes it roll. That takes planning. Lots of planning. This, says Arandi from Washington, DC, "means learning and improving your financial literacy — either that or, at the least, being able to select the right financial adviser and asking the right questions! Asset allocation, SRI performance, etc. These things count."

Arandi is a great source of inspiration. She has been working in economic development for nearly twenty years in areas including fair trade, microfinance, and youth development. Using the environment as an example, Arandi is all about minimizing negative externalities of business, or at least having the business pay for them until net environmental damage is zero. Perpetuating awful social impacts, she believes, can also be avoided and is a basic "social responsibility" she feels deeply.

"On the personal side it's been a lesson in learning about investment," Arandi recounts. "I got divorced a few years back, and prior to that my husband took care of all the finances. He had been to business school and his forte and passion was financial management and investments. We got married right after school, and it was a good division of work. I didn't mind him doing that either! I trusted his asset allocation decisions and kind of went along with what he decided. It was okay, you know: long-term, value-oriented, with a good amount of savings for retirement.

"When we separated, I had to take responsibility for these things. For about six months or so I left the portfolio as it was .... It's not like something I wanted to do in my free time. But little by little I started spending time on my investments, every quarter, as a habit. I wanted to get a handle on my finances, but it was a process. I even got my friend to help a bit!

"I never seem to spend enough time on it to get to the level of comfort I want. What does that mean, get a handle? At first, all I wanted to do was to understand what was in my portfolio. And I wanted to know what the returns had been over time. Then I wanted to see what to do with the cash I had available so I could start to optimize my investments.

"Each quarter I look to see how I am doing, not to try to replace low-performing things. I am more of a set-it-and-forget-it kind of gal. So far, I only have 5% of my assets in SRI. To be honest, I am not really focusing on that yet as I am still trying to learn and get a basic handle on portfolio. I am in it for safety and long-term return, so there is time.

"It may sound corny, but for me, my investments are all about retirement. That's important for me. I want my independence. I want to maintain a middle-class lifestyle in retirement, and for that, I need *at least* market-rate returns. I've looked at investment calculators, and they seem a bit rosy. I even went to a financial adviser and paid for his services, but really, I didn't find his recommendations to be illuminating.

"My vision in retirement is to do the things I've learned through life I would love to do. I can imagine a lot of things! But I don't need a ton of money. So many people seem to be miserable, and being rich is such a relative concept. This is the time, and more SRI is to come."

Living in the Midwest, Marissa takes the same view to visioning a different lifestyle than the norm. Marissa is a sustainability social media pundit, and passionate about the environment: "We need to protect healthy clean water and air.... Obviously social issues are very important, but I am most passionate about the environmental side of things. Oil, coal, natural gas, and all that, not an option. We need clean technology, especially in the developing world, where new energy development is needed. In developing countries, they are not talking about important social issues like transgender rights, gay marriage, and such — folks in the developing world are consumed with plain survival. My hope is that if we can remedy environmental problems, we will have the time and resources to address these pressing social concerns....

"I have thought about sustainable investments. Maybe I am not the best person to give answers on that topic though. We don't have too many investments because we don't make a massive income. I just love what I do, so that is compensation! We do have some savings and my husband manages them. My husband invests our 403(k) (403[b] OR 401[k]) with different mutual funds with a long-term view. We don't actively manage; they just sit there and do their well-diversified work for us!

"We've yet to have a full discussion on sustainable investment, even though these concepts constantly surround me. My husband is of the same mindset, though, and really understands where I am coming from.

"You know, we talk to people like my dad; he was always invested in BP and Chevron, and even he knew that solar was the next thing. Our financial goals are simple — we want safe investments to slowly grow our wealth. We want to retire well, but don't care about being millionaires. You know — afford things we need, kids to college in fifteen years or so, live a comfortable life with a vacation from time to time! Happiness!"

Vision sustains interest, but planning executes it. Few people interviewed for *ILYGAD* have really got to the point where they fully connect the dots. Jessie, late of Washington, DC, now living in Europe, has managed to do what most want to do: fully link his values with his investments. Jessie makes it sound easy to do to. But he has come a long way from small town in West Virginia, growing up, as he puts it, comfortably poor.

"When I think about my own habits... I believe that doing anything well, to have lasting merit, should be done sustainably and should be beneficial for more than just myself or my family. This translates into working for a foundation trying to unbend poverty. I've been at that for over twenty years.

"Along the way, I hope I have learned a bit about the application of capital to sustainable development. Whatever I do, I want it to be sustainable, something of lasting nature that creates a healthy ecosystem around whatever it is that gets done, something with long-term, harmonious, mutual reinforcement for good things intended and unintended to spring forth! For me, it's about every little thing you do, and not just a series of actions, it's a mindfulness about the environment and others around you.

"It blows me away all the amazing people I've met over my career — so aware, so forward thinking when it comes to their investment portfolio. They just won't buy Exxon, for example, but they want to invest well for themselves and to support Greenpeace!

"We are hopefully coming out of Caveman Capital into the era of Camelot Capital, or capital that is a driving force for building the kind of world we want. It's something by design and not what we have now, which is the default, proven fatal for our species and that of many, many others. It's a time to be intentional about the world we want the kids to live in. Fear of the default, I fear, is not enough.

"Exceptionalism just doesn't work anymore. Used to be, not that long ago, that old behaviors — go out gambling, hire prostitutes, bribe officials, etc. — were common. You would go to church, contribute, and all is good. Capitalism works the same way — rape, pillage, and plunder and atone through donations, which can never repair the social and environmental damage. It's a dumb way to work.

"Conscious capital, on the other hand, has none of this nonsense, and we can see that in the great performance of some SRI funds, which thoughtfully aligned values to their investment decision-making.

"When I was at my last job, our 401(k) wasn't really SRI. Managed by a competent conventional fund manager, there were some elements that were small cap, international investment, or some proxy SRI, but nothing intentional. When I left, I had my IRA rolled over, most of my funds into the Pax World.... Free at last! I also have an investment in Oiko Credit, a Dutch-based international development social enterprise investment fund, and the rest is in my local credit union, which also does some good social investments.

"The Pax World fund tracks a peer Vanguard fund, which is important to my wife. She is smart, engaged, and gets this stuff, and she looks out for the family. Our investments are very important to her as well. But when you talk about retirement, you must have the conversation about SRI and conventional, especially because, and this is notable, SRI does not have the whole infrastructure set up to sell, with built-in incentives, millions of financial advisers, etc.... Without all that, it can be an intimidating thing, especially if you have come from the poverty both my wife and I know all too well."

Jessie is considering making more impact investments, noting tongue and cheek that while SRI mutual funds serve a purpose, their "best-of-class approach seems likely to only keep the axe murders out of the party, but the drug dealers and car thieves are more than welcome.... Pick your criminals?"

Jen is an editor/ journalist on the West Coast and, like Jessie, has given a good deal of thought to SRI. Like most (late!) Millennials, she feels her small family of one daughter and a numbers-oriented significant other don't have enough money to risk. "We are, after all," she says, "involved in a small business venture, and our financial investments is about protecting our family's future.

"My husband works in a bigger, more stable company than I do, and there we do the 401(k) Vanguard thing. If we had a private asset manager, we might be able to move toward a more sustainable portfolio, but we are not there yet, given our choice of jobs. So it's a normal boring mutual fund for us, and not necessarily what I would recommend to others!"

But Jen proceeded to drop a very cool impact investment bomb on me. "I've always believed what motivates people are the things that they can see or touch, or somehow touches them in a personal way. 'On me, in me, and around me' — that's what connects, and that is why local is so tangible; it affects parts of your life. It also really makes movements go and is at the core of behavioral change.

"That is why we made an investment in a local company's direct public offering, or DPO. A DPO is like an initial public offering but for a private firm. The company we invest is a San Francisco-based food venture company that sells things like wine, beer, cheese, and snacks. The offering we took part in was for a total of $600k, with an annual return of 4%. We can take our money out only after three years, but that's ultra-local investment for you! And it's so much nicer than money in the stock market.

"There was a bunch of legal things to go through to do it, and we couldn't do more than 10% of our net worth. But it was just a bunch of regular people coming together in a cool project. It will never be a billion-dollar company, as much as we would love to imagine that, but it's a real business that takes a loan from customers and creates local economic well-being. We go by for snacks and drinks frequently, talk to the owners, and it's like we feel a part of what is going on! These tangible benefits aside, we also get a financial return! It is working so well; the company is opening a second store.

"I try not to preach too much, but it is curious how sometimes you find people just need a bit of connection. The other day I went to my eyebrow plucker and we got to talking. 'What do you do?' she asked me. 'I am an environmental journalist,' I told her. She said 'Oh! I don't believe in climate change.'

"Akkk! I thought of stopping and changing pluckers then and there. But as she had only done one brow, I was stuck. But we got to talking, and I soon learned that she bought most food locally, organic, free range eggs, etc., very high quality and not cheap! So even in her own way she was living a more sustainable life than a lot of others and was part of the climate change solution!"

Sampriti, whose story was partially told in Chapter Thirteen, thinks finding passions and connecting is a good way to go. She talked about some crowd-sourcing funding ideas as ways to experiment with SRI impact market. "You can," she says, "put your money where your causes are through initiatives like KIVA, where you lend directly to women or micro enterprises in developing countries. It's sort of like an investment and a donation. It's similar in many ways to Save the Children, where you provide a monthly amount to a child overseas, except your money goes to an entrepreneur via a pre-qualified microfinance institution."

Rick of Georgia also wants to invest in high-impact ways, not only through his investments but also through his life work. He entered the field of sustainability by way of the Great Recession: "I always knew what I wanted to do with my life, and that was to make it meaningful. So I started work with *Let My People Go Surfing*, which uses business to solve environmental and social problems. Then I did some solar panel installation out west, and once I had enough of that, I went back to school for a sustainable business MBA.

"The next challenge was to pay my student loan. I lived in Jackson Hole for a while, getting involved in the local community, did some time at a biodiesel manufacturing start-up, but it went under within a year. Then I went on to create a sustainability program for community development organizations and did a bit of consulting for an energy project in Savanah. I also did some work building a data base of green building materials, and now I am with a sustainability solutions software company.

"I've had some kind of career so far! But sustainability drives me, my career, my consumer decisions, and will direct my investing too. Pundits say Millennials are more engaged and purpose minded. I like to think I am, but when I think of my circle of friends, I am the only one like this! Everyone else seems like they are just out there trying to make a living. Jobs are a means to an end, keep the lights on, the kids fed…. I read about Millennials, and yes, personally, I am purpose driven. Maybe it's a regional thing, but down here in the deep Southeastern USA… well, when I came back from Wyoming my best friends were saying like 'Solar? are you serious? Does that work???'

"That was six years ago, and now it's a bit different. There is still that 'If you are a sustainability type (aka hippie) you are a freeloader and don't like to work' mentality. There is big resistance to change. Hey, I grew up in a conservative family where we were taught to work hard and pay our taxes. We were also taught that if you are a Democrat, you don't want to work and are always trying to restrict me from making a living for my family.

"This is the real tragedy of the commons. It is shocking, but it is changing, especially and paradoxically because we are starting to see some huge solar initiatives in Georgia and South Carolina! It's a conversation door opener now! Clean energy now means jobs, clean air, and has massive social and health implications, another wedge…. people respond to things that affect their welfare."

Beth works in DC and inherited a work ethic from her mother, growing up in a household with the mindset that "to whom much is given much is expected" and that we have responsibility for ourselves and to others. She was also a 2008 Obama campaign organizer, which was "life-changing" as it exposed her to all types of people and ways of organizing people with shared values, no matter their class, culture, or income. She learned how a "campaign transformed social issues to personal agency, how important collaboration was… the simple coming together of people from all walks of life, with the purpose of creating a better world."

"Is SRI transformational?" she asked. "Everyone has time, intellectual capacities, heart, and relationships, and it's how we look at all those assets at our disposal for the greater and greatest purpose.

"Maybe SRI is a bit like a campaign. Impact investment is on the one side and looks more at the power of our individual assets — time, money, and influence. SRI funds help us link value-based assets with those of others to create a whole much greater than the parts. If I put my limited assets into a product I believe in, start to create more capital, that makes a difference, and if that business is responsible in some identifiable way, we can say we've had an influence on value creation. That is more than just a return on our capital investment. It's a broader influence on value creation.

"Personally, I like to look at all the decisions I make to use my free time, money, purchases…. It's a holistic picture. I am not a billionaire, but I want do something to push sustainability along — things that I believe create value.

"That said, for the first two years at [my new] job in impact investing, I didn't even look at my own portfolio! My mother manages my savings accounts and it took a lot of convincing for her to look at SRI and impact investing, but my mother loves me, so she did it. She did it despite the discomfort or 'newness' of SRI for her, a traditional investment adviser.

"And she did it despite the small size of my portfolio. She first examined what was in my portfolio. It turned out most of the things in there I didn't want. So, Mom went out and found different fund options for me, which I went through using my SRI criteria until I felt I was 100% values aligned. The options were mostly mutual funds. But I did want some impact or alternative investment and got placed into the Calvert Foundation Community Investment Note®, which invests in community and economic development.

"SRI takes time to do, no doubt, and most people I imagine don't want to allocate time to their investments. The way I figure, unless you have a great mother to do it for you, you have go in baby steps, looking at one or two products at a time… small on-ramps so it stays interesting and fulfilling, and not overwhelming."

Kate from the West Coast took a different and equally successful approach. She has had "a financial adviser for eight or nine years. I said to him

I didn't want to be in companies with bad human rights records; nor did I want my money to make guns, dig up coal, or mess with the environment generally.

"The guy knew his work, I will give him that. But he didn't know how to invest sustainably. He said so, and I told him I don't have the time to do the research myself, so you do it or I leave. We agreed that he would he filter funds through my criteria and then recommend some new ones for me to approve. He warned that returns would have a higher chance of being lower than my old funds. I said, it's okay I don't want a world with guns, cigarettes, and abused people. I was putting my money where my values are."

Organic Lettuce and Baby Steps Toward Great SRI

What excites people enough to do something that seems as difficult as aligning their values with their investments?

Clearly for those who have done it, in part or in full, the force of their passion for the environment, for vibrant communities, human rights, and all the other good stuff that makes up sustainability is the primal goo, the origin.

There is a correlation too, it seems, between people who link SRI investments to the rest of their lives. Buying your first organic lettuce may just be the first baby step toward reassessing your portfolio. You don't have to be like Rick in Georgia, whose inspirational employment history makes me entirely jealous and wishing I was young again!

Be it gang-pressing your mother's help or telling your financial adviser to do it or get lost, there are ways to get over the information asymmetries between you and your dream SRI portfolio.

Take heart as did Beth. If you have the will, it's just one patient baby step after the next, and sooner than you might notice, you have the sustainable investments you truly want.

She will get there and so will you!

CHAPTER FIFTEEN

Stomping the Devil of Inertia
and Joining the Sustainability Investment Tribe

INERTIA. It's an interesting word. It's a word linked to physics and causes most of us to think about the time we didn't quite put the parking brake on full, much to the distress of our garbage cans.

But did you know that *inertia* comes from the Latin word for idleness or laziness?

That's why Johannes Kepler, in his 1621 *Epitome Astronomiae Copernicanae*, got the physics ball rolling by defining inertia as "resistance" to movement. He thought that the natural state of things was to be at rest, a fact so obvious that it needed no further explanation. Or so he thought.

Sir Isaac Newton didn't agree. He thought inertia was an "innate force" inherent in matter that resisted any acceleration — image yourself lying on the couch after a hard day at work, and you get the point. If something or someone doesn't push you off the couch, there you will stay, for what is at rest (or in motion) stays that way unless upset by some external force.

But wait! That's not all. Enter Einstein. Yes, Einstein! Einstein's theory of relativity radically redefined the concept of inertia to include not just mass (you on the couch) but energy as well. Seems our energy is either moving or not.

Now, if you look up the meaning of inertia in psychology, you find it indicates an indisposition to change. More colloquially, we can get stuck in a state of mind. Even if we want it, change is hard to achieve. Think of diets, exercise, disciplined work habits, tidiness etc. All infuriatingly unidirectional and usually away from where we want to go!

> *Inertia — the tendency of people, having once established a life trajectory, to continue on that course unless acted on by a greater force.*

From time to time, we can summon the energy or take a bump from someone or something to change our ways. But it seldom works for most of us. And even if we do happen to shake off whatever habit we don't want, at some point we usually revert to the mean (as in the average) of our behavior.

Getting people to change their habits is tough even when clear and present personal danger is involved. Take health care. Everyone who smokes now knows tobacco causes cancer, but millions continue to smoke. Not taking all our prescribed antibiotics was once thought to cause a relapse of symptoms, yet how many bottles half full of pills do we have in our medicine cabinets? Seems we are bound by inertia to do nothing about things we know will hurt us.

Self-destructive inaction happens for many reasons.

People don't like medicine or doctors' offices, or maybe they can't afford to take care of themselves. The bigger part of the challenge is not, however, rooted in rational thought but "in the powerful cognitive bias against change." It seems unless forced to do something differently, we keep repeating behavior that dooms us in doses large and small.

Take the experiment where dozens of participants were told they had a 90% chance of *not* getting a big-ass electrical shock in ten seconds unless they pressed a little button.[52] Shockingly, more than half the participants waited to get their shock!

Sound like our collective approach to climate change? Once again, I digress.

Another group was instructed to push the button to protect themselves from a pending shock *prior* to the experiment beginning. Of those who did the warm-up-button calisthenics, almost all of them took the 90% no-shock option during the experiment. Seems simply pushing a button was enough to redirect their psychological inertia and make a rational decision.

> So many fail because they don't get started — they don't go.
> They don't overcome inertia.
>
> — Ben Stein

The upshot: When faced with a choice requiring a proactive decision, people often do nothing, even when the simplest of actions could clearly improve their current or future state of being. But how to change?

Doctors sometimes break the ice of psychological inertia by administering a first dose of a medicine, arranging a free workout session, or walking to the drug store with the patient to get that nicotine patch. Psychologist Kurt Lewin argued over fifty years ago that individuals who remain "frozen in place" even when presented with attractive opportunities can be helped into a new direction. All they need, he posited, was

- Some sort of disruption, a shock to get unstuck and moving,
- To realize they desire change because of the disruption, and
- To get restuck in a new and different state and direction.

Seems once you are bumped into acting, once movement is initiated, inertia helps you to keep moving in a new direction. Just a little nudge can get you off the proverbial couch.

Stomping the Devil of Inertia and Getting Unstuck

The trick to getting off the proverbial conventional investment couch is to get moving, directing your energy and mass into a more and better SRI direction.

My Stomping the Devil of Inertia process for more SRI has seven steps. Each step requires just a little work, each designed to motivate a small change and give you a boost of energy, scooting you toward putting your values into action.

> *The Devil.*
> *An imaginary externalization of human evil used as an excuse for immorality.*
> *As in the devil made me do it :(*
>
> — Urban Dictionary

You can decide the amount of time to take between steps, but you need to know that, according to Sir Isaac and millions of failed dieters, anti-inertial forces lurk to slow your process. Set reasonable, life-manageable timeline targets for getting each step done, but don't let things slide so long that you lose that righteously won momentum.

If it's important, you will make the time. If not, stop reading now, knowing your sustainability impact is lost to humanity forever, and that the Devil and immorality have won the day....

Kidding — I would never try to guilt you into this really... Really, I wouldn't.

(Before you enter this process, know that it is designed to have you make investments, or at the least direct your financial planner/ broker to do so for you. If you are not up to doing this while meeting your financial and/or investment goals, do not, I repeat, DO NOT EVEN TRY! But you don't get a refund on this book either, so don't ask.)

1.0 Connect with A Single Value

Go somewhere quiet. Meditative. Then reflect on the values you care about most deeply. Connect with them, really connect. Connect in a deeply personal, visceral way.

Connect to something you care about so deeply it sends you mad, glad, or sad when you think about it and all the things companies are doing to make it more of a mess. Or think about how you could address this profound value to right wrongs and make things better.

If you have a significant other, get them to join you. Contemplate, mediate. Then both write your top three choices down on a slip of paper. From each other's slips, choose the one you least identify with. Do it again. Then again. Now of the two remaining issues, choose one. If you choose the same one, great. If not, figure it out. I can't get you any closer than this!

A single-issue focus can be quite powerful. My friend Simon has worked in SRI for years, sustaining his vision of sustainability by fighting against heartbreaking human rights violations in Burma-Myanmar. Heather has been motivated for years by factory workers' rights in China. (She and Lynn Zhang produced an amazing documentary, *Complicit.*) For me, it's been how our transportation systems have ruined cities, wreaked havoc on communities, and fouled our environment.

But why just one issue?

What I have found through advising hundreds of people on sustainability, finance, and economics over the years is that we all have so many different issues we care about, the complexity of it all can make doing something about it all just too hard. Narrowing your issues down to one you really feel for makes action easier. I did this in my own portfolio makeover a couple of years ago, and it worked charms. After I sold my first awful stock and bought trains... Wow — was I motivated to think about the next, and then the next, etc.

When you are done finding your issue, congratulate yourself, this step is done.

Tell family, friends with similar interests, the barista at your favorite café, anyone willing to listen. Scribe your issue on a piece of paper and tuck it into your wallet, post it on the fridge, or write it on the mirror in your bathroom. It's important!

Now, make an inviolate date with your computer in one week. The state of humanity hangs on your ability to make this date.

2.0 Make a Sustainable Investment

Now that you have waited a week, you are going to make an SRI that matches your values.

TODAY.

Right now, in fact. It will have nothing to do with your asset allocation, nothing to do with your retirement. Nothing to do with anything except the deeply held value you defined last week. Take out the paper you stuck in your wallet (or peel it off the fridge, or wipe it off the mirror). Time to get excited.

Go to your computer. Now type SRI and your value into your browser search engine. Do not look for a HUG (an investment with Huge Uncomplicated Gratification). Look for something simple, like one of the many SRI index or mutual funds.

When you find a fund or investment you like, don't worry about the fees or making the wrong decision. Fill out the forms, get out your card, and buy fifty dollars' worth. (Note that some funds have minimum investments, so check that out before getting too excited.) But if you can, get fifty dollars worth, no more, no less.

If you don't have an online investment account, there are many to choose from. E-Trade, for example, allows you to set up an account with which you can trade for free for six months without a minimum deposit, after which you need to put in five hundred dollars. If you don't want to keep the account, you can withdraw the money. If you can afford the five hundred dollars, then by all means keep the account running!

If you have a financial adviser managing your portfolio, call them. They might try to talk you out of it. Tell them you respect their advice and services, and that they are a good adviser, but you are working on a project to save the world and they should support you. Be clear what you want.

Don't argue, don't proselytize. Tell them you don't want to pay for the trade either.

The simplest, and in my mind best, way to do this is by going to the Calvert Foundation website. Once there, look for the Invest button, click it, then click Community Investment Note. From there it will take you through a less-than -five- minute registration process.

Push the "Buy" button, and have fun!

However you do this, once done, print out a copy of your investment receipt. Pin it to the wall, tape it to the fridge, or paste it to the mirror in the bathroom. If you have a used frame about, frame it. Put it somewhere you and, importantly, others will see it all the time.

Now write three friends and tell them what you did. If they write back saying you are nuts, or great, or unbelievable, invite them for coffee, so you can tell them about it. Don't proselytize, but if they ask.... Or go to a BBQ, cocktail party, soccer practice, and brag. You are now, even more than before, part of the solution!

But right now, go have chocolate or cheesecake or a beer or something. Celebrate your second step toward more of the kind of world you want for your kids, your grandkids. Think of all those marmots, polar bears, fungi, communities in Africa, etc., you might save through your investment.

Finally, read the next step below. Once you are done, define a date for taking it.

3.0 SRI Asset Allocation Tool

If you have not done your SRI and/or financial asset allocation homework, do it now — both financial (Part Two) and SRI (Chapter Twelve). If you have already done them, celebrate and go to the next step, or just celebrate! If you decide on the latter, set a date to do Step 4.0.

4.0 Arm Yourself for Action

This step is the simplest and the hardest. Through it, you must find where you keep your investment information. Once you have, and I understand this may take a moment for some and hours for others, you are going to get organized to use the SRI asset allocation tool from Chapter Eleven.

If, like many others, you have investments held in different places, and the records are spread out among different folders — electronic or otherwise — you might have to make an Excel spreadsheet to list them all. The list should include the basics for now: name of holdings, value of holdings, the number shares/ units you own, asset allocation type, and any applicable fees. (See Appendix Five for fee information.)

If you are lucky like me, and all your investments are listed in one accessible place (my online brokerage account) and you can remember the password (I keep all my passwords in a super-encrypted file), bookmark the page on your browser: You are going to be checking it more often.

If you have a financial adviser, tell them you want this list. If they can't do this for you, wonder why they can't, and/or why you are paying for their services. Let them know what you are wondering about. The list should come *pronto*.

As per Step 1.0, meditate on your summary list. Wonder what is in each item. Wonder about their performance.

That's all you need to do for now.

You are done.

Have a sustainability treat of organic coffee or wine, or maybe get your SO who didn't do all this work to take you for dinner. Or just dance around a bit. You must CELEBRATE because YOU are once again an even bigger part of the solution!

5.0 Its Time to Learn to Buy

I hope it's a rainy, late Sunday afternoon, or maybe early morning as the sun is coming up. A quiet time. Open your investment list.

Mediate for a minute and then repeat: Ignorance is not bliss. Information and knowledge are power. This is your mantra. Say it a few times because the objective of this step is to learn and then find and make one or two real SRI investments.

First, take out the spreadsheet of your investment holdings. Look at them one at a time. If they are mutual funds, describe them, each of their holdings. If they are stocks and bonds, what companies or governments do they belong to? Go to Morningstar to get free basic descriptions of the funds and/or securities if you need to.

Do you see what you like? Anything jump out? Research each fund or security as much or as little as you like (hint: a bit more is better). Make a note or two as you go through them and reflect on your values.

Now spend thirty minutes researching an SRI alternative to the one or two funds or securities you don't like the most. Assuming you have the asset allocation you like, you will need to have an alternative in the same asset class.

There are many ways to do this. Morningstar has sustainability ratings for many securities and funds. A general browser search will also yield great treasures of information. Appendix Six has a list to get you going as well. You can check out performance on Morningstar, or go to the company website. Remember to check fees.

If you are looking for securities, you can go to the SRI fund holdings of a desired asset class and see if it's there or not. SRI index funds, or ETFs, have good listings, but remember the screens applied are not aggressive and may be too generalized for your liking. You can get more information on the screens either directly on the site, or you may need to read the prospectus.

Remember to check the financial asset class of the security, including if it is large, medium, or small cap. Check out reviews of fund or stock performance. There are many good and free sites with historic performance analysis.

Pick one or two SRIs you would like to make. The list can include getting rid of something you don't want! Check against your financial asset allocation to make sure it's in line with your risk and return needs.

If you have a financial adviser, I recommend you do this step anyhow. Then call them and tell them what you did, how easy it was, and that you expect them to know about SRI if only because SRI investments assets total over $6.7 trillion. If they don't know or care, why are you using their services again?

Yeah! Now go talk with a friend about the investments you want to make. Maybe you can convince them to do the same! Take them for lunch; get them to be part of the solution. Personally, I would buy them a copy of this book. Tell them I said Hi!

Now I am going to recommend you slow your inertia down just a bit. Take a couple of weeks or so to think about your list. At the end of the gestation period, decide which to buy or sell. Best make the decision on a Tuesday one or two weeks hence, because you are going to buy an SRI on Wednesday after 11 am, when buying is theoretically and historically at its best! Best to watch the news the night before and mid-morning in case there is some market-shaking news going on. If there is, wait another week.

You are almost there! Contemplate life as an SRI investor, as it will soon come to be!

6.0 Find a Benchmark Investment and Watch it Grow

This step is not so hard to do. You can do this as a part of the previous step or you can do it in the week(s) you are thinking about whether you really want to buy a fund/stock or not.

Once you know the type of SRI asset you want to buy, simply type into your browser the benchmark for your investments: "asset type X."

If it is a fund, type "benchmark for XX type fund or stock" (e.g. international large capital equity fund). The query will give you a fund or stock market index against which to assess your stock/fund performance. (See Appendix Seven for some examples.) For example, I hold MSCI KLD Social 400 ETF, which holds 400 U.S. large capital companies and benchmarks against the MSCI USA IMI.

Fast forward to the Wednesday of your choice. Cue up the investment buy button up at 10:30 am. At precisely 11 am, push "Buy" and make a REAL SRI investment. Or call your financial adviser to do the same.

You've done it! A real SRI!! You are my new hero.

Go out to a local brew pub or organic garden market, or do something with lots of sustainability HUGs to celebrate. You must do this and you need to take your SO or a good friend. Tell them what you did: Relatively speaking you are an SRI pro now, so don't let 'em go; get them on our team.

7.0 SRI Asset Reallocation Repeat Steps

For most of you, the steps above will take between one to three months. Any more than this leaves you open to any number of things that can bump your mass and energy off from where you want to go!

Don't be the *Titanic*! Now that you have moral and physical inertia high ground, the Devil sulking away in some faraway corner, you can repeat Steps 4.0 through 6.0, replacing your funds and securities one at a time, as I like to do, or all at once. Before you know it, you will have a resplendent SRI portfolio. If you are training your adviser, it may take longer, but they will get on board — or you can find one that will!

Be very careful to do your asset allocation work. As mentioned earlier, in my haste I once bought far too much transportation stock, and when transport went into the "ditch" I was stuck with losses that are taking some time to bounce back. So pay heed; take your time. Unless you know something other stock pickers don't, you don't need to time the market. I advise taking a week to gestate on every selection. If nothing dramatic happens during that week, it's okay to buy.

Do the process until you are done reallocating everything in your portfolio, from conventional burn-the-world-securities and funds to great, green, vibrant, and harmonious SRI.

If you are a "Buy-and-Hold Polly," you are done for a year, after which you may have to rebalance your allocations. If you are a bit more active like Joe or me, you can muck about daily, weekly, or whenever!

Finally, if you don't feel you can do this and meet your financial and investment goals —

DON'T EVEN TRY! Get a professional to help.

BONUS HUG (Huge Uncomplicated Gratification investment)

If avoiding tobacco or dropping Coca-Cola from your portfolio just isn't enough, you can do what Jennifer on the West Coast did and go for a big HUG. Remember, most HUGs are packed with potent social impact possibilities but also often have tons of risk or turgid liquidity.

Start small if you can, never ever more than 10% of your assets, and less if you can, at least to start. Even if you have lots of money you could happily lose, start small. Being a responsible sustainability investor is important to the success of HUG-like investments. They need informed and active investors to ensure they perform.

I always looked at HUGs as either safe and below market returns, or amazing potential returns but with risk that makes me think of them as a donation. Look at Calvert Foundation or one of the many community development fund investment options. Investing in a local credit union is also a good way to support local investments. Some have long-term certificates of deposit that are fairly liquid, and you don't always have to be an active member, or even a member of their geographic community, to join or buy.

Some companies, like Veris Wealth Managers, have great depth of experience in HUGging but tend to work with larger clients. Many of the First Affirmative Financial Network advisers also know about HUGs, as do several advisers in Progressive Asset Management, Walden, and others. All good folk, but do your due diligence on any adviser before signing on the line. (See Bonus Chapter for some considerations on how to select an adviser.)

Whatever you do, look for the HUG that suits your passions! The HUGs I made in the 1990s in funds supporting labor in new tech ventures and preferred shares in a community credit union gave me tons of happiness. Remember, too, that I lost some money as well as well as making some, so be careful.

Most conventional financial advisers will not likely be able to help you find a HUG. This is one occasion where I would not even ask why they are your adviser. What they can and should do, however, is advise you on how a specific HUG will fit in your long-term investment plan, as well as asking all the right risk, allocation, and liquidity questions. If they don't, why are you using their services?

YOU ARE NOW DONE!

When you have done Steps 1 to 7, your investments will be in full balance with your values.

Your mass and energy will not only be pulsing hot happy but will be pushing you toward your own chosen sustainability destiny. You will also be part of a great energy force pushing millions of other sustainable and responsible investors toward creating a more just and sustainable world.

You are now a full member of the SRI Tribe. Celebrate that.

Chapter Sixteen

Sustainability Portfolio Makeovers for the 21st Century

M OST OF US RELATE MAKEOVERS to those gaudy television shows where people who don't fit Barbie and Ken cultural "norms" are shift-shaped, outfitted, and spray-painted into looking like a magazine model or movie star. The popularity of these shows is a little insulting, and I always wondered why so many take a primal pleasure from what we perceive to be the misfortune of others (i.e., they look so bad). Then bam, they become one of us.

Psychologists will tell you we love to mire in *schadenfreude* because the misfortune of another person makes us feel somehow superior. I always used to think schadenfreude was a shot of nasty liquor you drink upside down at party. Now I know better. It literally means *damage and joy*.

Wow.

When it comes to people makeovers, that's harsh. But maybe it's not such a bad feeling to have when looking at conventional investment portfolios and thinking about a makeover: the damage they do, and the joys of *sustainabilitizing* them.

Not sure I like people conforming to the norm through a makeover. But I do like the idea of a conventional investment portfolio makeover to fit SRI tribal norms. I'm not going to mince words. SRI is morally, metaphysically, naturally, and spiritually more fulfilling, and dare I say, the right thing to do.

After so many years of working in all sorts of crazy places around the world, I have given up on relativism. We live in a global society now, and sustainability must be the norm. I will not boast of moral superiority. But I humbly invoke the superiority of sustainability. It is in this spirit of makeover — damage to joy — that I offer you the makeover of two conventional portfolios, one for a Gen Xer and another for a Millennial.

Gen X Portfolio Makeover

James and Charlotte are a fifty-five- and fifty-three-year-old couple with two children, one just in and the other just about to go to university. They have managed their own portfolio for a dozen years after leaving a major brokerage, which they said just didn't pay attention to their needs.

Look at the list of holdings in their portfolio, below. If you've done your own financial asset allocation exercise and you are Gen X, you should note right away that this portfolio may be a bit financially aggressive for a couple their age, with a total of no fixed income assets and 91% in Growth securities, much of it rated higher risk by Morningstar. But James and Charlotte want to slow down the work thing in less than ten years, so it is time for a financial as well as an SRI asset reallocation.

Gen X Portfolio — Original Portfolio						
Security	Symbol	Asset Class	Risk Level	SRI Asset	$ Value (000s)	% Portfolio
Alibaba	BABA	Growth	Average	Low	8.7	7.6%
Mueller Water Products	MWA	Growth	High	High	7.5	6.6%
Headwaters	HW	Growth	High	High	15.6	13.7%
Domtar	UFS	Growth	Average	Medium	6.7	5.9%
Dow	DOW	Growth	Average	Medium	19.7	17.3%
Vanguard Total Market Index ETF	VTI	Growth	Average	Medium	9.8	8.6%
Stryker Corp	SYK	Growth	Average	Low	9.8	8.6%
Wells Fargo & Co	WFC	Growth	Average	Low	6.2	5.4%
BMG Bullion Fund	BMG100	Growth	High	Low	20.1	17.6%
Cash		Cash			10.1	8.8%

Charlotte wanted to keep a strong potential for equity appreciation as her risk tolerance is far above that of James. But after working through their financial planning exercise in Chapter Six, they settled on keeping good growth potential as an overall strategy. It helps that they don't plan to fully retire soon and that they have some real estate investment earning solid income. This means it's unlikely that they will dip into their investment fund until they reach their late sixties.

Their financial asset allocation makeover goal is staying with good growth stocks/ funds, but with less risk. They also wanted some fixed income, while keeping about the same cash for buying opportunities but not so much that they lose to inflation.

After working through the SRI Asset Allocator, they realized that they had much less impact than they wanted. Some investments they inherited from their conventional brokerage adviser had just stuck around. "We had always intended to swap these stocks out," said James, "but just never seem to have gotten around to it"

"The Dow stocks were gifted to us by a friend after we helped her out financially for a while," Charlotte related, "and while Dow is trying to do some good sustainability things, we never felt all that comfortable with a global chemical company. Just a personal feeling." Both liked the sustainability angle of their two water stocks, Mueller and Headwaters, but as smaller companies, they tended to be a bit too sensitive to market

Gen X Portfolio — After Makeover							
Security	Symbol	Asset Class	Risk Level	SRI Asset	% Portfolio	$ Value	Source
Amazon	AMZN	Growth	Average	Medium	4.5	3.9%	Domini
Guggenheim S&P Global Water ETF	CGW	Growth	Average	High	8.2	7.2%	Morningstar
Greenbrier	GBX	Growth	Average	High	6.5	5.7%	Own
IBM	IBM	Growth	Low	Medium	6.7	5.9%	Own
Vanguard Total Market Index ETF	VTI	Growth	Low	Medium	19.7	17.3%	Own
IShares MSCI KLD 400 Social Index Fund	DSI	Growth	Low	Very High	22.1	19.4%	Morningstar
TD Bank	TD	Growth	Low	Medium	6.2	5.4%	Own
Pax Ellevate Global Women's Index Fund	PXWEX	Growth	Low	Very High	8.5	7.4%	Morningstar
Domini Impact Bond Fund	DSBIX	Fixed Income	N/A	Very High	20.1	17.6%	Morningstar
Vanguard Municipal Money Market Fund	VMSXX	Cash	N/A	Very Low	11.7	10.2%	Own

movements. Neither James nor Charlotte could remember why they were holding BMG Bullion.

After their makeover, they said, "Our new portfolio felt relieving." The bulk of their holdings are now in low-fee exchange trade funds (ETFs). Their financial asset allocation has fewer higher-risk securities, is more diversified, and with 72% in growth securities or funds, still has good potential for capital appreciation. This mix fits James and Charlotte's near-term growth goals with a start down the path toward more fixed-income securities.

They increased their holding of Vanguard because they liked the fact that as unit holders they get some share of the fund's profit. James liked the efforts of John C. Bogle, founder of Vanguard, to "democratize" capitalism a bit: "Imperfect, I know, but I like the effort, and the performance is good and steady." The company does not, however, do much in the way of other types of SRI and tends to vote with management on sustainability issues (i.e., against them!)

The additions they liked the most are the two Domini funds. "The Domini family of funds have been around for a long time and the company has always been a leader in SRI. It's owned by Amy Domini; she once won *People's* woman of accomplishment award or something like that, a bonus!" said Charlotte. The Ellevate Global Women's Index Fund Institutional Class was a little light on growth potential, but both James and Charlotte see supporting women in business as a way to bring more sustainability issues into the workplace and corporate boardrooms while making a strong statement buy.

Guggenheim S&P Global Water ETF swapped out the two smaller water stocks for a fund with much larger companies and geographic di-versification. James and Charlotte bought four other stocks for different sustainability and financial reasons: the Greenbrier company for sustain-ability in transportation, IBM and Amazon for sustainability in technology, and TD for sustainability leadership in the financial sector.

The comparative SRI impact before and after the makeover is nothing short of exciting for the couple. "We went from too much financial risk and too little SRI performance to more comfortable risk and greater SRI im-pact!" The research took about seven hours, which they did together, each taking a security type they liked the most, with the overriding objectives of women, water, and transportation.

Gen X - SRI Asset Allocation

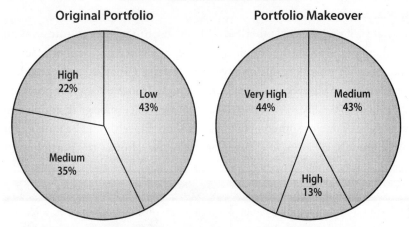

Gen X - Financial Asset Allocation

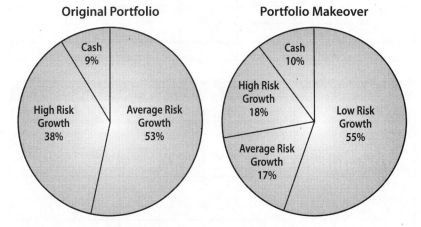

Millennial Portfolio Makeover

Bennet is from the Southern U.S. and lives with his girlfriend Julie. Both in their early thirties, they have been together some time now but have only just begun to invest together. Bennet is self-employed, and Julie works in the service industry. Income is erratic but enough for their low-consumption lifestyle.

Bennet managed to invest $22,000 in a 401(k) he had while working for a company his first few years out of college. When he started the job, like many others, he asked around a bit about a fund box he should check on the 401(k) application. Ultimately, he went for something standard, a

Fidelity Fund, which "performs okay, but nothing better than any other similar fund."

Late last year, Bennet inherited $20,000 in Citibank shares from an aunt, to add to the $16,000 the couple had saved for a down payment on a house, apartment, or small organic hobby farm property. (They still can't decide!)

Doing a makeover, "We realized a couple things about our portfolio that we didn't really like. The first was that we didn't manage it, and the results were blah. For someone our age, we thought we should be looking for more growth. We were so focused on saving for a house, the portfolio just

Millennial Portfolio Original Portfolio					
Security	Symbol	Asset Class	Risk Level	SRI Asset	$ Value (000)
Fidelity Blue Chip Value	FBCVX	Growth	Medium	Low	22.6
Citi	C	Growth	Medium	Low	19.9
Cash		Cash			16.2
					58.7

Millennial Portfolio After							
Security	Symbol	Asset Class	Risk Level	SRI Asset	$ Value	% of Portfolio	Source of Research
Pax Small Cap Individual Investor	PXSCX	Growth	Medium	High	15.2	25.9%	Morningstar
Pax Global Environmental Markets Fund	PGRNX	Growth	High	High	10	17.0%	Morningstar
Domini Impact International Equity Fund	DOMIX	Equities	Medium	High	12	DOMIX	Domini
Whole Foods Market (NASDAQ)	WFM	Growth	High	High	5.2	8.9%	PAX
Natus Medical (NASDAQ)	BABY	Growth	High	High	5.9	10.1%	Own
Calvert Foundation	N/A	Fixed Income	Low	Very High	2.1	3.6%	Advisor
Self Help Federal Credit Union	N/A	Cash	Low	Very High	20.3	34.6%	Advisor
				Total $	58.7	100.0%	

got lost. When we got the inheritance of the Citi shares, we were unsure what to do, and that's when we thought, Citi, really, is that us?"

In the makeover, they decided to keep saving toward their real estate dream, so increased their cash position in the Self Help Federal Credit Union. They didn't have a local credit union they liked, so they opted to invest in the SFCU, as it accepts members from anywhere in the country but still works hard to support local communities.

With the Pax World funds, they got increased exposure to higher-growth securities but within the context of a diversified fund. "We just couldn't see ourselves selecting individual companies for most of our portfolio," Bennet

Millennial - Financial Asset Allocation

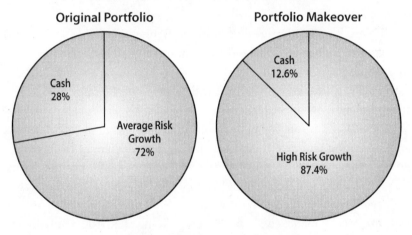

Original Portfolio

Cash
28%

Average Risk
Growth
72%

Portfolio Makeover

Cash
12.6%

High Risk Growth
87.4%

Millennial - SRI Asset Allocation

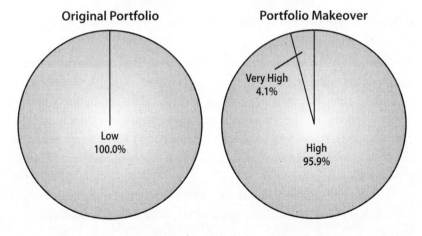

Original Portfolio

Low
100.0%

Portfolio Makeover

Very High
4.1%

High
95.9%

explains. "The Domini Impact International provides the good international-al exposure our adviser recommended we have; given 40% of market value lies outside the U.S. we thought that it was important. That the companies in this fund are mid to large cap and across Europe and Asia Pacific lowers the risk but keeps it growth oriented."

That said, Bennet and Julie both really wanted to invest in healthy food options and saw Whole Foods as a bit of a higher-risk stock market HUG. The investment in Natus, a medical firm focused on infant care, was motivated by family experience. The Calvert Foundation's low financial return and very high SRI impact gave them exposure to a range of social enterprise, housing, and community development investments in both the United States and in developing countries which, as confirmed globalists, was appealing to them.

The resulting financial reallocation had Bennet and Julie go from con-servative to higher growth (and risk), more aligned with their age and investment horizon. Eventually their cash will go toward a more conser-vative asset — real estate — which will balance out their portfolio to suit their moderate risk appetite.

The SRI allocation saw tremendous improvement in potential impact and, as important, gave them great joy by better aligning their portfo-lio with their values. "We love all the investments, really, but the Natus, Calvert, and the Self-Help Credit Union we love the most. It makes us feel connected, even though they (the last two investments anyhow) are the least important financially!" said Bennet. "Going from 100% very low to almost 90% very high SRI allocation is a total high!"

Why Do A Makeover Now?

The image I keep getting after reading over these portfolio makeovers is the one, you know, where the once unconventional man or woman is finally unveiled to family and friends.

I can't help it, but maybe like many or most of us, I feel better about the person even though we are applauding convergence toward a norm that basically has us screwing up as a society. If you don't agree, fine, but for me, one of my favorite songs will always be "No Mirrors In My Nana's House" by Sweet Honey in the Rock.

Or perhaps I err in using the term makeover and should have used makeunder, a less known concept and the antithesis of makeover. One where the artificial is peeled back to allow the natural to emerge. Seems a bit more fitting — conventional portfolio makeunder to reveal natural SRI attributes.

Pie in the sky, hopeful, or visionary objective? No damage, just joy.

I would humbly submit that the spirit of an SRI makeunder provides a superior return to conventional investment approaches. Financially, the returns from a well-selected SRI portfolio should be about the same as a conventional portfolio, or even better over the long term. Spiritually and existentially, SRI only adds to our joy of life, our sense of well-being and contentment. It's a partial contributory force for good for family and tribe.

Final Word: Giving a Damn is Great

From the days before digital, when filing cabinets stored the data that is now the bedrock of SRI analysis, SRI professionals have borne constant ridicule and criticism to build a $6.7 trillion investment movement... a movement that is changing the very nature of capitalism.

In the battles for legitimacy in the oh-so-conservative world of finance, the priests and priestesses, witches and warlocks, and the odd buttoned-down type, fought off the urge to become dominated by narrow issues to prove SRIs broad-based approach to sustainability and its financial competitiveness. They have fiercely advocated on behalf of thousands of concerned investors and collaborated heart and soul with other aligned social, economic, and environmental movements, all the while developing an enviable range of exciting products and services, just for You.

Yet, despite all they have done, and despite success both broad and profound on so many sustainability issues dear to us, SRI remains something of an institutional movement.

Supply has done more than its fair share. Demand, it's your turn now.

Individual investors, millions of you with shared sustainability values, it's time to rise up! There is no excuse. Whether you are a Gen Xer moving toward the Great Long Slowdown or a Millennial just starting out, SRI has what you need.

It is time you set your Economic Being free to do what it wants to do, which is save the world. As Yoda once (might) have said, "Sustainability values of ours, let them guide you, let them guide you." I hope *ILYGAD* showed you it is possible, desirable even, to save for your financial goals, save to avoid consumption, and save to invest the very most you can. I also hope it showed you that it is possible to align your financial goals and sustainability values in allocations that meet your goals as an investor and as a guardian of sustainability.

Use other books, use other guides, find SRI financial advisers — they are out there waiting for you. Do your work and then get your friends, family, community of faith, and others to come along. Brag at every cocktail party and BBQ about your incredible SRI portfolio; and not just the Huge Uncomplicated Gratification investments but your mutual and index funds as well. Yes, brag about the heroic shareholder advocates working on your behalf to change the world!

And yes, take the Devil of Inertia and shake him loose; you don't want or need him anymore. Do the relatively modest amount of work and shove off in the right direction. I guarantee you, paying attention to your finances can never be a bad thing. Do it cautiously, get help as you need it, but do it and you will sleep better at night, Do it, and like inspirational *ILYGAD* interviewees, you will excite others with hope and action for the future.

Live well, live sustainably, and Invest Like You Give a Damn.

Choosing a Financial Planner

Why have a Plan?

THERE ARE MANY REASONS to create a financial plan. One of the most important is that it can help you set and stick to a long-term vision, which in turn informs more immediate, day-to-day decisions. Very few people like financial limitations and discipline in the present, but when you can literally see yourself and/or your family moving toward your financial and life goals, inch by inch or by leaps and bounds, it helps to assuage, even make happy, our immediate gratification glands! A plan keeps you on track toward your financial goals.

Many are tempted to DYI their plan. This can work, but sadly, history shows it works best for only a very few. Taking up with a professional adviser might be a better option, giving you the added "umph" to make more of the right moves to reach your financial and sustainability vision.

Writes Lisa Wright of the *Toronto Star*: "It's a bit counter-intuitive for a lot of people because everything is about avoiding the middle man and going direct — robo-advisers and all the online stuff. The pendulum has really swung but professional advice has gotten more valuable because managing money is more complex than ever. There's a difference between information and knowledge. So, information is plentiful. Knowledge, even, is abundant. There are a lot of knowledgeable investors but are they wise? And that's the key — the wisdom."[53]

> *There is a difference between information and knowledge*
> — Lisa Wright in the *Toronto Star*

Certainly, DYI is an option, but what's the chance of you having all the knowledge to understand the intricacies of investment, accounting, tax, retirement, legal, or estate planning? Very few financial planners can provide all these services.

So, just as you can drive your car with your foot, you can DYI your financial planning and management. But does that necessarily make it a good idea? If you have the knowledge, or the time and ability, and if it is what cranks your gears, then by all means, give it a go. For most of us, the continuous effort to stay current with changing products, services, and financial and tax regulations is just not what the weekends were made for.

Also, as you have likely sensed from *Invest Like You Give a Damn*, financial planning and management are as much about psychology as finance. Several ILYGAD interviewees noted that, even if you don't like the advice of an outside perspective, it can provide reflection points for your own interests, needs, and possibilities. The adviser of the future, says Wright, "is going to be that hybrid between money manager, wealth planner and that little bit of life coach to help people really articulate what their dreams and goals are, and using money to facilitate that."[54]

> *A successful adviser doesn't have to look for clients. Clients seek her or him out.*
>
> — Sue Orman[55]

Financial planners can play schoolmaster, helping you stay disciplined. You can even empower them to make some of your financial moves once a direction is set (e.g., securities selection), or you may simply ask them to bug you (with appropriate input!) to take steps and make decisions. As my favorite Scottish poet long ago said, the best laid plans gang aft agley: Things that can go wrong often do, through lack of time, procrastination, poor intel, etc. This can hurt in the wallet and on the balance sheet of finance and life. It can also lead to the lost opportunity of potential not pursued. Someone helping you walk the line can really help.

As argued throughout *ILYGAD*, you need to be on top of your own financial situation. You can't delegate that responsibility to an adviser. You need to know some of the basics, and, more importantly, care about what is going on in your portfolio. The money you might spend to get help may seem inordinate, but if you are going to meet your goals and contribute the most to making the world more sustainable, a financial adviser of one type or another can likely help you save or make more money than you might on your own. Don't confuse cash today with income tomorrow.

Fiduciary versus Suitability Standard

The fiduciary standard means an adviser must act in the best interest of his or her client at all times. They must provide objective and unbiased information that service the client's needs first. This means the adviser is, for example, prohibited from selling a client one investment over another similar investment simply because it offers higher commissions. It also means advisers must do their best to offer sound and appropriate investment advice, acting only on accurate and complete information. Avoiding conflict of interest is key, and something fiduciary advisers must transparently disclose. Additionally, advisers must place trades under best execution standard, or the best security for the lowest cost. Financial advisers charging a fee for service, including CFPs, follow the fiduciary standard.

The suitability obligation ensures that an adviser's recommendations are consistent with the best interests of a client. This requires advisers to make recommendations that suit client needs, without necessarily putting their interests below those of the client. An adviser must be reasonably sure their recommendations are suitable for their client (in terms of financial needs, objectives, and circumstances). All things being equal, an adviser can, for example, sell the higher commissioned of two similar funds that suit the client's needs.

Many Reasons to Seek a Financial Adviser

There are many practical reasons for deciding to go out and find a financial planner. There are also some important financial, life-defining moments that literally beg you to seek the wisdom of a financial planner. Here is a short list in no order:

- Want to manage your finances better but are unsure where to start.
- Time is short, why do your own financial planning and management?
- You want professional input to your own DYI plan.
- You lack the expertise on one or more important areas of planning (e.g., investments, insurance, taxes, retirement).
- You have an immediate financial need or unplanned life event.
- Recently married or co-habiting and want to bring your financial lives together.

- Starting or expanding a business, changing career, or want to gig it free-lance with all the tax and cash-flow-management considerations.
- Added to the family? Taxes, college savings, estate planning, enough said.
- Sale or purchase of a big asset in the pipeline (e.g., house, a roof for a house, second property etc.).
- You hit an unexpected jackpot, won lottery, inherited money, etc.
- You feel "lost" in finance.
- You know impartial, independent input and strategy would be good!
- You are getting old, wealthier, and things financial are getting complicated.

Testing Character

There was a commercial for a financial planning company on the TV awhile back where clients, so happy with their advisers, would invite him or her to family events and picnics. Oh, what joy! My experience, and that of many *ILYGAD* interviewees, was not so much like that. It turns out that finding a financial adviser is harder than one would imagine.

Besides, I would argue, you don't need to *like* your adviser in this way. *Au contraire*, "all business" is better. That way you can "yell" at them when they do dumb things or admonish them for things done wrong. Okay, that's hyperbole to make a point. What I do want is to deeply respect my adviser and to trust they or I can speak truth to power in our relationship.

Several key characteristics to consider:

- Depth and breadth of professional experience.
- Diverse life experience and wisdom that has tested their personal mettle.
- Been through market upswings and downturns that tested their financial planning fortitude.
- Know what they know, know what they don't know (usually comes with experience).
- Well-reasoned and rational… especially as it relates to their financial planning and investment philosophy and biases.
- Provable record of accomplishments in financial planning and beyond.
- Not a family member or friend. Not a family member or friend. (I said that twice, and you know why.)
- They have life experiences you can relate to.

There are, however, a couple of characteristics that simply cannot be rendered in a bullet.

Take **trust**. You must trust your adviser. This is the only way you can develop a long-term relationship. Trust is born of confidence, which in turn will allow them to successfully develop a financial plan and management strategy for you. You are going to have to share a lot of private information about yourself and your family if the relationship is to work. And you are going to have to trust your adviser to always act in your best interest. This may cause you to look for someone who understands your life experiences, philosophy, and vision, and thus could lead you to working with an adviser of the same gender, sexual orientation, or cultural and social sensitivities. (But remember they must also be eminently qualified… more on that below.)

Financial advisers are people too, so they will have their planning and investment biases. Getting to know their investment approach and philosophy is key. You need to divine and understand this thoroughly *before* committing to using their services. (See list of questions above.) Are they a Buy-and-Hold Polly? Or are they Treasury Bill Conservative?

To get an idea about this, ask who their typical client is and see if it sounds like you. Experience and practice makes perfect, so if they have other similar clients they will likely be able to relate stories of successes, challenges, and even failures. They should be able to tell you about investments that would be of interest to a portfolio like your own.

Beware of anyone who claims to always do better than the market: No one does. A good adviser will focus on how they will help you meet your needs within your personal risk level comfort zone and time horizon, with your goals in mind. They should use plain language so you can easily understand their message. If an adviser leaves you feeling dazed like we all used to feel (pre-GPS) after getting complicated directions from some random guy on the corner, unable to respond for fear of demonstrating ignorance, run.

An adviser should also be a skilled listener. Rule of thumb: 10% questions, 90% listening during a preliminary interview. An adviser may offer an insight or two, but until they really know you and your financial situation, why would they dare to give you advice?

A personalized plan and management strategy takes time, and they need more than a short conversation to "get" you. You and they should discuss goals and objectives first and they should explain what you will get and how from developing a relationship with them. More information is required to get to nitty gritty recommendations that will work for you: It's called due diligence!

At this point, the adviser should clearly state cost of services, disclaimers to what they are responsible for or not, and give you a sense of the risks that come along with their approach. They should clearly mention potential conflicts of interest as well (e.g., if and how they are compensated for any product/ service or strategy they recommend). Some professional designations like the Certified Financial Planner (CFP) are required to disclose conflicts. (See box above on Fiduciary versus Suitability, and Appendix Five on fees.)

It's a bad sign if an advisor pressures you or pushes a decision faster than you want to make it. Remember, you set the pace, so set one that is manageable and meaningful to you, not them. It's your business that counts, not theirs.

Finally, you will probably visit potential advisers at their office a couple of times before deciding to use their services. Seeing their place of work will help you measure their character. Pay attention to how their offices is kept; is it neat and tidy? Confidential client files left out in the open? Is it appropriately busy and are you comfortable with the general atmosphere?

A final note on privacy: You are going to have to regularly provide a bunch of personal and financial information to the financial adviser of your choice. Some designations, like the CFP, must keep all information confidential, sharing it only to manage business on your behalf with your agreement (or when the courts tell them too). Not getting a confidentiality agreement in your contract must be a deal breaker.

Types of Services Offered

Anyone who wants to can hang out the financial adviser shingle, but a shingle alone does not an expert make. Some advisers may have a bunch of designations, some more confidence building than others. But what are all these acronyms and what do they mean? This section deals with how to distinguish between designations and how to check their validity.

As noted above and throughout *ILYGAD*, financial advisers come in various shapes and sizes. Some are built for more generalized tasks. Others are more specialized. Some plan but don't provide investment services.

Others manage or sell investments, but don't do much financial planning. Retirement income planning is the focus of some; others may focus on the saving phase of life. Accountants could lower your tax bill and insurance agents can sell you a policy, but both are likely not able or interested in advising your broader financial picture.

You may, in fact, need more than one adviser. Financial planners can provide guidance on how to save, invest, and increase household asset value. They can help you toward meeting specific financial goals, from buying a house to taking an extended leave from work. But the rewards for having and following a good plan can all be undone if you don't have equally good tax advice. Your adviser should know what they know and know what they don't know, and get you the advice you need from the experts that can provide it (e.g., attorneys, estate planners, and accountants etc.).

Knowing how each potential type of adviser can meet your needs, and their motivation for doing so, is important. Here are the main types of advisers you may have to consider:

Financial Advisers/Planners focus on all aspects of your financial life, such as how much to save and what type of insurance you need — it is not just about the investments.

Investment advisers offer advice on all types of securities and must be registered with the Securities and Exchange Commission (SEC) and/or a state securities agency. Investment advisers recommend the buying and selling of securities for their clients. Financial planners will often also advise clients on their portfolio allocations, and many are also registered investment advisers.

Investment advisers must have a security license and cannot legally sell securities products without one. If an adviser you are speaking with doesn't have a license, they can use third party stockbrokers. Stockbrokers are also licensed by a state and generally earn transaction-based commissions. They or their company must be a registered member of the Financial Industry Regulatory Authority (FINRA). This requires passing the FINRA securities exams.

Retirement Planners are focused on the whole Social Security, tax, investment, pension, retirement dance. Us older folk near retirement might find it helpful to consult with someone specialized in this area. Some designations signaling this expertise include Retirement Management Analyst (RMA) or a Retirement Income Certified Professional (RICP).

Accountants provide tax advice, including the preparation and submission of tax returns. Certified Public Accountants (CPAs) are licensed by the state in which they work. CPAs must pass a grueling set of Personal Financial Specialist course work and exams administered by the American Institution of Certified Public Accountants

Attorneys. Few attorneys offer financial planning services. If they do, they normally focus on estate and tax planning. Your financial planner could need help from an attorney on highly specific issues requiring legal advice or legal document preparation (e.g., wills, trusts, or business related issues).

Estate planners can give you estate tax or other estate planning issues advice, including how to manage your assets after you've departed this Earth. Remember, no matter who provides estate planning advice — attorneys, accountants, financial planners, insurance agents, trust bankers, etc. — you will need a lawyer for all estate-related legal documents (e.g., wills, trusts and powers of attorney, etc.).

Insurance agents are state(s) licensed to sell a range of insurance products (e.g., life, health, property, casualty, etc.). Financial planners can be licensed to sell and/or give insurance advice, and many are. Any good financial planners will assess your insurance situation and advise you on what you might need. Remember, independent insurance agents sell products for multiple insurance providers, while others sell just for one company.

Alphabet Soup and Credentials

Broad knowledge, formal and informal education, and passion for their craft is a sign of a good adviser or financial planner (or any other type of adviser for that matter). Longevity, integrity, goals, and (humble) confidence also count. These qualities, together with credible professional designation and current membership in relevant associations, all suggest an adviser is keeping up their chosen profession.

Of course, having a designation alone does not prove an adviser is competent. Some designations are easy to get, requiring minimal effort; memberships, for instance, are often simply a matter of paying the requisite fee. Others, like Certified Financial Planner and Certified Public Accountant, require ongoing education to maintain certification.

I would urge anyone to consider that your adviser be a **Certified Financial Planner.** This is not a simple designation to get. It requires two years of course work and many hours of annual education requirements.[56] CFPs also take ethics classes and are required to complete three years of work to finally earn the designation. All this is no guarantee a CPA will automatically give you great service. You need to be vigilant and rigorous in your selection process to verify that the skills of a given financial adviser will meet your need and quality standards.

The **CFA** or Chartered Financial Analyst designation is another designation you will encounter, though with a bit less frequently than the CFP. The CFA program is one of the most respected and recognized investment management designations in investment and financial planning. Completing it requires mastery of a broad range of portfolio management and advanced investment analytical skills. The qualification includes having a bachelor's degree or equivalent and at least four years of professional work experience. There are three levels of exams to pass (and from what I heard these are very hard). Once complete, the CFA must maintain membership in the CFA Institute.

Other designations you might find include the following:

Certified Investment Management Analyst® is an advanced investment consulting designation offered by the Investment Management Consultants Association. CIMA certification holders have at least three years of financial services experience, have passed background checks, completed a graduate-level program, and have passed a comprehensive exam.

A Certified Public Accountant (CPA) has passed the exceedingly challenging CPA exam. They are licensed by one of the fifty states and require constant education to maintain their status. The intense course work is developed and managed by the American Institute of Chartered Public Accountants (AICPA).

Charter Life Underwriter (CLU) is for individuals specializing in life insurance and estate planning. They must successfully undertake several core and elective courses and get past eight two-hour exams!

Certified Private Wealth Adviser (CPWA) is a credential for advisers targeting high-net-worth individuals with more complex financial planning needs. The CPWA focuses on a client's wealth life cycle from accumulation to preservation and distribution. The Investment Management Consultants Association offers the designation.

Chartered Financial Consultants (ChFC) is a credential introduced in 1982 as an alternative to the CFP. It has the same core curriculum, plus other elective courses focusing on personal financial planning issues. Advisers complete eight courses over two to four years.

Investment Adviser Representatives (IAR) are state registered and make securities recommendations, manage client investment accounts, determine security recommendations or advice, solicit or offer investment services, or supervise employees doing any of the above.

A **Master of Sciences in Financial Services** (MSFS) requires substantial coursework and prepares advisers in a range of general and specialized financial services.

The **Personal Financial Specialist** (PFS) certification is offered by the American Institute of Certified Public Accountants (AICPA) to CPAs specializing in individual financial and wealth planning (e.g., estate planning, retirement planning, investing, insurance). PFS professionals must complete sixty hours of continuing professional education every three years.

Registered Investment Advisers (RIA) must pass the Series 65 (Uniform Investment Adviser Law) exam administered by FINRA. The test covers federal securities law and other topics related to investment advice. RIAs must be registered with the SEC or in the state(s) in which they do business. This is not required if the adviser's investment services or advice is purely incidental to their main business.

Registered Financial Consultants (RFC) have met the requirements of the International Association of Registered Financial Consultants. The designation is given to a financial planner who meets several academic and on-the-job qualifications.

Retirement Management Analyst (RMA) is offered by the Retirement Income Industry Association and is available to financial advisers with three-plus years of experience. The designation certifies mastery of the retirement planning advisory process. Courses are taught at accredited universities.

Retirement Income Certified Professional (RICP) is offered by the American College of Financial Services and focuses on clients transitioning from asset accumulation to "creating a sustainable livelihood for clients in retirement." Three courses with exams must be completed.

These titles provide some comfort that the adviser is actively trying to improve his or her skills and knowledge. But again, neither the credibility of the designation nor years of experience necessarily mean their service provision will meet your needs.

Sustainable and Responsible Investment Credentials

Unfortunately, sustainable and responsible credentials available to advisers are limited, and SRI is mostly an on-the-job gig. But there are some basic SRI courses that financial planners can take to ensure a minimum level of knowledge.

The **US Forum for Sustainable and Responsible Investment** (SIF) Foundation and the Center for Sustainable Investment Education offer *Fundamentals of Sustainable and Impact Investment.* This is an introductory course intended for investment advisers, financial planners, and other financial professionals wanting to understand the basics of sustainable, responsible, and impact investment. The course offers instruction and scenario learning aimed at enhancing a professional's capacity to integrate sustainable and responsible investment data in investment decision-making. The course offers continuing education credits for several professional designations (e.g., CFA, CFP, CIMA, CIMC and CPWA).

The **Responsible Investor Association** (RIA) offers a Canadian Responsible Investor Fundamentals course for financial advisers, investment specialists, and individual investors who want to enhance their knowledge of SRI. The RIA also operates the PRI Academy, which focuses on environmental, social, and governance issues affecting shareholder and stakeholder value. The RIA offers Responsible Investment Adviser Certification (RIAC), Responsible Investment Professional Certification (RIPC), and Responsible Investment Specialist (RIS) designations via third-party certification.

Several universities also have basic to mid-level courses. There are a few conferences offering good points of SRI knowledge. The SRI Conference hosted by First Affirmative Financial Network is the oldest (more than twenty-five years). The SIF USA and the RIA also host regular conferences. All of the conferences offer course credits for CFP and other designations. Some conferences are open to the public and are great places to meet financial advisers.

But unfortunately, most SRI experience must be learned on the job. Ask your potential adviser about their volunteer, other career, or educational activities to plumb their SRI experience. Look for community organizations, particularly those engaged in economic and social justice work. Check for humanitarian and other types of volunteer work, and ask what role they have played. In some cases, they will be responsible for advising investments and finances, or strategy and leadership. These are all good signs.

Finding your Adviser

There several tools online that can shorten your search for a financial adviser. A few are listed here to get you on your way.

The **Financial Planning Association** allows you to search for CFPAs via their Certified Financial Planner data base. You can search by name or by state. You can also find CPAs with the Personal Financial Specialist credential at the American Institute of CPAs.

The **National Association of Personal Financial Advisers** (NAPFA) is the national association for fee-only advisers (i.e., advisers who do not sell any products on commission). The NAPFA has a name and zip code advisory search engine.

Another search engine, **Boomerater**, offers a host of online services focused on, you guessed, it Boomers. It has a useful search engine for legal and financial services, including listing of financial planners and financial advisers across all geographic areas, searchable by zip code.

The **Garrett Planning Network** is a network of several hundreds of hourly based, fee-only financial planners. Their search engine uses zip codes to provide a list of financial advisers who offer financial planning on an hourly basis.

Paladin Registry is a financial advisory that background-checks financial adviser credentials, ethics, business practices, and services. The firm offers a free search engine as well as fee-for-service checks. It also has other resources to help you better understand the search process, including some tips and traps to watch for. All the advisers in the Paladin registry are pre-screened to meet their selection criteria.

The **RIA** in Canada provides an interactive map showing the location of their professional and institutional members. The **SFI USA** has a list of institutional members. The First Affirmative Financial Network also has a search function for their SRI adviser network. Social Funds, a private website, provides an SRI financial professional search function by state.

Checking up on an Adviser's Credentials and Record

Many designations sound impressive but may only take a couple of hours to get, so be careful with the alphabet soup that comes after an adviser's name.

Checking personal and professional credentials, along with maintaining certifications and designations compliance, is very important. Much of this can be done online.

CFP professionals cannot offer investment advice or buy and sell securities unless they are licensed to do so. Ask which securities licenses a potential adviser holds, if any, and check out their validity at either the SEC for companies (not individuals unless they own a registered investment advisory) with more than $100M in assets managed or via FINRA for those with fewer. The SEC maintains two years' worth of data for sales representatives who let their licenses expire and a permanent file of complaints. There is a Central Registry Depository; every adviser with a securities license has a unique CRD number, which allows you to check their status at FINRA.

Remember, advisers selling insurance must have a state insurance license. A CFP cannot be a broker (i.e., someone licensed to buy and sell investment products). You can verify a CFP status and background with the CFP Board of Standards at cfp.net.

If the adviser is also an investment manager, make sure they are registered with the appropriate securities agency and have an unblemished record. Investment advisers charging fees must be registered with the SEC and/or Financial Industry Regulatory Authority.

Background checks are normal

This part of selecting and adviser is not much fun, but you must run a background check on your potential adviser. Some suggest starting with two tough questions: Have you ever been charged and/or convicted of a criminal activity and have you been investigated by any association, regulatory organizations, or investment-industry group?

The CFP Board, FINRA, and state insurance and securities departments keep disciplinary histories of financial planners and investment managers. You can check the SEC Investment Advisor Public Disclosure database to see if your potential adviser is a licensed investment adviser. The database also includes information on any investigations, charges, convictions, disputes, bankruptcies, and liens.

While CFPs aim for high standards of professional conduct and are obligated to uphold "principles of integrity, objectivity, competence, fairness, confidentiality, professionalism and diligence," this is not always the case.

The CFP has a set of rules of conduct that insist CFPs put client interest before all. CFPs violating these rules can be sanctioned by the board.

Treat any disclosures you might find as a madly waving red flag warning. Be aware that not finding "bad things" doesn't guarantee an adviser is competent, qualified, honest, or smart. Remember Bernie Madoff? He had a perfect reputation — until he got caught.

The Adviser Selection Process

The sales pitch. It is designed to make you buy. There are many types of pitches, and you should suffer none of them if you are looking to work with an SRI-oriented adviser.

Unfortunately, people being people, you will likely encounter a pitch of some sort, for which the only remedy is to be prepared. The information found in the sections above provides an overview of how to get ready, but like any list it cannot be complete. Do your homework long before walking into the first interview with your potential new adviser.

The process is simple:

1. Make a short list of advisers based on broad criteria of credentials, education, services offered, use friends, colleagues, and online resources.
2. Do basic research on individual and/or firms to check credentials, compliance, and for any past monkey business.
3. Speak to potential advisers to make sure a basic match is possible vis-à-vis quick assessment of character, experience, services, and fees.
4. Do in-depth interviews to assess their approach and see if there is a match between their character and services and your needs.
5. Check references and do in-depth online research to confirm adviser's information.
6. Have a final interview to get more detail on their recommended approach to meeting your service needs.

Interview Questions You Should and Ask Questions They Should Ask You

You need to prepare your interview questions to ask your potential new adviser. This will let them know you are serious. It will also help you to judge their character as they respond. A good adviser should have clear, well-thought-out answers to any question you might have. They should answer honestly and frankly, admitting when they don't know something, but letting you know how they might find out if it is important to serving you.

Questions to ask a Potential Financial Adviser

An adviser should be willing to tell you what they can do, what they can't, and what they don't do. Some questions to ask are listed below. You will want to add to these questions I am sure, and can order them in a way that makes you feel most comfortable.

Experience and credentials

- What is your experience?
- What qualifications do you have?
- What credentials and licenses do you have, and where can I check on them?

SRI

- What does SRI mean to you?
- What is your SRI philosophy?
- What are the values you hold most dear?
- Who are your typical clients?
- What types of SRI are you familiar with?
- Can you explain your approach to financial planning?

Services

- Which services, financial and non-financial, do you offer?
- What services would you recommend for me?
- Do I need comprehensive financial planning or just help with specific aspects?
- Will you have or use other professionals on my account?
- What do you charge and why?
- What's the worst/best financial decision you have made personally?
- Can you tell me about a client who has experienced a transformation because of your services? (Remember privacy laws!)
- Can you give me a sample of client communications, portfolio reviews, and ongoing communications?
- Can you give me two or three references of clients like me?

Answering your questions is only the half of it. You can also judge the nature and quality of an adviser based on the questions they ask you. A good SRI-oriented financial adviser should ask good questions. Some may include the following:

- What's your relationship with money?
- What feeds your soul?
- What types of SRI are you most interested in?
- What is your experience in engaging a financial adviser?
- What is your health like and that of your significant other and/or any dependents you might have?
- What levels of debt do you have?
- Do you save and how much for your kids' education?
- Do you take care of parents (emotionally and/or financially)?
- Are you saving for or do you need to make major expenditures soon? Extended work absence, new business start-up, second property?
- Have you started retirement planning?
- At what level are you funding your retirement?
- Have you organized your will? Do you have a trust fund? An executor, and/or designated legal representative?
- Are you in line to inherit money?
- What types of insurance do you have?

If you can, assess the adviser's own financial status and that of their company. If an adviser is unpressured by personal financial obligations, they will be better placed to serve you well. This is not to say that advisers, young and older, or just starting out will not provide good service. Rather, just remember to watch out for this type of pressure and factor it into your assessment.

Appendix One

Sample Household Income and Expense Spreadsheet

INCOME	
Income One	
Income Two	
Other Income	
Other Income	
Total Income	
EXPENSES	
Housing	
Mortgage	
Utilities	
Repairs/Renos	
Property Tax	
Other	
Household	
Food	
Furniture	
Art	
Clothing	
Other Home Articles	
Cleaning & Maintenance Supplies	
Phone / Internet	
Cleaning / Maintenance Services	
Other	
Lifestyle	
Entertainment	
Eating Out	

EXPENSES cont.	
Activities / Events	
Gifts	
Special Event (fund or actual costs)	
School fees and/or other School Costs	
Courses / Activities / Memberships	
Medical\Dental	
Personal Care (e.g., salons, massage etc.)	
Child Care (include babysitting)	
Parental Care (personal expenses)	
Pets	
Other	
Transportation and Travel	
Car Payments	
Car Insurance	
Insurance	
Licensing (car and personal)	
Maintenance / Cleaning	
Fuel	
Vacation Travel	
Other Travel	
Finances	
Debt Costs (not including mortgage)	
Student Debt	
Other Loans	
Investment Savings	
Emergency Savings	
Bank Service Fees	
Kids Savings	
Alimony	
Parental Care (financial only)	
Financial Advice / Services	
Donations	
Other	
Insurance	
Personal Insurance	
Home Insurance	
Health Insurance	

EXPENSES cont.	
Other	
MISCELLANEOUS	
Miscellaneous (10% of all expenses)	
TOTAL EXPENSES	

Appendix Two:
Financial Planning Monthly Meeting Agenda

1. **Check In! 5 minutes**

   Take a moment to unload your day and let yourself or your significant other know what mood you are in, and why. Let it all go in a big breath, and then get ready to begin.

2. **Income (Yeah!) and Expenses (!) — 20 minutes**

   2.1 Go over income for the month, including any unexpected income, small or large.

   2.2 Next go over expenses for the month, including any unexpected costs or costs that were anticipated but put off.

   2.3 Discuss what to do with extra income, or what to do with unexpected costs.

   2.4 Discuss any changes to the household budget that may be required.

   These two items can be in as much detail as you wish or in order of magnitude. Use your family budget as a guide.

3. **Balance Sheet Stuff (!) — 20 minutes**

   3.1 Detail and discuss value of assets (i.e., things you own and can sell for cash), reset value as needed.

   3.2 Detail and discuss liabilities (things you owe!), reset liability cost as needed.

   3.3 Review investment portfolio, discuss allocation and holdings, decide on changes if necessary.

   3.4 Discuss savings, retirement, debt reduction goals.

4. **Financial Planning and Management — 10 minutes**

   4.1 Identify and discuss any outstanding planning or management tasks that need to be done.

4.2 Review financial management responsibilities, and redistribute if necessary.

4.3 Review new documentation process, passwords, etc.

5. **Other financial issues ....** (e.g., insurance, will and testament, etc.)

Appendix Three:
List of Retirement Calculators

THERE ARE MANY DIFFERENT TYPES of retirement calculators available. The ones listed here are web-based and free. Many of them were assessed by Darrow Kirkpatrick of caniretireyet.com in a terrific article called *The Best Retirement Calculators* (first posted in 2014 but updated since; the site is good too).

Two calculators that provide more sophisticated estimates of retirement income are the Ultimate Retirement Calculator by Financial Mentors and the Personal Capital Retirement Planner.

Sample Retirement Income Calculators	
ARRP	Easy to use with different scenario planners for lifestyle.
Bloomberg	Nice interface, very simple to use but not particularly complex; only one income, no life-changing income or expenses.
CalcXML Retirement Savings *	Simple input. Income replacement. Social Security estimate/override. Spouse. Graphical/tabular output. PDF report.
cFIREsim *	Spouse. Asset allocation including gold. Rebalancing. Financial events. Spending policies. Graphical/tabular output. Dip analysis. Investigate scenarios. Save data. Support forum.
Chase Retirement Calculator *	Nice interface. Simple input. Social Security estimate. Spouse. Graphical/tabular output. Explore Options offers more parameters and simple scenario comparison.
CNN Money	Very simple and fast calculator, no bells and whistles.
Dinkytown.net Retirement Planner *	Nice interface. Income replacement. Social Security estimate. Retirement work. Graphical/tabular output. Well documented.
Fidelity Retirement Income Planner *	Nice interface. Detailed expenses. Social Security estimate/override. Spouse. Multiple accounts. Asset allocation. Rebalancing. Real estate. Financial events. Retirement work. Scenarios. Tax calculations. RMDs. Annuities. Graphical/tabular output. Today's dollars option. Save data. Well documented. (Requires signup.)

Sample Retirement Income Calculators cont.	
Financial Mentor Ultimate Retirement Calculator *	Simple input. Social Security override. Financial events. Retirement work. Tabular output. Computes savings/ contributions needed to fully fund plan.
New Retirement *	Nice interface. Simple input. Social Security override/ optimization. Spouse. Multiple accounts. Real estate. Financial events. Retirement work. Scenarios. Tax calculations. RMDs. Annuities. Graphical/tabular output. Save data. Well documented. (Requires signup.)
Personal Capital Retirement Planner *	Nice interface. Simple input. Social Security override. Spouse. Multiple accounts. Asset allocation. Real estate. Financial events. Retirement work. College saving. Annuities. Graphical/tabular output. Today's dollars. Save data. Well documented. (Requires signup.)
Scottrade Retirement Savings Calculator *	Nice interface. Simple input. Social Security override. Multiple accounts. Retirement work. Graphical output. Today's dollars. Well documented.
SmartAsset Retirement Calculator *	Nice interface. Simple input. Social Security estimate. Multiple accounts. Tax calculations. Graphical output.
T. Rowe Price Retirement Income Calculator *	Nice interface. Simple input. Social Security estimate/override. Spouse. Asset allocation. Rebalancing. Scenarios. Graphical output. Today's dollars. Save data. Well documented.
Vanguard Retirement Nest Egg Calculator *	Nice interface. Simple input. Asset allocation. Graphical output. Well documented.

Sources

* Review taken from *The Best Retirement Calculators*, Darrow Kirkpatrick, on the Can I Retire blog, November 22, 2014 (caniretireyet.com/the-best-retirement-calculators;)

aarp.org/ work/retirement-planning/retirement_calculator.html/

money.cnn.com/calculator/retirement/retirement-need/

Appendix Four:
Common SRI Categories
and Issues to Guide Your Passions

T HE CATEGORIES AND ISSUES below provide a wide range of issues commonly used or referred to in SRI. Given the nature of sustainability there are many others you may wish to apply. Strongly held religious beliefs, for example, are not represented.

1. **Alcohol**

2. **Animal testing and welfare**

3. **Community and Local**
   - Local supply chain
   - Hiring locally
   - Community development initiatives

4. **Defense**

5. **Employment**

6. **Environment**
   - Clean energy
   - Green technology
   - Climate change/carbon
   - Pollution
   - Biodiversity
   - Environmental management
   - Waste management
   - Water use
   - Forestry
   - Mining
   - Nuclear power

7. **Fair Trade**
   - International development
   - Minority-owned firm sourcing

8. **Gambling**

9. **Governance**
   - Board structure
   - Board diversity
   - Executive remuneration
   - Avoidance of bribery and corruption
   - Good practice marketing
   - Irresponsible marketing or advertising

10. **Human Rights**
    - Child labor
    - Diversity
    - Equal opportunities
    - Food supply
    - Human trafficking
    - Immigrants and immigration
    - Lesbian, gay, bisexual, and transgender
    - Slave labor
    - Sexual harassment
    - Sexual exploitation in the travel and tourism
    - Women

11. **Impact Investing** is investing in companies, organizations, and institutions aiming to solving social or environmental problems with market-oriented solutions.

12. **High-Impact and community investing** is investing in social, environmental, or economic activities that will benefit individuals, communities, and/or businesses with a social, environmental, or economic justice purpose.

13. **Labor Relations**
    - Right to affiliate with associations, groups, unions, etc.
    - Work-life balance
    - Fair wages
    - Decent working conditions

14.Proxy Voting

15.Tobacco

16.Social Enterprise is investing in businesses with a clear social, environmental, or economic justice purpose.

17.Sustainable agriculture
- GMO-free
- Local produce
- Free range/ naturally raised
- Organic

Appendix Five:
Watch Out For Those Fees

FINANCIAL ADVISERS are paid in various ways, and it is in your interest to be conversant with how they are remunerated and how that biases their recommendations or not. Some advisers are paid on a commission basis, while others charge a fee. Some use a combination of both.

The main distinction is found in the technical terms of whether an adviser employs fiduciary or suitability standards to their practice.

A **fiduciary standard** is when an adviser is bound to give you advice that fits your specific needs. As a fiduciary, they cannot, for example, sell you any financial product or service unless it is in your best interest. For example, a fiduciary standard adviser cannot buy mutual fund A over mutual fund B, even if both meet your needs but A offers higher commissions. Nor can they advise you to sell an asset to increase the size of your investment portfolio if the only result is increasing their fee as a percentage of assets under management. Fiduciaries as a result are typically fee-only advisers.

The **suitability standard** is one where advisers must recommend products and services that are suitable to your overall needs. Suitability advisers often work on a commission basis, typically paid by the funds and/or other product providers. Some believe that suitability advisers aren't required to choose your best investment options. While this may be technically true, choosing a higher-commission product while serving your needs is not necessarily mutually exclusive. Few sustainability investment advisers will steer you the wrong way unless, of course, they don't want a long-term relationship.

As with any economic decision, you need to be aware of what motivates an adviser's financial interests. While it's true that suitability advisers have different standards and motivations, most are not out to cheat you. They may guide you to investments that pay them more or are part of their company's offer, but they will want repeat business. Shop around, bust the fee numbers, and decide what serves you best.

Fee-based advisers have different motivations you will need to know as well. Say they get 1% of your asset base under management as an annual fee. This could cause them to hesitate before advising portfolio liquidation for buying a house, investing in your own business, or taking a year off to wander the Himalayas.

Each type of compensation has its pros and cons. If you are just starting out, you may wish to pay for a bit of up-front advice, and then use a commission-based adviser to purchase funds or securities. (This can be cost effective if you plan to hold them for long time.) But if you are the type that really wants to get to know your adviser, a fee-based professional may be the best for you.

Fee Structures

Fee or commission based, your (potential) adviser should be clear about services and transactions costs. They must also tell you what they will be paid personally for taking care of your business.

There are no such thing as standard fees in financial planning. As noted, some advisers charge fees only, while others entirely on commission. Many do both. There is no right or wrong, and it is your responsibility to understand and feel comfortable with an adviser's proposed compensation. If after several tries, you don't understand their explanation, or they don't try to explain, run.

> *Note to watch for: If you have compared fee-based advisers' costs, and one is much lower than others, it may be they are compensating with more commission-based income.*

Fee-Only versus Fee-Based

You will want to know if your adviser charges *fee-only* or is *fee-based*. The big difference: Fee-only advisers do not make commissions, whereas fee-based advisers might and probably do!

Fee-only advisers typically work for a percentage of your portfolio. The fee should range from between 1% to 2% per year. The more the assets you have, the lower the rate (typically!). When your portfolio grows in value, your adviser makes more; of course, the opposite is true if your portfolio value shrinks.

Or you can pay by the service. Many advisers will charge you a one-time-only fee for a financial plan. Others might, like a lawyer or accountant, charge an hourly rate.

There are many variations. Some advisers may charge a percentage of your net worth, which would include your real estate, business(es), etc., with the idea of increasing your overall worth. Others might take a percentage of your gross income, offering a broader set of recommendations on your career, business, and other activities to increase your overall income.

Fee Types

Hourly rate

Charging by the hour usually secures you the most objective advice, as an adviser is not bound to purchase any given investment for you. As with lawyers, fees vary. More experienced advisers, advisers with a highly-specialized field, or advisers with a good deal of success will charge more per hour. Advisers with less experience will typically charge less.

Flat fee

This kind of fee is usually charged for a specified project, such as a financial plan. Flat-fee services are not linked to your portfolio value, asset base, or any product purchase. This increases the chance of getting purely objective advice.

Retainer Fees

Perhaps your financial situation is tricky or sophisticated. It may be that you have a small business and rental properties that need financial management support. You may need income on a regular basis from your investments (which requires more attention), or may have exotic stock trading activities (e.g., calls and puts). If any of these are the case, you may require ongoing advice and may be best served by a retainer fee. Not linking your adviser's compensation to assets or to the buying or selling of financial products can help ensure greater objectivity and attention to your business.

In any fee-based relationship, you will need to remember that many advisers may be acting on a fee basis. They can still give you "objective" advice, but they may recommend one product or service over another based on their commission. Again, this is not necessarily bad, just something to watch for. Whatever you ask for, an adviser should tell you in clear, jargon-free language what you are getting up-front, the proposed fee, and their own compensation.

The adviser should also detail any "conflicts of interest," in writing, where this applies. Think insurance policies, securities via a third-party broker, or mutual fund commissions. Your adviser may, for example, recommend you get help from an attorney, accountant, or insurance agent. If so, they should tell you if they stand to gain from this referral, be it cash or in kind (e.g., the "I refer you/you refer me" network). If a referral fee or other kind of compensation is in place, this is a conflict of interest and needs to be discussed. Again, not necessarily bad if you know about it, but suspicious if you are not fully informed.

Commission-Based Fees

Commissions are paid to advisers for the sale of a financial product or service. They are one of the most common forms of remuneration in the finance industry. Again, not necessarily bad, as commission-based advisers will want continued business from you. Beware to distinguish between someone who is a good financial adviser and someone who is simply good at sales.

Expect to get "The Suggestion" from a commissioned adviser that you buy one of their products. That's how they make money. The adviser needs to demonstrate that whatever they are hawking is not only suitable for you but a good buy! Remember, commission-based advisers will get higher commissions from one product or others, and they need to tell you how their advice could affect meeting your financial goals.

Common Costs to Investments

It is very important to make sure you understand just how much you are paying for your investments. If you are buying a single security, the fee, either to your broker/adviser or your online trading service, is simple to determine.

Funds are a different beast all together. According to Brett Carson, the average mutual fund expense ratio (see definitions below) according to Morningstar was 1.25% (2014 numbers). Seems low, right? But get this, Carson calculated this low fee would cut your savings at retirement from around $945,000 to $757,000. Increase the fee another 0.25%: you lose another $30,000![57]

Wait — there are can be more costs associated with mutual funds, which bring the average estimated cost to the share/unit holder to around 4% annually (for a taxable account).[58]

There are two broad types of fund fees: fees you pay when you sell or buy a fund's shares (transaction fees, aka loads) and ongoing fees, which are usually charged annually.

Loads and Shareholder Fees

Loads are one way that funds compensate brokers and marketers for selling. Sales loads are paid when you buy or sell units or shares in a fund. There are three main types of fees, and they can be used alone or in combination:

- **Front-End fees** are charged when you buy into a fund, by being deducted from the amount you invest.

- **Back-End fees** are charged when you sell shares or units from a fund. These fees can decrease over time with some funds, providing shareholders with an incentive to stay in the fund.

- **No-load funds** have no commission or sales charge, though some do charge purchase, redemption, exchange, or account fees.

There are also **redemption fees**. These are charged when investors sell or redeem fund shares or units. This sounds like a back-end fee, but technically it is not, because it is used to cover the administrative costs of the shareholder's sale. The fee is limited to 2.0% by the SEC.

Similarly, funds can charge a **purchase fee** to cover administrative costs of your purchase. This fee is paid to the fund, not to a broker, and as such is not considered a sales load.

Some funds also charge a **transfer fee** when a shareholder transfers money from one fund within a family of funds to another (e.g., shifting from an equity to a bond fund as part of your portfolio asset reallocation strategy).

Loads are simply sales commissions and, as with maintenance fees, there seems to be no correlation between higher load fees and performance. So don't be fooled! Shop around; chances are you can find funds with similar risk profile and performance with different fee structures.

Ongoing Fees

Mutual funds have what is known as an **expense ratio**, or a management expense ratio (MRE). This is the cost of actively managing a fund. Money is taken out of fund assets to pay the MRE. As an investor, you don't pay the fee directly, but it is a cost to you because it reduces the profit you make. Like all costs, the MRE can be found in the fund prospectus, usually as "Annual Fund Operating Expenses."

The MRE includes all **management costs**, including hiring managers, which can cost from 0.5% to 2% of total fund assets. This cost does not always correlate with better performance, so much so that the Securities and Exchange Commission website warns, "Higher expense funds do not, on average, perform better than lower expense funds."

MRE also includes an ongoing expense ratio that pays the commission, advertising, and promotions cost of the fund. The SEC does not limit the size of this fee, but the Financial Industry Regulatory Authority says it cannot "exceed 0.75% of a fund's average net assets per year." Some funds also charge a "service fee" as a part of the MRE. This will include such things as marketing materials and making and sending out prospectuses, and may include the cost of buying and selling securities. These fees cannot exceed 0.25%.

There can be other expenses. **Account fees** can be charged on shareholders with less than a stated minimum of a fund (e.g., a pre-set dollar amount). Fees for legal and custodial charges, record keeping, accounting, and other types of administrative work can also be paid separately.

Passive index funds, which are not actively managed, can have low expense ratios (0.25% of assets). Fees for funds that trade securities more actively can go as high as 2.0%, with an average equity mutual fund being about 1.3%–1.5%. You will also pay more for specialty funds, or funds with more international holdings.

The average expense ratios for basic types of fund are

- Large-cap stock funds: 1.25%
- Mid-cap stock funds: 1.35%
- Small-cap stock funds: 1.40%
- Foreign stock funds: 1.50%
- S&P 500 index funds: 0.15%
- Bond funds: 0.90%
- Index funds: 0.2%

Averages vary by type because each requires different levels of management and research. Index funds have the lowest expenses because they are mostly passively managed (i.e., they don't buy and sell a lot of securities). This keeps the fund's management costs low compared to more actively managed funds. Most index funds will have expense ratios of around 0.20% or lower. Some exchange-traded funds have even lower expense ratios.[59]

Sources of Fee Information

Morningstar Fee Information (basic free service)			
Load	Total Assets	Expenses	Fee Level
None	$35.3 bil	0.77%	Below Average

Morningstar provides simple-to-read information on fees and loads for all funds listed on it site. You will still need to read the fund prospectus and/or check with your adviser or sales agent about the "all-in price" and any other relevant details (e.g., declining back end loads).

FINRA also has an online tool that shows fee costs (and other data) on over 18,000 mutual funds, exchange-traded funds, and exchange-traded notes.

End Note

Prior to formalizing a relationship with an adviser, or deciding to buy any product or service, you must have your adviser or sales agent provide full and complete disclosure on how they will be compensated. They must also tell you about any conflict of interest they may have in their proposed compensation package.

You should not have to ask for this information, and is a pretty bad sign if the adviser does not put fees and compensation issues up front.

Some other considerations:

1. If you don't need to, don't let your adviser have control (or custody) of your assets. This will give them the ability to make decisions with your money from withdrawals, transfers, trades, etc.
2. Don't write a check or transfer funds to your adviser, save to pay for their services (unless it is automatically withdrawn annually as per your contract). Send money directly to the third-party service providers (e.g., brokerage, insurance company, accountant, lawyer etc.).

At the end of the day, you need to read the fine print on any contract you might enter or product/service you may buy. This overview is intended to provide the basics you need to develop a "fee radar," and is not complete in terms of the types and nature of all fees possibly charged.

Appendix Six:
Example U.S. and Canadian SRI Funds

T̲HE̲ ̲U̲.S̲.̲ ̲A̲N̲D̲ ̲C̲A̲N̲A̲D̲I̲A̲N̲ ̲F̲U̲N̲D̲S̲ ̲L̲I̲S̲T̲E̲D̲ here are a sample of the growing number of SRI funds. The U.S. list is taken from the SRI Forum USA website, Wikipedia, Morningstar, and Social Funds.com, among other sources. The Canadian list is from RAI Canada.

U.S. Funds

iShares MSCI USA ESG Select ETF
iShares MSCI KLD 400 Social ETF
Access Capital Strategies Community Investment Fund
ACWI Low Carbon Target ETF
AHA Diversified Equity Fund — Institutional Class
AHA Diversified Equity Fund — N Class
AHA Full Maturity Fixed Income Fund — Institutional Class
AHA Full Maturity Fixed Income Fund — N Class
AHA Limited Maturity Fixed Income Fund — Institutional Class
AHA Limited Maturity Fixed Income Fund — N Class
AHA Socially Responsible Equity N
AHA Balanced Fund — Institutional Class
AHA Socially Responsible Equity I
Alger Green
American Century NT Equity Growth
American Century Sustainable Equity
American Trust Allegiance
Appleseed Fund
Ariel Focus
Ariel Focus Fund
Ariel Fund

Ariel Appreciation Fund
Azzad Ethical Mid Cap Fund
Azzad Ethical Income Fund
Barclays Return on Disability ETN
Barclays Women in Leadership ETN
Baywood Socially Responsible
Boston Common US Equity
Brighter Student Fund
Calvert Capital Accumulation A
Calvert Capital Accumulation B
Calvert Capital Accumulation C
Calvert Conservative Allocation Fund
Calvert Large Cap Growth A
Calvert Large Cap Growth B
Calvert Large Cap Growth C
Calvert Large Cap Growth I
Calvert Mid Cap Value Fund
Calvert Moderate Allocation Fund
Calvert New Vision Small Cap A
Calvert New Vision Small Cap B
Calvert New Vision Small Cap C
Calvert Small Cap Value Fund
Calvert Social Index A
Calvert Social Index B
Calvert Social Index C
Calvert Social Index I
Calvert Social Investment Balanced A
Calvert Social Investment Balanced C
Calvert Social Investment Bond A
Calvert Social Investment Enhanced Equity A
Calvert Social Investment Enhanced Equity B
Calvert Social Investment Enhanced Equity C
Calvert Social Investment Equity A
Calvert Social Investment Equity C
Calvert Social Investment Equity I
Calvert World Values International A
Calvert World Values International C

Calvert Aggressive Allocation Fund
Calvert Global Alternative Energy Fund A
Calvert Global Water Fund
Calvert International Opportunities Fund
Clear Bridge Sustainability Leaders
CRA Qualified Investment
DFA US Sustainability Core
Domini European Social Equity A
Domini European Social Equity I
Domini Institutional Social Equity
Domini PacAsia Social Equity A
Domini PacAsia Social Equity I
Domini Social Equity A
Domini Social Equity I
Domini European PacAsia Social Equity A
Domini European PacAsia Social Equity I
Domini Social Bond
Dreyfus Third Century
EcoLogical Strategy ETF
Epiphany Faith and Family Values 100 Fund — C Class
Epiphany Faith and Family Values 100 Fund — N Class
Epiphany FFV
Epiphany Faith and Family Values 100 Fund — A Class
Etho Climate Leadership US ETF
Flex Total Return Utilities Fund
FlexShares STOXX Global ESG Impact Index Fund
FlexShares STOXX US ESG Impact Index Fund
Gabelli SRI Green Fund, Inc AAA
Gabelli SRI Green Fund Inc C
Gabelli SRI Green Fund Inc I
Gabelli SRI Green Fund Inc A
Global X Conscious Companies ETF
Global X S&P 500 Catholic Values ETF
Green Century Equity
Green Century Balanced [19]
GuideStone Funds Growth Equity
GuideStone Funds Value Equity

Integrity Growth & Income
Integrity Growth & Income Fund
Invesco Summit
iShares MSCI EAFE ESG Select ETF
iShares Sustainable MSCI Global Impact ETF
Legg Mason Prt Social Awareness Fund B
Legg Mason Prt Social Awareness Fund C
Legg Mason Prt Social Awareness Fund A
LKCM Aquinas Catholic Equity
MMA Praxis Core Stock Fund B
MMA Praxis Growth Index Fund A
MMA Praxis Growth Index Fund B
MMA Praxis Intermediate Income A
MMA Praxis Intermediate Income B
MMA Praxis International A
MMA Praxis International B
MMA Praxis Small Cap Fund A
MMA Praxis Small Cap Fund B
MMA Praxis Value Index A
MMA Praxis Value Index B
MMA Praxis Core Stock Fund A
NB Socially Responsive Fund
New Alternatives Fund
NuShares ESG Large-Cap Growth ETF
NuShares ESG Large-Cap Value ETF
NuShares ESG Mid-Cap Growth ETF
NuShares ESG Mid-Cap Value ETF
NuShares ESG Small-Cap ETF
Oppenheimer Funds ESG Revenue ETF
Oppenheimer Funds Global ESG Revenue ETF
Parnassus Endeavor Fund
Parnassus Small Cap Fund
Parnassus Core Equity Fund
Parnassus Fund
Parnassus Income Fixed Income
Parnassus Mid Cap Fund
Pax ESG Beta Quality Individual

Pax World High Yield
Pax World Value Fund — Institutional Class
Pax World Balanced
Pax World Growth
Pax World Value Fund — Individual Investor
Pax World Women's Equity Fund — Individual Investor
Pax World Women's Equity Fund — Institutional Class
Portfolio 21 Global Equity Fund Class R
Portfolio 21 Institutional
SEI Large Cap Diversified Alpha (SIIT)
Sentinel Sustainable Emerging Companies Fund
Sentinel Sustainable Core Opportunities Fund [30]
SPDR Gender Diversity Index ETF(SHE)
SPDR MSCI EAFE Fossil Fuel Reserves Free ETF
SPDR 500Fossil Fuel Free ETF
SPDR S&P Fossil Fuel Reserves Free ETF
Steward Large Cap Enhanced Index
TIAA-CREF Social Choice Equity Fund
TIAA-CREF Social Choice Lw Crbn Eq
Timothy Plan Large/Mid Cap Growth
Touchstone Premium Yield Equity
Vanguard FTSE Social Index Fund
Walden Equity
Walden Social Equity Fund
Walden Social Balanced Fund
Winslow Green Growth Fund
Workplace Equality Portfolio ETF

Canadian Funds

iShares Jantzi Social Index ETF (XEN) BGI043
Blue Heron Canadian Focused Equity
Blue Heron Global Dividend
Blue Heron Global Equity
Blue Heron Income
Clarington Inhance Monthly Income SRI Fund F6
Desjardins Environment
Desjardins Environment C

Desjardins Environment F
DSC GWL Ethics (G) NL
Global Equity Balanced NEI Ethical Select Growth Portfolio Series A
Global Neutral Balanced SocieTerra Growth Portfolio
GWL Ethics (G)
GWL Ethics (G) 100/100
GWL Ethics (G) 75/100
GWL Ethics (G) 75/75
GWL Ethics Fund (G) DSC
GWL Ethics Fund (G) NL
IA Clarington Inhance Canadian Equity SRI Class A
IA Clarington Inhance Growth SRI Portfolio Ser F
IA Clarington Inhance Monthly Income SRI Fund FE
International Equity NEI Ethical International Equity Fund Series A NEI
Ethical International Equity Fund Series F
Jantzi Balanced Fund Series F
Jantzi Canadian Equity Fund Series
Jantzi Canadian Equity Fund Series D
Jantzi Canadian Equity Fund Series I
Jantzi Global Equity Fund Series F
LON Ethics (G) 100/100
LON Ethics (G) 75/100
LON Ethics (G) 75/75
London Life Ethics Fund (GWLIM)
Meritas Canadian Bond Fund Series F SRI302 NEI Canadian Bond Class A
Meritas Growth & Income Portfolio Series A
Meritas Growth & Income Portfolio Series F
Meritas Growth Portfolio Series
Meritas Growth Portfolio Series F
Meritas International Equity Fund
Meritas International Equity Fund Series F
Meritas Jantzi Social Index Fund
Meritas Jantzi Social Index Fund Series F
Meritas Monthly Dividend and Income Fund
Meritas Monthly Dividend and Income Fund Series F
Meritas U.S. Equity Fund Series A
Meritas U.S. Equity Fund Series F

NEI Canadian Bond Class F
NEI Ethical American Multi-Strategy Fund Series F
NEI Ethical Canadian Equity Fund Series A
NEI Ethical Canadian Equity Fund Series F
NEI Ethical Global Dividend Fund Series F
NEI Ethical Global Equity Fund Class A
NEI Ethical Global Equity Fund Class F
NEI Ethical Select Balanced Portfolio Series
NEI Ethical Select Balanced Portfolio Series F
NEI Ethical Select Growth Portfolio Series F
NEI Global Strategic Yield Fund Series A
NEI Global Strategic Yield Fund Series F
NEI Global Strategic Yield Fund Series T
NEI Global Total Return Bond Fund Series A
NEI Global Total Return Bond Fund Series F
NEI Global Total Return Bond Fund Series T
PH&N Community Values Bond Fund Series C
PH&N Community Values Bond Fund Advisor Series
PH&N Community Values Bond Fund Series D
PH&N Community Values Canadian Equity Fund Ser O
PH&N Community Values Global Equity Fund Advisor
RBC Jantzi Balanced Fund Advisor Series
RBC Jantzi Balanced Fund Series A
RBC Jantzi Balanced Fund Series D
RBC Jantzi Balanced Fund Series I
RBC Jantzi Canadian Equity Fund Advisor Series
RBC Jantzi Canadian Equity Fund Series A
RBC Jantzi Global Equity Fund
RBC Jantzi Global Equity Fund Advisor Series
RBC Jantzi Global Equity Fund Series D
RBC Jantzi Global Equity Fund Series I
Social Housing Canadian Equity Fund Series
Social Housing Canadian Short-Term Bond Series B
SocieTerra Growth Plus Portfolio
U.S. Equity NEI Ethical American Multi-Strategy Fund Series A

Appendix Seven:
Example Investment Benchmarks

Aᴄᴄᴏʀᴅɪɴɢ ᴛᴏ Iɴᴠᴇsᴛᴏᴘᴇᴅɪᴀ, a "benchmark is a standard against which the performance of a security, investment fund, or investment manager can be measured. The objective of a benchmark is to give investors a point of reference against which to assess or evaluate financial performance."

Morningstar, for example, employees the Standard & Poor (S&P) 500 for "stock-oriented funds, including domestic-hybrid, international-hybrid, and convertible-bond funds." The S&P 500 is often a full-market index as it holds 500 stocks of the biggest companies on U.S. stock markets. The index is market-cap-weighted, that is, the importance and impact of each stock depends on its market value: A small or large percentage change of a larger company's stock value will have a bigger effect on the S&P average than that of a smaller company.

A benchmark can include indexes that measure various investments and segments of various stock markets. Indexes that measure both the broad market and specific segments are regularly used to assess and modify portfolios on an ongoing basis.

Benchmarks help investors understand their performance and can also provide a reference point for desired returns (e.g., I want to beat the "X" benchmark). The benchmark used must reflect the risk an investor is willing to take and should be mirrored in a portfolio's holdings.

This means each type of investment vehicle, from mutual funds to index funds to a single stock, can use different indices to benchmark a portfolio's performance.

Major Benchmarks

Barclays Capital U.S. Aggregate Bond Index (e.g., Lehman Brothers Aggregate Index, aka "the BarCap Aggregate) is a broad bond index covering most U.S.-traded bonds and some foreign bonds traded in the U.S. It consists of approximately 17,000 bonds, hence the name "total bond index" for those index funds that track it.

For most investors, the Index is to fixed income what the S&P 500 or the DJIA is to stock investment. It is used to benchmark the performance of bond and fixed income portfolios/investments, and many index funds and exchange-traded funds track its performance. The index is weighted to market capitalization (i.e., according to market of bond categories, e.g., treasury securities, foreign bonds, mortgage-backed securities, government agency bonds, corporate). Bonds are medium term and have an average 4.57-year maturity, representing approximately 8,200 fixed-income securities of about $15 trillion, or 43% of the U.S. bond market. Bonds have investment grades (i.e., Baa3/BB or more) as rated by Moody's and S&P rating agencies, though around 80% of bonds on the index are AAA.

Dow Jones Industrial Average or DJIA is a stock market index of 30 large publicly owned U.S.-based companies. Established in 1885, the industrial portion of the name is now historical as many of the industrial sectors in the index have little (or nothing) to do with heavy industry. The average is price-weighted, and to compensate for the effects of stock splits and other adjustments, is currently a scaled average.[60]

Lipper Indexes are a series of indexes tracking the financial performance of different types of mutual, allowing investors to benchmark mutual funds of certain types against an index of 30 funds belonging to each major investment style (e.g., value and growth funds, small- and large-cap funds). An investor can benchmark their small-cap mutual fund, for example, against the Lipper Small-Cap Index, which is a combination of 30 of the largest small-cap funds (by asset size).

The **MSCI EAFE Index** tracks the performance of about two dozen developed countries in Europe, Australasia, and the Far East. The index was developed by Morgan Stanley Capital International (MSCI) to measure the equity performance of select emerging markets worldwide. It has large- and mid-cap stocks from 23 emerging market economies (Brazil, Chile, China, Colombia, Czech Republic, Egypt, Greece, Hungary, India, Indonesia, Korea, Malaysia, Mexico, Peru, Philippines, Poland, Qatar, Russia, South Africa, Taiwan, Thailand, Turkey, and the United Arab Emirates). It is thought to capture not just the market but political, economic, and currency risks associated with emerging markets as well.

The **MSCI World Index** is an equity index capturing large- and mid-cap funds across developed markets in countries around the world. It includes about 85% of the free float-adjusted market capitalization in each developed country represented (Austria, Australia, Belgium, Canada, Demark, Finland, France, Germany, Ireland, Japan, Israel, Italy, Netherlands, Norway, New Zealand, Portugal, Singapore, Spain, Switzerland, United Kingdom, United States).

Russell 2000: U.S. Small-Cap Stocks is the benchmark commonly used to assess U.S. small-cap stock performance. The index is composed of 2,000 small-cap companies (of less than $1.3 billion in market capitalization). If a company grows beyond the small-capitalization categorization, the stock is removed and replaced with another firm to maintain the integrity of accurate small-cap measurement.

The **S&P 500** is used as benchmark for individual large-cap stocks and large-cap-focused funds. The 500 companies included in the index must meet various criteria, including having a market capitalization greater than $4 billion and consistently reporting positive earnings.

Wilshire 5000 — originally an index of 5,000 publicly traded companies, the Wilshire now counts over 6,700. Companies must be headquartered in the United States, be traded actively on an American stock exchange, and have widely available pricing information. The Wilshire 5000 is a market capitalization-weighted index, which gives greater weight to companies with a larger firm value and underweights those with less. It is one of the broadest indexes available, designed to track the performance of American stock markets. This index is commonly used in broad market benchmarking.

For more information and definitions, see Investopedia at investopedia. com.

Notes

1 Sustainable and Responsible Investment Forum (SIF USA) US at ussif. org/performance.

2 Daniel Gilbert. "Exxon CEO Joins Suit Citing Fracking Concerns." *Wall Street Journal*, February 20, 2014.

3 My recounting of SRI will be different from others', and this little stroll through history will be, well, a bit unique. I want to assure you, it's neither comprehensive nor a tale my SRI friends will all be pleased with. Such is the interpretation of history. I do, however, want to assure you that those SRI professionals and companies mentioned, or the many I haven't mentioned, contributed with their hearts and souls one and all; such a dedicated group of people you can only hope to meet in this life time.

4 See Wikipedia: "Socially Responsible Investment;" and, "The Impact of Sustainable and Responsible Investment," The Sustainable and Responsible Investment Forum, USA, 2014.

5 For some interesting treatment of the effects of psychology on our social and economic outlooks see "A Sideways View: New Stirrings in Business Psychology" at Psychology Today.

6 Gwen Sharp, PhD. *"Changing U.S. Racial Demographics."* Sociological Images, May 8, 2013.

7 Studies done by the Pew Charitable Trusts, the American Enterprise Institute, the Brookings Institution, the Heritage Foundation, and the Urban Institute challenged the notion that each generation will be better off than the one that preceded it. For an overview see John Morton and Isabel V. Sawhill, "Economic Mobility: Is the American Dream Alive and Well?" May 25, 2007. Brookings Institute.

8 Derek Thompson. "The Unluckiest Generation: What will become of Millennials?" The Atlantic, April 26, 2013.

9 "MILLENNIALS: A Portrait of Generation Next Confident. Connected. Open to Change." Pew Research Center, February 2010.

10 Carlo de Bassa Scheresberg."College-Educated Millennials: An Overview of Their Personal Finances." TIAA-CREF Institute, 2014.

11 Ibid.

12 Ron Alsop. "The Trophy Kids Grow Up: How the Millennial Generation is Shaking Up the Workplace," Jossey-Bass, 2008.

13 Kate Lyons. "Generation Y: a guide to a much-maligned demographic." *The Guardian,* March 7, 2016.

14 Rob Asghar. "Gen X is from Mars, Gen Y is from Venus: A primer on how to motivate a Millennial." *Forbes,* January 1, 2014.

15 Ibid.

16 Kate Lyons. "Generation Y: a guide to a much-maligned demographic." *The Guardian,* March 7, 2016.

17 Carlo de Bassa Scheresberg. College-Educated Millennials: An Overview of Their Personal Finances." TIAA-CREF Institute, 2014.

18 Derek Thompson. "How to Freak Out About Millennials in a Statistically Responsible Manner." *The Atlantic,* July 3, 2014.

19 Generation Y. See Value Options at: valueoptions.com/spotlight_YIW/gen_y.htm.

20 Barbara Dafoe Whitehead and David Popenoe. "Sex Without Strings, Relationships Without Ring." See the National Marriage Project.

21 According to the Urban Institute, cited in "Revealed: The 30-year economic betrayal dragging down Generation Y's income." *The Guardian,* March 7, 2016.

22 Paris Lee. "Millennials Are Idiots." *Vice,* June 20, 2014.

23 Brianna Ehley. "Irresponsible Millennials Saving More than Almost Every Other Group." *The Fiscal Times,* February 25, 2015.

24 Samanta Sharf. "he Recession Generation: How Millennials are changing Money Management Forever." *Forbes,* July 30, 2014.

25 Stephen Koukoulas. "Millennials Should Stop Moaning: They've Got More Degrees and Low Rates." *The Guardian,* April 04, 2016.

26 Kimberly Palmer. "Why Millennials Still Don't Save Enough." *US News,* June 18, 2014.

27 Terri Friedline. PhD, and Stacia West. "Financial Education Is Not Enough: Millennials May Need Financial Capability for Healthy Financial Behaviors." AEDI Working Paper, (cited on the FINRA

Investor Education Foundation website), 2015.

28 Nathaniel Popper. "Why Millennials are in no hurry to take on debt." *New York Times*, August 14, 2016.

29 Caelainn Barr and Shiv Malik. "Revealed: 30 Year Economic Betrayal Dragging Down Generation Y Income." *The Guardian*, March 8, 2016.

30 Carlo de Bassa Scheresberg. "College-Educated Millennials: An Overview of Their Personal Finances." TIAA-CREF Institute, 2014.

31 Sonya Stinson. "What Gen X Can Teach Boomers about finance." *Forbes*, March 5, 2014.

32 J. F. Coughlin and Lisa D'Ambrosio. "Seven myths of financial planning and baby boomer retirement." *Journal of Financial Services Marketing*, March 7, 2009.

33 Ginita Wall. "Love & Money: 25 Financial Tips for Couples." Women's Institute for Financial Education.

34 Brian Stoffel. "The Average American Has This Much Saved in a 401(k) — How Do You Compare?" The Motley Fool, Jan 5, 2015.

35 See the 2017 federal income tax calculator at CalcXML.com. For poverty levels see US Department of Health and Human Services, at aspe.hhs.gov/2015-poverty-guidelines#threshholds.

36 I like the Bloomberg calculator, not just for political purposes either, you can see it at bloomberg.com/personal-finance/calculators/retirement/.

37 Tom Lauricella. "When Should Retirees Downsize Homes?" *Wall Street Journal*, January 25, 2014.

38 Kate Lyons. "Generation Y: a guide to a much-maligned demographic." *The Guardian*, March 7, 2016.

39 Blake Ellis. "Average American inheritance: $177,000." *CNN Money*, December 13, 2013.

40 David Weliver. "The 2015 Millennial Money Survey: How much do 20-Somethings Earn and Save?" *Money Under 30*, May 18, 2015.

41 Greg B. Davies. "Overcoming the cost of being human (or, The pursuit of anxiety-adjusted returns)." Barclays, 2013.

42 Greg B. Davies. "Why Millennials Still Don't Save Enough." *US News*, June 18, 2014.

43 Carlo de Bassa Scheresberg. "College-Educated Millennials: An Overview of Their Personal Finances." TIAA-CREF Institute, 2014.

44 Samanta Sharf. "The Recession Generation: How Millennials are changing Money Management Forever." *Forbes*, July 30, 2014.

45 Ron Lieber. "Zen and the Art of 401(k) Maintenance." *New York Times,* August 5, 2016.

46 This was calculated for the 90 years ending 2015! See David A. Levine. "The Goldilocks Strategy for Prudent Investors." *New York Times,* July 1, 2016.

47 Investopedia, Asset Allocation, investopedia.com.

48 Definitions from investopedia.com. Barclays U.S. Aggregate Bond Index data from thebalance.com. Good sites, full of great information!

49 See Smart Asset Allocation Calculator at: www.smartasset.com.

50 See CNN Money, asset allocator tool at money.cnn.com/tools/asset allocwizard/.

51 sec.gov/spotlight/jobs-act.shtml.

52 Adam Gaha . "Inertia and Decision Making: The need to take the first step with someone in order to change their habits." September 13, 2013, posted at summarizedreading.com/2013/09/inertia-and-decision-making-need-to.html.

53 Lisa Wright. "How to pick a financial advisor." *Toronto Star,* March 24, 2017.

54 Lisa Wright. "How to pick a financial advisor." Toronto Star, March 24, 2017.

55 See Sue Orman's blog at suzeorman.com.

56 CFP professionals must pass the comprehensive CFP Certification Exam, which tests their ability to apply financial planning knowledge to real-life situations. The exam covers the financial planning process, tax planning, employee benefits and retirement planning, estate planning, investment management and insurance. The average pass rate for this difficult exam is only 55%. This comprehensive exam ensures that CFP professionals are highly qualified to develop a plan for your finances.

57 Brett Carson. "Barely noticeable mutual fund fees could cost you more than $500,000 over a lifetime." *Business Insider,* March 17, 2015.

58 "The real cost of Mutual Funds." *Forbes,* March 4, 2011.

59 Data from The Balance www.thebalance.com/average-expense-ratios-for-mutual-funds-2466612.

60 See Dow Jones Industrial Index in Wikipedia.

Index

RICP, 184
RIPC, 185
RIS, 185
risk, 98, 99
    assessment of, 110
    and asset allocation, 111
    and company size, 110
    and geography, 111
    and investment types, 108–109
    necessity of, 105
Rita and Al, 81–82
RMA, 184
Roth fund, 79, 87
Russell 2000: U.S. Small-Cap
    Stocks, 221

S
S&P 500, 221
Sanders, Bernie, 45
savers, as category, 58, 60
saving
    among Millennials, 50–52, 94
    automatic investment, 75
    for investments, 56–57
    for retirement, 67–68, 70,
        75–79
savings accounts, 97
Schueth, Steve, 3
Scottrade Retirement Savings
    Calculator, 198
screened mutual funds, 19–21
SEC Investment Advisor Public
    Disclosure, 187
Securities and Exchange
    Commission (SEC), 181
Series 65 (Uniform Investment
    Adviser Law) exam, 184

SFI USA, 186
Shared Interest, 22
shareholder activism, 14–16
shareholder fees, 207
shock experiment, 154
shorting stocks, 100
SIF, 185
single-issue focus, 156–157
Slater, Ross, 67
Slow Food movement, 19
SmartAsset Retirement Calculator,
    198
Smashing TVs, 17–19
Smith, Cheryl, 131, 139
Social Funds, 186
Social Investment Forum (SIF),
    2, 5
Social Investment Organization, 3
social security, 73–74
Soros, George, 116
South Africa, 12
SPDR Gender Diversity ETF, 23
spenders, as category, 58, 60
spirituality
    SRI motivation, 17–19
    SRI roots in, 12
spreadsheet, 191–193
SRI
    allocator tool, 120–127
    baby steps, 151
    beginnings of, 9–11
    Canadian funds, samples,
        215–217
    categories, 199–201
    challenges to the industry,
        132–133, 138–139
    cocktail party test, 16–17

About the Author

MARC DE SOUSA-SHIELDS is an international sustainable development and investment consultant. He co-founded and was first Executive Director of the Social Investment Organization (SIO) of Canada. He has been an advisor to the United Nations and was a member of the US Social Investment Forum International Committee. He wrote *Sustainable and Responsible Investment in Emerging Markets* for the World Bank-International Finance Corporation and led a USAID project on *Transitions to Private Capital.* He has written for leading on-line corporate sustainability magazines including *Triple Pundit* and *Sustainable Brands* and is author of *The Sustainable Century by Design or Disaster* (forthcoming), TheSustainableCentury.net blog, and the Sustainable Century Podcast. The hardest things he has done are convincing his mother-in-law to make social investments, and organic urban gardening in a semi-tropical climate. He has worked and traveled in over 80 countries and, when not on the road, Marc lives in Mexico.

A Note about the Publisher

NEW SOCIETY PUBLISHERS is an activist, solutions-oriented publisher focused on publishing books for a world of change. Our books offer tips, tools, and insights from leading experts in sustainable building, homesteading, climate change, environment, conscientious commerce, renewable energy, and more — positive solutions for troubled times.

 We're proud to hold to the highest environmental and social standards of any publisher in North America. This is why some of our books might cost a little more. We think it's worth it!

- We print all our books in North America, never overseas
- All our books are printed on **100% post-consumer recycled paper,** processed chlorine free, with low-VOC vegetable-based inks (since 2002)
- Our corporate structure is an innovative employee shareholder agreement, so we're one-third employee-owned (since 2015)
- We're carbon-neutral (since 2006)
- We're certified as a B Corporation (since 2016)

At New Society Publishers, we care deeply about *what* we publish – but also about *how* we do business.

New Society Publishers
ENVIRONMENTAL BENEFITS STATEMENT

For every 5,000 books printed, New Society saves the following resources:[1]

26	Trees
2,327	Pounds of Solid Waste
2,560	Gallons of Water
3,339	Kilowatt Hours of Electricity
4,230	Pounds of Greenhouse Gases
18	Pounds of HAPs, VOCs, and AOX Combined
6	Cubic Yards of Landfill Space

[1]Environmental benefits are calculated based on research done by the Environmental Defense Fund and other members of the Paper Task Force who study the environmental impacts of the paper industry.

MIX
Paper from responsible sources
FSC
www.fsc.org   FSC® C016245

new society
PUBLISHERS
www.newsociety.com